The Hoarding Handbook

THE HOARDING HANDBOOK

A Guide for Human Service Professionals

Christiana Bratiotis

Cristina Sorrentino Schmalisch

Gail Steketee

OXFORD
UNIVERSITY PRESS

Oxford University Press, Inc., publishes works that further Oxford University's objective of excellence in research, scholarship, and education.

Oxford   New York
Auckland   Cape Town   Dar es Salaam   Hong Kong   Karachi   Kuala Lumpur   Madrid   Melbourne
Mexico City   Nairobi   New Delhi   Shanghai   Taipei   Toronto

With offices in
Argentina   Austria   Brazil   Chile   Czech Republic   France   Greece   Guatemala   Hungary   Italy
Japan   Poland   Portugal   Singapore   South Korea   Switzerland   Thailand   Turkey   Ukraine   Vietnam

Published by Oxford University Press, Inc.
198 Madison Avenue, New York, New York 10016
www.oup.com

Oxford is a registered trademark of Oxford University Press

Library of Congress Cataloging-in-Publication Data

Bratiotis, Christiana.
  The hoarding handbook : a guide for human service professionals / Christiana Bratiotis, Cristina Sorrentino Schmalisch, Gail Steketee.
    p. cm.
  Includes bibliographical references and index.
  ISBN 978-0-19-538551-9 (pbk. : alk. paper) 1. Obsessive-compulsive disorder.
2. Compulsive hoarding. 3. Social service. I. Schmalisch, Cristina Sorrentino.
II. Steketee, Gail. III. Title.
  RC533.B735 2011
    616.85'227—dc22   2010054219

1 3 5 7 9 8 6 4 2
Printed in the United States of America
on acid-free paper

FOREWORD

My first foray into the world of hoarding occurred nearly 20 years ago when, as part of a research project, I visited severely cluttered homes that were stuffed with treasures. I remember being astonished by the value these objects had for their owners and equally amazed by the openness these people displayed in sharing their stories with me. Not long after that, in a study of hoarding cases investigated by health departments, I received quite a different picture from health officers frustrated and angry with people who, in their minds, not only denied a problem with hoarding but refused to cooperate with orders to correct serious fire and health code violations. Interestingly, a few of these cases were the same people I interviewed earlier.

The experience taught me something about hoarding. There are perspectives about this problem that vary widely. The client or sufferer's perspective was the first to capture the interest of researchers. What do all these things mean to these people, and how do they view their behavior? Soon after, the therapist's perspective became a topic of great interest. Informed by the client's perspective, therapists have developed effective ways of treating hoarding with cognitive-behavioral therapy. The third perspective is that of family members who often grew up amid a cluttered home or must try to ensure that their aging family member has a safe and healthy home. Though limited, there is a growing literature on the impact hoarding has on families.

For each of these perspectives, there is not only research, but books designed to help. Missing from this literature, however, is the perspective from arguably one of the most important groups—human service personnel. Employees of agencies dealing with health, housing, the elderly, child neglect and abuse, fire, police, and even the law view hoarding cases frequently, probably more often than do mental health professionals. Until now, few published resources were available for them.

This is the first book about hoarding designed for human service personnel. It provides a comprehensive and detailed resource for all agency officials who deal with hoarding. It is a valuable tool for learning not only how their agency can work with cases of hoarding, but also about the role other agencies and officials play in dealing with it. Bratiotis, Schmalisch, and Steketee have been at the forefront of developing community interventions for hoarding. They have worked with a wide variety of agencies on cases of hoarding and consulted with numerous hoarding task forces across the country. Their perspective is well-informed and practical.

Several things about the volume are noteworthy. The information on hoarding task forces and the Hoarding Task Force Intervention Model they present can shape a community's response to hoarding. People with hoarding problems lead difficult lives. Hoarding is usually not the only problem and often not the most serious one. Cooperation among agencies will be the only way to resolve many of these cases. This guide makes heavy use of case illustrations that provide clear examples related to each type of service personnel. The illustrations are rich with detail and highlight the remarkable complexity of hoarding. The Tips and Strategies section of each chapter offers welcome advice for service personnel, especially those new to hoarding.

The Hoarding Handbook: A Guide for Human Service Professionals will be valuable for service personnel of all sorts, from fireman to elder service workers, in solving this growing crisis. It will also be useful for mental health professionals who often are unaware of the role other agencies play in cases of hoarding.

Randy O. Frost, Ph.D.

ACKNOWLEDGMENTS

We acknowledge the many hoarding clients we three authors have met with and spoken to over the past 10 years. They have helped us immeasurably to understand the problem of hoarding and the complex human service responses that are needed. We also acknowledge our many professional colleagues from across the human service disciplines who have helped us work with hoarding clients, have trained with us and have raised the challenging questions we have tried to address in this book.

We especially thank Joanne Allison, Stefanie Belandis, Sarah Dowal, Jesse Edsell-Vetter, Anne Goodwin, Paul Halfmann, Kim Hubbard, Lynne Johnson, Kathleen McGrath, Jane Nathanson, Mark Odom, Gary Patronek, Terry Prince, Margaret Riley, Dianne Sandman, Frances Strassman and Sheryl Vito for their help with the content of this book. Oxford editors Maura Roessner and Nicholas Liu have been especially supportive in guiding us through the many challenges of developing the content for this work.

We also gratefully acknowledge the pioneering work on hoarding by Dr. Randy Frost and the consultation and support of research colleagues Drs. David Tolin and Sanjaya Saxena. We are honored to keep the company of hoarding research and clinical colleagues Drs. Jordana Muroff and Catherine Ayers, Jessica Rasmussen and Amanda Gibson, and countless others who have contributed to our work over these last several years.

Christiana thanks her parents Reverend Fr. George and Gloria Bratiotis for the wise council and sound encouragement and her sister Alexia for regularly extending love and good humor as the book evolved and now emerges. She is most grateful to her doctoral classmates who were present when the book project started and are standing by to celebrate its publication.

Cristina thanks her husband, Matthias, for 'standing like a wall behind her' in the long course of working on this book. She also thanks

Toni Tugenberg for her unflagging willingness to share her time and home to help move this work to completion.

Gail thanks her husband Brian McCorkle who has supported her throughout her work on hoarding and her family and friends who have so graciously lent their ears to this endeavor. This work would not be possible without her longstanding research partnership with Dr. Randy Frost.

CONTENTS

CONTRIBUTORS

Sarah L. Dowal
Boston University
Schools of Social Work and Public Health
Boston, Massachusetts

Jesse Edsell-Vetter
Metropolitan Boston Housing Partnership
Boston, Massachusetts

Randy O. Frost
Smith College
Northampton, Massachusetts

Paul Halfmann
Massachusetts Department of Public Health
Boston, Massachusetts

Gary Patronek
Animal Rescue League of Boston
Boston, Massachusetts

INTRODUCTION

This handbook for human service professionals is a compilation of research findings, information garnered from colleagues in a range of professions, and the collective reflection of our extensive practice with people who hoard. Writing this book grew from the synergy of the three authors working together as professionals in various stages of their careers. All three of us are clinical social workers who share a commitment to advancing clinical and community responses to this challenging problem. Our approach to hoarding derives from a mental health perspective, with a strong focus on how professionals, agencies, and communities address this problem. In the course of working together on a variety of hoarding cases, we have often interfaced with the human service disciplines described in this book.

ABOUT OUR BOOK

Writing a book with close colleagues who, for a time, all worked at the same institution and still live in close geographic proximity is a unique experience. We sat together for much of the writing of this book, collectively gathering thoughts, checking facts, and discussing the current state of the knowledge. Much of the practice wisdom shared in the text draws from cases in the Northeast part of the United States where we live and work. We used examples shared by colleagues from different areas of the country and incorporated terminology that we believe generically represents human service terms, although regional nuances in the language sometimes posed a challenge.

Throughout this book, we tried to reference the latest research when it was relevant to the topic. Material in the text that does not contain citations reflects the authors' practice and clinical experience and we have tried to indicate this clearly. The Tips and Strategies sections of Chapters 6–13 derive from recommendations by professional colleagues in the relevant human service disciplines. Occasionally we provide recommendations and suggestions that we believe represent current best practices for hoarding. At the same time, we understand that these practices are constantly changing.

ABOUT THE AUTHORS

Christiana Bratiotis, Ph.D., is a clinical social worker with practice experience in leading multidisciplinary community collaborations. Her training in the clinical treatment of hoarding disorder, combined with her interest in regional policy development and implementation, led to a pioneering study of the formation and operation of community hoarding task forces. This research was the impetus for the current volume and is the source of much of the book's information about community intervention by human service professionals. Christiana provides consultation to families and communities as they plan and carry out hoarding interventions. She presents and trains internationally on these topics.

    Cristina Sorrentino Schmalisch, Ph.D., is a clinical social worker with a research background working in private practice. Cristina has 5 years of experience delivering specialized cognitive-behavioral therapy for hoarding. She works closely with a wide range of human service professionals on shared cases of hoarding and provides community intervention referrals. Cristina provides community training on hoarding with specific emphasis on communication strategies, empathic intervention, and multisystem involvement.

    Gail Steketee, Ph.D., is a clinical social worker and an established researcher in the field of anxiety disorders. With over 30 years of clinical research on obsessive compulsive disorder, Gail began research on hoarding disorder in the mid-1990s. She has written over 50 published works on the nature and treatment of hoarding. Along with colleague Dr. Randy Frost, she developed a conceptual model of hoarding and the specialized cognitive-behavioral treatment for hoarding disorder discussed in this book. Gail is a member of the Scientific Advisory Board of the International Obsessive Compulsive Disorder Foundation that sponsors the virtual Hoarding Center noted in the section on Resources. She presents internationally on hoarding disorder and has mentored and trained students in a range of mental health disciplines.

TERMINOLOGY

Throughout this book we most often use the term *hoarding* to indicate a situation characterized by the accumulation of excessive clutter that precludes ordinary use of the living spaces in and around the home. As detailed in Chapter 1, other hoarding symptoms include difficulty parting with objects and excessive acquiring, problems that are typically accompanied by strongly held beliefs about objects and cognitive features such as difficulty making decisions, procrastination, and lack of motivation to change the hoarding behavior.

In contrast to this general term, *compulsive hoarding* has been used in much of the mental health literature to signal the clinical nature of this problem. Media sources, taking their cue from the academic literature, often use this term when reporting on cases of hoarding. In this book we have omitted the adjective *compulsive* because it is likely to be replaced with the currently preferred diagnostic title *hoarding disorder* to help distinguish it from a different mental health problem, obsessive compulsive disorder. Chapter 1 mentions and Chapter 5 describes in more detail the proposed diagnosis of hoarding disorder, which is currently under consideration by the American Psychiatric Association for inclusion in the 5th edition of the *Diagnostic and Statistical Manual of Mental Disorders* (*DSM-V*). However, as this is not yet a formal diagnosis, we generally use the term *hoarding* to refer to the broad signs and symptoms mentioned above rather than to a mental health disorder.

HUMAN SERVICES FOR HOARDING

In our experience, many types of human service professionals become involved with hoarding clients. Examples include housing staff (landlords, inspectors in public buildings), public health and safety officials (public health and fire department officers) responding to reports from neighbors or family members, and protective service workers alerted to possible problems with children, elders, and disabled adults living in the home. Although sometimes those needing protective service are themselves hoarding, often they are bystanders in a home in which the primary caretaker and/or his or her partner have lost control of clutter. When animals are hoarded, the first professional to encounter the problem may be an animal control officer or a member of the local humane society. Occasionally, the initial human service professionals to see a home will be health care providers sent to provide personal or family care services—for example, visiting nurses, paramedics, occupational therapists, home health aides, personal care assistants, and even primary care providers who make home visits. Their initial discovery of massive clutter that prevents effective functioning can trigger additional service contacts to address the hoarding itself. Finally, neighbors and family members often serve as first entry points when they contact agencies directly, seeking help for themselves or for the person who hoards.

Many agencies receive referrals after the hoarding has been discovered. Such secondary care systems include those mentioned above, as well as mental health services, public health departments, fire departments, legal systems, and professional organizers. Among mental health providers are public agencies such as state departments of mental health with case management staff as well as therapists and counselors. Likewise, private care providers may become involved. The disciplines represented among mental health providers are wide ranging and can include psychologists, psychiatrists, social workers, psychiatric nurses, mental health counselors, and pastoral counselors. Clergy may be drawn into hoarding problems when the person who hoards is a member of a religious group or of the community served by that group. Public health and fire officials must act to ensure that the home is brought into compliance with relevant health and safety codes. Legal professionals (lawyers, judges) may enter the picture at the public or private level—for example, when eviction proceedings are initiated by a public housing site or by a private landlord, or when neighbors seek legal solutions to unsightly exterior clutter. Often their role is to assist inside and outside the courtroom on the side of the plaintiff or defendant during adjudication relevant to evictions, property clean-up, damages sought, and/or other punitive actions. Professional organizers may play a role, sometimes called directly by hoarding clients or concerned family members and sometimes asked to assist one of the other human service professionals mentioned above.

In these service contacts, the initial interaction between the provider and the hoarding client typically sets the stage for future cooperation or lack thereof. In communities in which task forces have been established, services are nearly always coordinated across providers, often pitting an enforcer against a helper by asking one agency to wield the regulatory "stick" while the other offers a service "carrot." Whether coordinated through a single agency or across multiple providers, most interventions for hoarding are necessarily delivered in the home in which the clutter and disorganization occur. This presents a problem for some health and mental health care professionals who typically work within an office setting, as there is little evidence to date that services delivered outside the home have a lasting impact on the hoarding problem. Such health care providers may be able to partner with professionals such as visiting nurses or home health aides who can visit the home.

HOW TO USE THIS BOOK

This book is designed to provide a comprehensive look at service delivery systems for serious hoarding problems, with the goal of providing effective services across the myriad potential providers. To use this book most effectively, we recommend reading Chapters 1–4 thoroughly, as these set the stage for understanding hoarding, including interpersonal aspects, assessing the severity of risk, and determining the best strategies for collaborating with other service delivery groups. We also strongly recommend reading Chapter 5 on mental health aspects of hoarding to ensure a clear understanding of how people who hoard think and feel and why they behave as they do. This will set the stage for better coordination across service systems described in subsequent chapters on housing, public health and safety, protective services, animal hoarding, the legal system, medical aspects of hoarding, and the role of professional organizers. In the final chapter of this book, we consider ongoing challenges and strategies for solving this widespread, complex, and difficult problem.

We strongly recommend that readers learn who becomes involved in hoarding cases within their own community to better understand points of entry that might best facilitate successful resolution of hoarding in its many manifestations. At the end of this book you will find a glossary of terms, a list of resources and referral options that are current at the time of the publication of this book, and an Appendix containing instruments to assess hoarding. Those that were developed and tested in our research projects and those of our close colleagues can be downloaded from the Oxford University website at www.oup.com/us. We hope these will be updated regularly on the International Obsessive Compulsive Disorder Foundation website at www.ocfoundation.org, which has undertaken to provide ongoing resources to people with hoarding problems and their families. For readers interested in thoroughly understanding how to intervene with hoarding clients from a mental health perspective, we recommend the Therapist Guide and Client Workbook in Oxford University Press's *Treatments that Work* series: Steketee, G., & Frost, R. O. (2007). *Compulsive Hoarding and Acquiring: A Therapist Guide*.

The Hoarding Handbook

CHAPTER 1

Hoarding and Its Effects

Hoarding is a complex problem that compels attention from a wide range of providers of human services. It is no surprise that understanding this syndrome is critical to providing effective services. This chapter defines hoarding, describes its symptoms and features, and notes the multiple roles played by human service professionals who encounter serious hoarding. Service providers are most helpful when they understand how to differentiate hoarding from related and sometimes associated conditions (for example, squalor and animal hoarding) and are aware of common comorbid mental and physical health problems. This knowledge can enable responders to triage cases based on severity and other features that might affect the other intervention strategies needed.

WHAT IS HOARDING?

"Compulsive hoarding," as it has been labeled in recent psychological literature, was defined by Frost and Hartl (1996) as having three main features:

1. the accumulation of and failure to discard a large number of objects that seem to be useless or of limited value,
2. extensive clutter in living spaces that prevents the effective use of the spaces, and
3. significant distress or impairment caused by hoarding.

People who hoard differ from collectors who deliberately accumulate and maintain specialized collections of objects that are generally well organized and considered by most people to be interesting and valuable

(Danet & Katriel, 1989). Instead, people who hoard acquire many things seemingly at random and without regard to available space in their homes. Furthermore, the acquired objects become disorganized and even chaotic clutter that interferes with everyday living and is often dangerous. The Internet is a gateway to descriptions of unusually severe cases of hoarding, including the classic case of the elderly Collyer brothers in New York City that captivated the public for weeks in the late 1940s. To this day, hoarding clients are known as "collyer cases" in New York City. Hoarding can result in serious and even life-threatening problems and the syndrome appears to worsen as people age (Grisham, Frost, Steketee, Kim, & Hood, 2006). Most people who seek help for hoarding are middle-aged, averaging about 50 years, according to our research and the research of others. Unfortunately, we know relatively little about people who do not seek help voluntarily but are discovered and reported by others.

Nearly all people who hoard *acquire too many things*, whether purchased items or free things such as newspapers, advertisements, giveaway items, and street trash. Their acquiring is associated with positive feelings and even with a "high" that reinforces the behavior and makes it very difficult to stop. Sometimes, acquiring episodes are intended to help sooth negative moods (Kyrios, Frost, & Steketee, 2004). A principal feature of hoarding is *difficulty discarding* objects that most others would view as unneeded, worthless, or useless. Those who hoard consider their accumulated possessions to have sentimental (emotional), instrumental (useful), or intrinsic (beauty) value, and in fact, most people also save things for these very same reasons. However, people who hoard assign great value to many more items (for example, outdated receipts, ordinary bottle tops, take-out food containers, parts of board games for which most pieces are missing), and they are therefore unable to discard most of them.

As they accumulate more things and cannot get rid of them, the hallmark feature of hoarding appears in the form of large amounts of *disorganized clutter* in most parts of the home. People who hoard also seem to be *unable to organize* their things (Wincze, Steketee, & Frost, 2007), perhaps because of problems with decision making and perfectionism described later in this chapter. As the clutter spreads, it *interferes with basic activities* such as cooking, cleaning, moving through the home, and even sleeping in the bed. In extreme cases, hoarding is a *dangerous and life-threatening problem* that increases the risk of home fires, falls, and bodily harm from floor collapse, health problems such as cardiopulmonary disease, and even suffocation from cascading piles of clutter. Elderly clients, small children, and people with physical disabilities are at special risk in severely cluttered homes.

Animal hoarding may be a subtype of hoarding, although the relationship between these two conditions is not yet clear. Animal hoarding has been defined by the following three conditions (Patronek, 1999):

1. The accumulation of a large number of animals, more than the typical pet owner has (more than 20), and usually not for the purpose of breeding and sale.
2. A failure to provide an adequate living environment for the animals, as indicated by overcrowded or unsanitary living conditions, inadequate nutrition, inadequate veterinary care, or evidence of unhealthy condition of the animals under the owner's care.
3. A reluctance to place the animals for adoption or into the care of others.

Animal hoarding is often identified through complaints by neighbors to animal control agencies. Typically the owner denies that the animals are suffering or that the living area is compromised. This behavior indicates an important feature of this problem—poor insight or limited awareness by the animal owner. See Chapter 9 for details about animal hoarding and intervention.

THE FEATURES OF HOARDING

Below we summarize the features of hoarding and refer readers to comprehensive reviews of this topic for further information (Pertusa, Frost, Fullana et al., 2010; Saxena, 2008a). Hoarding of objects occurs across western cultures, although it is not yet clear whether it is common in disadvantaged nonwestern cultures. Findings in the United States indicate that it occurs at similar rates in white and nonwhite samples. Epidemiological studies in the United States and Europe have indicated that hoarding occurs in 2–5% of adults. Beginning typically in the teenage years, hoarding appears to gradually worsen over the life span, with middle-aged and elderly adults most likely to have serious symptoms. Interestingly, prevalence studies have found that more men than women report hoarding problems, but more women than men seek help from mental health clinicians. Hoarding occurs across all socioeconomic strata, but is commonly associated with lower income levels and can be a cause of homelessness. Thus, it is not surprising that hoarding is also found among homeless people despite their limited space for accumulating clutter (Mataix-Cols et al., 2010).

The first encounter with serious hoarding and its main manifestation—mounds of disorganized clutter—is daunting for most human service professionals. The responder is "hit in the face" by the sight and sometimes the smell of piles of newspapers, magazines, old mail, clothing, boxes and bags of new and old purchases that were never used, containers of many types, including storage bins with buried lids intended to help the person get organized. The quantity and array of items are often overwhelming and provoke reactions such as "Why would anyone keep this stuff?," "What an awful mess!," and "How can anyone live like this?" It is immediately obvious that clearing out the clutter will be no easy task. Here are a few examples of first encounters.

The child and family service worker knocks on the door of a woman who has been reported to need services to protect the welfare of her children at home. The mother comes to the door but opens it only a crack. She peers out with anxiety and suspicion written on her face and in her body language. The worker explains the purpose of his visit gently but clearly, encouraging her to invite him into the home. This takes some back and forth dialogue until she relents and opens the door a little wider. It soon becomes apparent that the door will not open further because it is blocked by piles of newspapers and bags of unknown items. The worker squeezes through the door and sees narrow paths threading through knee high clutter. On moving further into the small apartment, it becomes clear that all of the rooms are cluttered, including the bedroom and play spaces used by the children. In fact, there is no clear space where the children could sit on the floor, play on their beds, or do their homework. The professional works hard to control his initial shock as he talks to the woman. He opens a new case file at the child welfare agency.

A middle-aged daughter calls the Department of Aging in a panic asking what to do about her 85-year-old mother who has been saving all of her delivered Meals on Wheels food containers for months and probably for years. According to the daughter, her mother's stove and refrigerator no longer work and are full of old food containers. Stacks of ancient newspapers are everywhere, and unopened mail and bills are piled up. The stairs are crowded with bags, papers, and magazines. The daughter who lives in another state reports that she is shocked. Although she has been in contact with her mother regularly by phone, she has not been to the home for 2 years. The clutter is much worse and very frightening now that her mother walks with a cane and is unsteady on her feet. What if she falls and breaks her hip? The Department of Aging professional recognizes hoarding as the main problem and provides the daughter with a referral to a nearby elder service agency that can send a staff member to the home to learn more about the situation.

The manager at a public housing building is alerted by a cleaning staff that one of the residents regularly comes to the dumpsters before trash day to rummage through the bins. This man puts many items into plastic bags and lugs them back to his apartment. In fact, bags and boxes have begun to accumulate outside the apartment door and other floor occupants have complained. One neighbor says that the apartment stinks, and she is convinced that the cockroaches in her own apartment are caused by this man's accumulated trash. The manager calls the housing inspector to ask for an annual inspection of the apartment. After some wrangling with the occupant who finally lets him in, the inspector finds the front hallway almost completely blocked, piles of trash bags preventing access to the windows, and the narrow galley kitchen filled with trash on the counters and in bags on the floor. Other rooms are slightly less cluttered but are very dirty, and the whole place smells. The inspector's report triggers a visit by the manager who threatens to call a cleaning company to clear out the apartment. The occupant becomes belligerent and a standoff ensues.

A nurse makes her first visit to an elderly man who has ongoing health problems and has recently been settled in an assisted living building. She finds that this gentleman's room contains considerable clutter in the form of magazines, advertising flyers, papers, newspapers, and mail. As she explores his health needs, he reports that he is out of medication. However, further questioning of resident staff members indicates that he often loses the medications in his piles of stuff. They also worry that his symptoms of cardio-pulmonary disease will worsen because of the dust and allergens in his room, which they cannot keep clean because of the clutter. Although they do their best to remove some of the clutter, he becomes very upset by this, and they are reluctant to do more.

The police department receives a call from a neighbor who complains about a house next door where the yard is full of trash and many cats and dogs seem to come and go from the home. She complains about the smell. The dispatcher reports the problem to the public health department, which sends an officer out to investigate. A middle-aged woman speaks to the officer through a closed door and refuses to let him in. It is clear from the trash-strewn yard, the odor of urine and feces, and the drawn shades pressing against the windows that something is seriously amiss. The officer is unsuccessful in gaining entry to the home. After completing his report at the office, he calls the local society for the prevention of cruelty to animals to inform them of his observations. They send an investigator to the private home, but again the woman refuses entry, forcing the agency to seek a court order to investigate the welfare of the animals.

These scenarios are typical initial encounters with hoarding by human service providers from various organizations. In most of these cases, the person who hoards is not seeking help voluntarily, but has been reported to the authorities by others. All too often, such nonvoluntary cases, especially those involving severe hoarding problems, become a serious economic burden on local social service agencies. One seemingly simple but often very costly solution is to clean out the apartment. Unfortunately, this strategy typically results in recidivism as the hoarding resident simply resumes acquiring and cluttering behaviors after the cleanout. In fact, one small town in western Massachusetts spent $16,000 to clear out a home, only to find they needed to repeat the process all over again a year and a half later (Frost, Steketee, & Williams, 2000). What is clear from the scenarios above is the need for human service agency professionals to work with their colleagues in other relevant settings to find workable solutions to these sometimes life-threatening situations. The first step in this effort is to learn more about hoarding as a mental, behavioral, and social problem.

DIAGNOSING HOARDING

Hoarding does not yet have diagnostic status as a separate syndrome in the *Diagnostic and Statistical Manual of Mental Disorders* (*DSM-IV*) established by the American Psychiatric Association (2000). [This is the "bible" used by trained mental health clinicians to diagnose mental disorders in the United States. *The International Classification of Diseases* (the current version is the *ICD-10*) is the World Health Organization's international diagnostic manual for physical and mental disorders. Diagnostic criteria from the *DSM* are usually very similar to those in the *ICD*. At this time, we do not know whether there are any plans to include hoarding in the *ICD* manual.] Currently, hoarding is listed as one of several symptoms of obsessive compulsive personality disorder on Axis II and is also mentioned as a subtype of obsessive compulsive disorder (OCD) in Axis I. However, neither classification seems satisfactory in the wake of research suggesting that hoarding and OCD differ in important ways (e.g., Grisham et al., 2005; Pertusa et al., 2010; Saxena, 2008b). Some reasons for this are given below and more detail is provided in Chapter 5. For example, obsessions and rituals are less clearly evident in hoarding disorder compared to the washing, checking, ordering, and repeating rituals that are common OCD symptoms. Demographic and symptom features also appear to differ—people who hoard tend to be older, less often married, and less insightful about their problem compared to those with OCD. Likewise, research points to biological differences between hoarding and OCD with regard to genetic heritability (different sites were involved) and biological features (different brain regions were implicated). However, as Pertusa, Frost, and Mataix-Cols (2010) have reported, some OCD symptoms (e.g., contamination fears, concerns about mistakes) can result in clutter when other defining features of hoarding, such as excessive acquisition and difficulty discarding, are not present. In such cases mental health clinicians should diagnose and treat OCD rather than hoarding disorder.

Within the psychiatric community, discussions are ongoing at the present time to determine whether hoarding should be classified as a separate mental health disorder (tentatively titled Hoarding Disorder) within the obsessive compulsive (OC) spectrum disorders. Recent discussions among members of the OC Spectrum diagnostic working group for *DSM-V* have resulted in the following tentative criteria to define hoarding disorder:

1. Persistent difficulty discarding or parting with possessions, regardless of whether they are perceived by others to be valuable or not. This difficulty is due to strong urges to save items, distress and/or indecision associated with discarding.

2. The symptoms result in the accumulation of a large number of possessions that clutter the active living areas of the home or workplace so intended use of at least some of these areas is no longer possible (e.g., unable to cook in kitchen or to sit in living room). If all living areas are uncluttered it is only because third parties have intervened (e.g., parents in the case of children, family members, cleaners, local authorities, etc.).

3. The symptoms cause clinically significant distress or impairment in social, occupational, or other important areas of functioning (including maintaining a safe environment for self and others).

In addition to these primary symptoms and features of hoarding, it may be important to verify that the clutter is not a temporary problem due to a recent move, major home renovations, or inheriting a large number of items. Trained mental health diagnosticians will also need to make a differential diagnosis regarding the following health and mental health conditions:

- The hoarding symptoms are not due to a general medical condition (e.g., brain injury, cerebrovascular disease).
- The hoarding symptoms are not due to another mental disorder (e.g., hoarding as a compulsion provoked by obsessions in Obsessive-Compulsive Disorder, lack of motivation in Major Depressive Disorder, delusions in Schizophrenia or another Psychotic Disorder, cognitive deficits in Dementia, restricted interests in Autistic Disorder,

food storing in Prader-Willi Syndrome). (Mataix-Coles, Frost, Pertusa, Clark, Saxena, Leckman, Stein, Matsunaga, & Wilhelm, 2010)

When hoarding behaviors appear to be caused by another medical or emotional disorder, we recommend that experts in those problems be asked to assist in assessing and recommending interventions for the affected person. Human service workers may need to interface with other experts to address the primary problem in order to manage the unfortunate effects of accumulated clutter.

Although excessive acquiring occurs in about 90% of people who hoard (Frost, Tolin, Steketee, Fitch, & Selbo-Bruns, 2009), it is not yet clear whether this common symptom will become part of the central features of hoarding or will be included as a specifier, as follows:

> *With Excessive Acquisition:* Symptoms are accompanied by excessive collecting or buying or stealing of items that are not needed or for which there is no available space.
>
> In addition, diagnosticians may be asked to rate the level of awareness of the problem:
> - *Good or fair insight*: Recognizes that hoarding-related beliefs and behaviours (difficulty discarding, clutter, or excessive acquisition) are problematic.
> - *Poor insight*: Mostly convinced that hoarding-related beliefs and behaviors are not problematic despite evidence to the contrary.
> - *Absent insight*: Completely convinced that hoarding-related beliefs and behaviors are not problematic despite evidence to the contrary.

Unfortunately, many people deny that acquisition or difficulty parting with items is either excessive or unreasonable. For this reason, we recommend asking family members, friends, or other informants familiar with the person and their lifestyle to help assess the context and extent of the hoarding problem.

Squalor

Although not part of the diagnostic criteria, squalid conditions may be present in hoarding homes in the form of human or animal waste, rotting food, insect infestations, and other conditions that contribute to severe odor and serious damage to the home. This has been called Diogenes Syndrome or severe domestic squalor (for a review see Snowdon, Shah, & Halliday, 2007). Individuals with these conditions may also display poor personal hygiene apparent in unpleasant body odor, unkempt appearance, and dirty clothing. Although squalor is often accompanied by evidence of hoarding, the reverse seems less common, and in fact, squalid home conditions have been relatively rare among hoarding participants in our research studies. Nonetheless, such conditions pose serious public health challenges that threaten occupants of the home or neighbors. In these cases, public health officials or other health organizations may need to be involved (see Chapter 7).

A MODEL FOR UNDERSTANDING HOARDING

Many people are simultaneously appalled and drawn to the stories of hoarding. Uninformed observers can jump to the conclusion that hoarding results from laziness or some moral defect. Although a few people who hoard might have such traits, our experience with hundreds of people who have participated in our research or requested information and referral suggests that the majority do not. Instead, they suffer from complicated and interwoven behavioral, emotional, and cognitive problems that appear to have multiple causes. Steketee and Frost (2007) described a theoretical model for understanding hoarding in *Compulsive Hoarding and Acquiring: A Therapist Guide* (New York: Oxford University Press). This manual provides training in how to gather clinical information to help individual clients understand their hoarding in order to plan effective intervention strategies. Many aspects of the model have been tested empirically, although some parts, such as family factors, remain insufficiently studied. The hoarding model is depicted in Figure 1–1 with arrows that indicate possible causal factors in the development and manifestation of hoarding symptoms.

According to this model, hoarding is thought to stem from several vulnerability factors. Especially important among these are *biological factors*, such as inherited genes or neurobiological structures and metabolism that might predispose a person to hoarding. Hoarding runs in families (see Cullen et al., 2007; Mathews et al., 2007; Samuels et al., 2002), and a number of researchers are currently studying the specific genetic markers for this problem and how genetic versus environmental factors influence hoarding behavior. For example, the chronic indecision that seems to interfere with normal discarding may be an inherited trait. In addition, certain brain structures (e.g., the prefrontal cortex) may affect acquiring and other behaviors in people who hoard. Hoarding that develops later in life may be a consequence of traumatic brain injury and/or dementia associated with frontal lesions (Anderson, Damasio, & Damasio, 2005; Saxena et al., 2004). Research suggests that patterns of brain activity in people who hoard differ from those in people with other mental health problems, especially OCD, and from those without apparent mental health problems (e.g., Tolin, Kiehl, Worhunsky, Book, & Maltby, 2008). Thus, biology undoubtedly plays an important role in the onset and persistence of hoarding symptoms. More detailed reviews can be found in Saxena (2008b) and Pertusa et al. (2010).

Another contributor to hoarding seems likely to be *family behavior and learned axioms*, some of which are also embedded in the person's culture. Although there is limited research evidence for this part of the model, reports from hundreds of clients indicate that hoarding is likely to be learned from observation of parental behavior as children grow up in households dominated by clutter with little opportunity to learn organizational and decision-making skills. Some people who hoard recall parental directives such as "Waste not, want not" and "Better safe than sorry." These engendered guilt and anxiety when trying to decide whether to keep or discard an item. One woman recalled being so well schooled to avoid wasting money that she felt truly anxious when she tried to purchase a well-made pair of shoes she could easily afford at a moderate price—they seemed an extravagance she did not deserve, even though she knew they would feel better and last longer. Thus, family experiences while growing up can establish long-lasting patterns of thinking (sometimes called core beliefs about the self, the world, and others) and behaviors that are hard to break, even when they no longer make sense during adulthood.

According to the hoarding model, *concurrent mental health problems and mood-states* such as depression and anxiety may play a role in the development or expression of hoarding. The most common comorbid mental

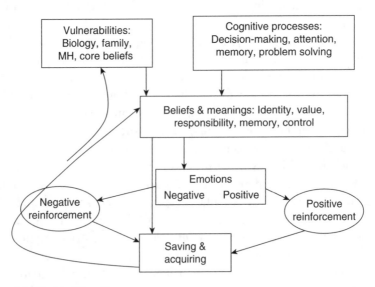

Figure 1.1: Model of Hoarding.

health problem is major depressive disorder, which occurs in more than half of the people who seek help for hoarding (Frost, Steketee, Williams, & Warren, 2000; Samuels et al., 2002; Steketee, Frost, Wincze, Greene, & Douglas, 2000). Such serious depression could play a causal role if the low mood prevents a person from making effective decisions or attending to everyday caretaking of their homes and themselves. Depression is also likely to be a consequence of severe hoarding as the problem becomes more and more debilitating.

Other common comorbid problems are anxiety disorders (Frost et al., 2000; Tolin, Meunier, Frost, & Steketee, 2010; Samuels et al., 2002). These include social phobia, which leads people to avoid social situations and perhaps to greater isolation, and generalized anxiety disorder, in which worry is the main feature. Certainly hoarding makes socializing in the home more difficult, but it is also possible that social anxiety could contribute to hoarding behavior. For example, one woman felt obligated to have things and information available in case someone might need it. Irrational though her fear was, she thought others would be upset with her if she did not have an everyday item they needed. On the other side of these negative mood problems are conditions such as bipolar disorder in which the manic phase might lead to excessive buying that adds to the accumulation of hoarded items. In a related vein, impulsivity associated with impulse control disorders (e.g., gambling, kleptomania) might lead to poor decision making and excessive acquiring. Furthermore, people with attention deficit and hyperactivity disorder (ADHD) may be more prone to hoarding if they are unable to focus on tasks such as sorting and organizing long enough to accomplish them.

Some *personality features* seem to contribute to hoarding as well (Mataix-Cols, Baur, Rauch, & Jenike, 2000; Samuels et al., 2002; Seedat & Stein, 2002). People with obsessive-compulsive personality disorder (OCPD) features may have concerns about waste and rigid thinking that impedes reasoned decisions about discarding. Perfectionism is a very common trait among those who hoard and seems to interfere with rapid decision making and add to negative moods as the person continually fails to meet his or her own inflated personal standards. We have sometimes seen paranoid personality features that lead people to be overly concerned about discarding materials with identifying personal information (magazines with address labels), even if this is very unlikely to result in a personal threat. Occasionally, a person will display dependent personality traits in which they defer decisions until someone else they trust can confirm the wisdom of the choice. Obviously, this makes it very difficult to discard items. Clients with borderline personality disorder traits experience fluctuating strong emotions that interfere with sorting, decision making, and discarding.

In the hoarding model, *cognitive processes* are thought to play a crucial role, and it is likely that these are inherited traits that derive from specific brain structures and brain metabolism. Chief among these problems with executive functioning is difficulty making decisions (Wincze et al., 2007), not merely about objects but also about ordinary everyday choices such as deciding what clothes to wear or ordering in a restaurant. As noted above, people with ADHD are likely to have difficulty sustaining attention on important tasks that affect clutter. Problems categorizing objects and papers can contribute to disorganization and difficulty recalling where objects were placed or where papers are filed. Most people who hoard do not appear to have significant memory problems, but rather are worried that they have a poor memory (Hartl et al., 2004). We have wondered whether people who hoard have somewhat different perceptual processes, seeing objects in a more complex light than most of us. For example, a pencil might be used to write, to prop up another object, as part of an art construction, or even other uses that most people would not have considered. This sort of thinking about alternative uses for objects, a form of creativity and complex thinking, may also be prominent among those who hoard, although this has not yet been studied.

The vulnerability and cognitive processing factors that predispose someone to hoarding behavior are thought to be mediated through various *beliefs and meanings* that people assign to objects (Steketee, Frost, & Kyrios, 2003). Research suggests that among these are *sentimental* attachments to objects because they represent a person's history. Objects may even be represented as people (with names, for example) or as having feelings, both forms of anthropomorphizing. Beliefs about emotion include the idea that objects provide comfort and/or safety and that the person might not be able to tolerate the distress of discarding something. A second group of beliefs refers to *instrumental* aspects of possessions, for example, their possible usefulness, the opportunities they present, the importance of the information they contain, or their potential future monetary value. A third group of beliefs concerns the *intrinsic* value of objects, for example, that they are beautiful, interesting, and/or fun. A more rare form of this idea is that items have special powers or effects, perhaps even magical ones. Other beliefs include the idea that the person must control his or her things to protect the objects or themselves and that the person has special responsibility for objects and/or for the people who may need them. One woman carried a wide variety of household objects around in grocery bags to make sure she had whatever someone she met might need that day.

According to the hoarding model, these personal beliefs produce both *positive and negative emotions*. For example, thinking about the beauty of items commonly leads to feelings of pleasure, excitement, or pride.

Thinking about protecting objects might engender relief or satisfaction. Recalling a sentimental attachment might produce fondness. Perhaps even more common are negative emotions that follow beliefs about possessions. These include anxiety following fearful beliefs, as in the case of the woman who thinks, "If I discard this, I will lose an important opportunity" and feels sadness or even grief about losing objects. Beliefs about responsibility for objects lead to guilty feelings, and thoughts about controlling possessions often produce anger or frustration when others touch the things.

In the final stage of the model, both the positive and the negative emotions *reinforce the beliefs and behaviors* they follow. As beliefs are reinforced, so are the acquiring and saving behaviors that are the hallmarks of hoarding and produce the excessive clutter. Furthermore, a home filled with clutter will tend to reinforce negative core beliefs that the person is inadequate or unworthy, and possibly contribute to other mental health problems such as depression and anxiety. At the same time, the hoarding behaviors interfere with functioning inside and outside of the home. For example, they often make it difficult to use the kitchen for cooking, food preparation, and eating; they interfere with using bathrooms, sleeping in the bedroom, finding clothing or important papers, doing laundry, and entertaining visitors. Unfortunately, some consequences of hoarding behaviors are dangerous, as when exits are blocked, structural damage is imminent because repairs cannot be made, fire hazards are evident in flammable materials near heat sources, and insect and rodent infestations endanger health.

Unfortunately, *insight and motivation* remain problematic among those who hoard. It is especially difficult to understand how those with severe functioning difficulties living in dangerous environments can remain convinced that their lifestyle is not problematic and flatly refuse to consider making any changes. This is perhaps the least understood aspect of hoarding. It is possible, of course, that people recognize that their lifestyle is abnormal, even problematic, but that they react strongly to other people's pressure to change because of intense fear of losing their possessions. Whatever the reason, this lack of insight and motivation makes it difficult for well-intentioned family members and service providers to accomplish change. For this group, motivational interviewing (see Chapter 2) is essential to help them move toward change rather than defending their right to keep their stuff.

At the same time that people who hoard present such problematic symptoms, many also exhibit remarkable *strengths*. We often encounter people who are quite creative, evident in their art or craft projects from earlier days before they were trapped by the clutter that prevents them from finishing almost anything they started. Some show special visual and perceptual talents and have strong associative thinking patterns, seeing features and uses in objects the rest of us do not notice. Unfortunately, there is as yet almost no literature that delineates these strengths, although we anticipate that such studies will be forthcoming in the next few years. Furthermore, many of those who hoard exhibit a strong sense of responsibility and concern about the environment and other people. They do not want objects to be wasted. Although their concern may be excessive, their strong sense of moral and social responsibility rails against the consumerism and wastefulness of our current "throw-away" society, a sentiment many ordinary people share.

With a good understanding of the sources of hoarding behaviors, service providers are likely to form effective client relationships that do not exacerbate the already limited self-awareness and motivation to resolve clutter problems. It is critical for human service providers to take a whole person view of hoarding rather than adopt a "medical model" perspective in which hoarding is viewed simply as a form of psychopathology and disease. Keeping the strengths in mind for this population will help human service providers form stronger alliances with these clients and persevere in the face of their limited insight and motivation.

CHAPTER 2

Special Challenges

Interpersonal Aspects of Working with Hoarding

Human service professionals who visit the home of someone who hoards often have strong reactions–disbelief, dismay, fear, and frustration. Such feelings are understandable given the very serious consequences that can result from severe hoarding. Nonetheless, it is critical for service professionals to show restraint in their expression of feelings or judgments about the living situation. As noted in Chapter 1, people who hoard have a mental health problem and usually feel considerable discomfort and shame when someone is in their home. Building a working relationship with them takes time and effort, and this investment can substantially increase the person's interest in and compliance with a plan to work on the hoarding problem. Assisting the person who hoards may also mean interfacing and collaborating with family members. The use of empathic language is essential to facilitate a positive interaction.

MANAGING INITIAL REACTIONS TO ENTERING A HOARDED HOME

- *Use respectful language.* Like anyone else, those who hoard will not be receptive to negative comments about the state of their home or their character (e.g., "What a mess!" "What kind of person lives like this?"). They also are likely to notice nonverbal messages that convey negative judgment, particularly facial expressions of frowns or grimaces. Imagine your response if someone came into your home and spoke in this manner, especially if you already felt embarrassed. It is important for service providers to use respectful language and to refrain from expressing judgment about the home, the individual, or the family, even nonverbally. At the same time, we know from experience that professionals who deal with hoarding on a daily basis need support, as hoarding is a challenging problem. We suggest that professionals identify helpful supporters and reserve their personal reflections for conversations with these colleagues.

- *Match the person's language.* People who hoard are often aware that others do not view their possessions and homes as they do. They can react negatively to references to their possessions that convey a negative judgment or devaluation of the possession. Words such as "trash" and "junk" clearly label items as having little or no value and should be omitted from your vocabulary while visiting the home. Using the words "hoarding disorder" or even "hoarding" is not advisable, at least at the outset of your work; many people who hoard view these terms as derogatory and stigmatizing. At the same time, hoarding clients often use words that reflect their positive perception of their objects—"my things" or "my collections." Providers can notice these words and use the same expression when referring to their possessions ("your things," "your collections"). This matching effort helps everyone get "on the same page."

Another important consideration as a guest in the home of someone who hoards is treatment of their possessions. For the person with a hoarding problem, each object is imbued with special meaning. The human service professional's unexpected handling of and suggestion about what to do with objects may be tremendously unsettling. To avert this situation:

- *Avoid touching objects in the home.* Those who hoard often have strong feelings and beliefs about their possessions. For example, they may view their possessions as extensions of themselves and/or experience feelings of comfort and safety in the presence of some possessions. Very often, when another person touches their things, they find this threatening and some report feeling "violated." They may also fear that the visitor will harm their possessions. Such strong emotions and beliefs lead them to seek complete control over their possessions. Visitors should avoid touching the person's belongings without explicit permission, although this is sometimes unavoidable when clutter is piled high and paths are not clear. When training new clinicians, we recommend that they take a notebook and pen to keep their hands occupied so that they are less tempted to touch objects.
- *Avoid making suggestions about the person's belongings.* Those who hoard often have extras of common items (e.g., multiple copies of the same

issue of a free newspaper, three blenders, dozens of toiletry items). They may also keep things they are unlikely to use in the near future, such as a walker for a middle-aged, fully mobile individual. Although it can be tempting to make well-intentioned suggestions about discarding (recycling, donating, selling, or disposing) some items, such direct suggestions are usually poorly received, especially early in the relationship when rapport is not strong and the person does not agree that discarding is necessary.

A premature emphasis on the removal of household items may cause undue stress and make it difficult to establish a trusting relationship with the service provider. To avoid this situation:

- *Focus initially on safety.* Discussion of the fate of the person's possessions will be necessary at some point, but avoid this during initial visits to the home if possible. At this time, service providers should clarify safety and legal requirements. As these become clear and intervention plans are made, a discussion of what to do with the possessions (donate, give away, sell, recycle, discard) will follow and may require the input of other professionals who can best guide this process.
- *Imagine yourself in the hoarding client's shoes.* Most of the above suggestions are recommendations based on how most people want those assisting them to behave. It is probably most useful to sit for a moment and imagine that you were the recipient of a visit because of the clutter in your home. How would you want others to behave toward you to help you manage your anger, frustration, resentment, and embarrassment? Insights from even a brief image of being on the other side of this relationship will undoubtedly be useful in guiding your empathic responses.

Not only can a premature focus on removing items make it difficult to establish a trusting relationship, it can also lead to detrimental and even deadly outcomes. On the island of Nantucket, Massachusetts, one health inspector experienced this unfortunate situation: "In all three instances of going in and cleaning these places up, within weeks of relocating the individual back into a clean environment, the individual passed away . . . it was such a dramatic change for them because we didn't realize the impact of the sociological change" (Brace, 2007).

Despite providers' best efforts to build a relationship and behave in a respectful and friendly manner, hoarding clients may nonetheless react negatively, evoking strong negative reactions even in experienced helping professionals. If you feel yourself becoming angry or upset, pause and take a deep breath. Remember that hoarding is a difficult problem to have and to fix. With whom might you discuss this situation later?

For people who hoard, it is helpful to acknowledge their feelings, especially when they seem upset (e.g., "I can see that having me in your home is difficult for you"). This can help them recognize their emotions and resulting behaviors and may help them calm down. Note, however, that actually telling the person how to feel (e.g., "Calm down, there's no reason to be upset") often has quite the opposite effect! Instead, speaking calmly in a conciliatory manner, while being firm about the changes necessary for health and safety, will help the person calm down. If the home dweller remains angry or upset despite your best efforts, indicate that you will not be able to continue the visit if he or she is not able to speak more calmly. If this does not deescalate the situation, arrange to continue the visit on another day. When rescheduling, ask if it would be easier to have a trusted friend or counselor present.

Family members of people who hoard may also demonstrate a strong emotional response. Providers may encounter frustration, anger, sadness, remorse, and other emotions in response to extended exposure to and attempts to intervene with their loved one and the clutter. Listening with empathy to understand the family's experience is important. Acknowledging that this is a normal response and suggesting counseling or other sources of support for family members can also be helpful.

DEALING WITH RESISTANCE

It is hardly surprising that people who hoard might not welcome a service provider into their home. In fact, they may not have allowed even close family members or friends into their homes for years. They may engage in behaviors that thwart or stall the intervention process by failing to respond to a request to schedule a home visit or refusing to open the door at the time of the visit. They may also become angry or distressed during the visit and argue or verbally confront the visitor.

These reactions can be extremely difficult for professionals to manage. Bear in mind that hoarding is a mental health problem. These are not lazy or immoral people who are being purposefully stubborn, difficult, or belligerent. They are trapped in a web of collecting, disorganization, clutter, and great difficulty letting go of things. Their problematic behavior is accompanied by anxiety and depression, problems with attention and concentration, and often a history of hoarding in the family. While others find the behavior baffling, those affected by hoarding almost invariably consider their possessions valuable. What may seem simply a bottle cap or an old receipt to someone else often holds special significance to a person with hoarding, on par with an important family photograph. Although those who hoard often deny that they have a problem, they are usually aware that others do not live as they do. It is little wonder that many who hoard have a strong desire to be left alone and find the necessity of having an authority figure visit or inspect their home highly aversive and anxiety-provoking, even if the person is legally mandated to do so.

Service providers can minimize conflict and obstructionist tactics by considering the behavior to be the person's best attempt to protect himself or herself against uncomfortable or painful feelings. People who feel attacked naturally defend or protect themselves, often by arguing or refusing to communicate. This keeps others at a distance, thereby avoiding unpleasant feelings. To address resistance, we recommend strategies used in motivational interviewing (see Miller & Rollnick, 2002):

- *Avoid persuasion and arguing.* It can be very tempting to try using logic and persuasion when attempting to motivate people to reduce the clutter in their home. No matter how well intentioned, efforts to persuade almost always elicit a defense of the opposite viewpoint. For example, comments that most people discard their newspapers within one or, at most, two weeks of receiving them or that people need only one blender make hoarding clients feel compelled to justify why they need to keep the newspapers ("they may have information that I need") or have three blenders ("in case one breaks"). Thus, trying to persuade them will have the opposite effect—the person actually talks himself or herself into keeping the items. That is, their verbal statements reinforce keeping rather than getting rid of items at a time when the professional wants to reinforce quite the reverse. So avoid arguments and even efforts to persuade as these simply encourage people to dig their heels in deeper, even when they do question the need to keep these items.

- *Use encouraging language.* When communicating about the consequences of hoarding, use language that reduces defensiveness and increases motivation to solve the problem. The following commentary recognizes progress, states the remaining problem in enough detail so that the client can understand the requirement, and asks for specific changes and ideas:

  "You've been able to make good progress clearing out your 'pit' [the client's name for a large pile of clutter in the living room]. I can see you've got more room in here now. I'm really glad. The next problem is removing some of these books because the inspector said they are too heavy for the floor supports, which could crack and fall through. That'd be pretty awful for you and me too. He said we [note the use of "we" to promote collaboration] need to remove about half of the books. I know someone who can help haul heavy things like books when we need him. What are your thoughts about how to remove some of the books?"

- *Highlight strengths.* All people have strengths—positive aspects of themselves, their behavior, or even their homes. A visitor's ability to notice these strengths helps forge a good relationship. For example, clients with hoarding may have rooms or areas in their home that are ordered and organized, even uncluttered—for example, a clean bathroom, or books neatly arrayed on shelves. They can be very creative and examples of their work might be found on the wall or among the clutter. They may take good care of a pet or their plants. Professional helpers can notice these positive features with statements such as, "I see that you can easily use your bathroom sink and shower," "What a beautiful painting!," or "I can see how much you care about your cat." Commenting briefly on these strengths helps clients understand that the visitor sees the whole person and is not concerned solely with problems in the home.

- *Praise change efforts liberally.* Individuals with hoarding are often habituated to hearing about what they are doing wrong or that their efforts are not good enough, whether from family members or authorities. Words of praise for their efforts to make changes and acknowledgment of progress go a long way to reducing resistance and motivating further change. Consider saying something such as "You've worked really hard today, well done!" "Great work on throwing out that newspaper!" Sometimes a simple thumbs-up gesture and a smile will do the trick. At the same time, we caution not overdoing it for clients who are depressed and unable to hear the positive statements, which do not match their own negative view of themselves. In such cases, avoid cheerleading but be sure to give modest compliments for clear efforts and accomplishments.

FAMILY INVOLVEMENT

Although approximately 20% of people who hoard live alone and are isolated (Samuels et al., 2008), others live with family members and/or are in frequent contact with family and friends. Accordingly, human service providers may also need to work with family members. The same strategies for communicating and intervening with the hoarding person are also valuable in interacting with family members. Family members' emotional reactions and beliefs about the hoarding, can range from identification to condemnation. The nature of these feelings is likely to influence intervention efforts, whether the family member is merely an outside observer or is directly involved in the work.

Spouses, partners, or other family members who live in the home experience the problems with clutter and collecting on a daily basis. Keep in mind that family members may themselves have hoarding traits or even a full blown problem, as hoarding does run in families. We have encountered situations in which both partners hoard, sometimes equally committed to doing so and sometimes divided on whether to seek help. Partners who do not hoard are often both deeply concerned and intensely frustrated by the problem. Efforts to help by clearing the clutter (especially if they do this surreptitiously) are inevitably received with hostility followed by difficult communication and disagreements. Those who try a softer approach by pointing out the problem may simply provoke denial of the problem or of its severity as their attempts to discuss the problem are met with resistance and anger. In some cases, spouses and partners may decide to separate from the person and problem, sometimes leading to divorce or permanent separation. In fact, it is puzzling that a surprising number of spouses/partners tolerate severe hoarding, choosing to remain amid clutter that is not of their own making. The reasons for this are unclear, but are likely due to a strong empathy with and commitment to the partner and/or strong discomfort with the possibility of separation. Whatever their reasons, these family members should be involved in the assessment and intervention process.

In addition to spouses and partners, other family members living in the home are often deeply affected. Minor children and older adults who are dependent on the hoarder may experience difficulty in family relationships, distress, embarrassment and shame, and even physical and mental health problems. In extreme cases in which children/adolescents, older adults, and people with disabilities live in the hoarded environment, protective services may need to be involved (see Chapter 8).

Adult children of people who hoard sometimes discover the problem in an elder parent and find themselves in shock—confused, embarrassed for their parent and for themselves, and chagrined that they were unaware of such a serious situation. Uncertainty about where to look for help complicates their anxiety. An all too common discovery scenario occurs when an elder parent is hospitalized following a medical emergency and the adult child visits the parent's home for the first time in many years. A typical initial reaction to finding unexpected mounds of clutter and unsafe and unusable living spaces is to begin an immediate clean-up of the home, whatever the financial and emotional cost. As later chapters detail, such unassisted clean-outs are not recommended until the parent is able to participate (although some unusual circumstances may necessitate this).

Family members of people who hoard are often altruistically well-intentioned. They sincerely wish to help their loved one live a better life—one that is free of clutter. Various family members, whether living in the hoarded home or not, have different ideas or approaches to helping with the clutter. Although generating ideas and strategies can be helpful, the person who hoards, especially if recently debilitated, can easily become overwhelmed and reject all offers of assistance. Family members who think that the best course of action is to clear the clutter without the permission of the person who hoards should be discouraged from this approach. In our experience, this strategy leads to resentment, hostility, and irreparable rifts in familial relationships. It is critical that the person who hoards be involved in the intervention efforts as much as possible.

ASSISTING THE FAMILY

Family members are often in the difficult position of trying to assess the level of risk or interference caused by the clutter. Human service professionals can be especially helpful in this regard. The determination is frequently made more complex by family members' lack of familiarity with the problem of hoarding and their inability to remain objective in determining severity. In fact, immediately after the initial discovery, family members are so shocked by the extent of the problem that they overreact, finding the clutter intolerable because it is such a departure from their values and lifestyle. This initial reaction will likely subside over time so the human service worker can engage their problem-solving abilities toward an effective but humane solution that will not destroy family relationships.

Some hoarding situations are sufficiently severe that they require immediate intervention because threats to individuals' or neighbors' health and safety are imminent. In these instances, families can directly contact human service organizations such as fire or public health departments or protective service agencies. Far more often, however, the clutter interferes with the dweller's daily functioning but there is no immediate danger. Accurately determining the immediacy of the need for intervention is of utmost importance in assisting family members and those who hoard. To obtain an unbiased assessment and guide for intervention, family members can enlist the help of community organizations and human service agencies. As mentioned in Chapter 3, many communities throughout the United States have organized hoarding task forces that are especially useful as a first contact for family members because of their ability to engage a broad range of services to assist with assessment and intervention. Alternatively, family members can contact departments on aging, protective services, and mental health professionals for help with hoarding assessment.

Human service professionals can assist family members first by listening closely as noted above, and then by recommending that they talk directly with their hoarding family member in a nonjudgmental way. This conversation can include talking about what the person owns and why they keep these things in order to better understand how the hoarding problem developed and what the owner most values in these objects. To facilitate these initial conversations and later intervention efforts, we strongly recommend Michael Tompkins and Tamara Hartl's book *Digging Out* (2009), written specifically for families of people who hoard. This comprehensive book approaches intervention with family members from a harm reduction perspective. That is, the goal is to first and foremost reduce danger and to accomplish this with the minimum removal of clutter necessary. If this is done respectfully, hoarding family members are more likely to be willing to take the next step of clearing more clutter. At this point, professionals can be especially helpful to family members by offering concrete assistance such as finding help with hauling, providing emotional support, and, if possible, serving as discarding/nonacquisition coaches.

STRENGTHENING CLIENTS' INTERNAL MOTIVATION

The willingness to address hoarding cannot be imposed from external agencies or persons. Professionals can find it tremendously challenging to assist people with hoarding to develop internal motivation to resolve the hoarding problem. This task proceeds alongside actual work to remove clutter and organize the remaining objects in an effective way. As noted above, strategies are drawn from Miller and Rollnick's (2002) client-centered, directive methods for enhancing internal motivation to change by exploring and resolving ambivalence. Motivational interviewing (MI) is a powerful approach that requires careful study and practice before applying it with clients. Some of these strategies are not intuitive, even for seasoned professionals, and are therefore best learned through specialized training. The 2002 motivational interviewing guide is accompanied by a series of audio tapes that are especially helpful in illustrating the methods, although professionals will need to consider how the material applies specifically to hoarding contexts.

Steketee and Frost's (2007) therapist guide presents summaries of motivational enhancement strategies for clinicians providing hoarding interventions. They include strategies such as asking for elaboration, looking forward and looking backward, affirming self-efficacy, asking evocative questions, and encouraging change talk. Tompkins and Hartl's (2009) *Digging Out* also contains specific strategies for family members to increase motivation to change. Although details of specific MI strategies for hoarding are beyond the scope of this volume, we provide a brief discussion of two primary areas of MI that we find useful for assessing hoarding and building motivation to change. These are (1) the client's perception of the importance of addressing the hoarding problem and (2) the client's confidence in his or her ability to change.

Importance of Addressing the Problem

Much of the time, people who hoard are not the ones most distressed by the hoarding and its effects. Although they may feel shame and other negative emotions, their awareness of the impact of the problem on their lives and the lives of those around them often seems surprisingly limited. Even when they are aware of the problem, addressing it may not be a priority. For example, in response to a clinician's query:

> "No, I didn't get to the homework of clearing off the mantel. I'm a very busy man. I have several groups I attend. I like to read the papers every day. I watch a little TV and then I doze off because I'm tired from being out and about. Then on the weekends I do things for church. It's a very busy time of year, you know. Well, and my son-in-law came into town and took me fly-fishing—that was a nice time. I like to be outdoors instead of stuck in the house doing all the cleaning."

Even when a professional draws attention to the importance of the problem and potential or even impending negative consequences, sometimes the person is still unable to recognize the urgency of working on the hoarding problem, unable to see it from anyone else's perspective.

> "Yes, I know the inspection is next week. That inspector—he has it in for me. I think the place is comfortable. It's a little cramped, but it's not a problem for me. You know, I like a lot of things around me and a person can choose how they want to live and this is how I want to live. That inspector needs to lighten up. It's his problem, not mine and I'll tell him so."

In such a case, it may be helpful to simply ask what the regulations are for the building or what the housing inspector specifically requested, for example, in relation to the possessions blocking the rear exit. This asks the client to state aloud the alternative perspective that he or she finds difficult to keep in mind and brings forward the idea of clearing the spaces. Further, it helps shift clients' thinking away from rehearsing their justifications for the current conditions.

To inspire internal motivation to address the problem, professionals can encourage the person to consider how a change in his or her hoarding would fit with the achievement of life goals. Consider the following reframe of the above commentary by a helping professional:

> "I understand that you are very busy with many things to do. I think it's great that you enjoy your life. I wonder, how would having a home in which it was easy to move around and use the furniture allow you to further enjoy using your home and to participate in the activities you like?" [Notice that the professional did not ask "Would having a home…" but instead asked "How would…."]

Encouraging Confidence in the Ability to Change

When people who hoard are aware of the impact of their hoarding and recognize the importance of addressing the problem, sometimes a lack of confidence in their ability stymies the efforts. Consider the following comment:

> "Yes, it is important, I agree with you and I really do want to live differently. This is just awful. It's no way for a woman my age to live. The thing of it is, I'm just not sure where to start. There are so many things everywhere and every time I get started, I end up stopping because I don't know where to put things. There's just too much and I get overwhelmed."

Encouraging the person to divide larger tasks into smaller, more manageable goals is an important step in encouraging confidence. Also useful are reminders that the person was able to achieve personal goals in the past and that the same tools and skills can be transferred to their decluttering goals.

> "I remember when you told me about how you implemented a filing system in your work office. I wonder if we might think through the steps you took to start that system. For example, how did you break the task into more manageable parts? Perhaps that would give you a way to think about establishing an organizational system here at home."

Enhancing motivation is a challenging, yet critical, component to setting the stage for change and sustaining efforts to address a hoarding problem. For the helping professional, many elements of assisting with hoarding present professional challenges. In this final section, we recommend methods for supporting human service workers.

SUPPORTING PROVIDERS AND MAINTAINING SAFETY

The demands on human service professionals are high and constant across multiple social problems. Hoarding is no exception. Many professionals anecdotally indicate that assisting people who hoard is one of the most demanding and time-consuming aspects of their work life. Not only is it a significant challenge to identify and implement necessary resources and supports, but the emotional demands on human service workers are significant. For professionals to meet the challenge of providing hoarding assistance that is empathic and goal-directed, we offer the following suggestions:

• Obtain collegial support and consultation
• Engage in regular supervision on hoarding cases
• Participate in multidisciplinary, collaborative community efforts to address hoarding, such as community hoarding task forces

Although the obstacles to successful hoarding intervention cannot be eliminated, they can be reduced. Professional helpers need to recognize the toll this work can take on their professional and personal lives to help them maintain their commitment to working with people who hoard. This means taking personal care of oneself while also giving care to others (see Murphy & Dillon, 2010). Supervisors also need to be aware of the toll that working with hoarding clients takes on staff and should plan to establish regular supervision times to allow frustrations to be aired and to help clarify what to do in confusing circumstances. We strongly recommend group supervision among those working on hoarding whenever this is possible.

In addition to professional supports, ensuring physical safety in a hoarded home is also a critical component that should not be underestimated. For example, when the home is exceptionally dirty or squalid conditions are present, workers should not be shy about wearing a face mask and/or gloves, while at the same time encouraging clients to use these protections during efforts to sort and remove items. If it is not clear whether the home has significant structural problems, the service provider can request an evaluation from a knowledgeable housing inspector who can clarify the extent of the suspected damage. Ideally, the inspector would have training in working with hoarding problems and be briefed in advance about the home. Such an inspection is needed both to ensure the safety of the home dweller(s) and of the service workers assisting them.

SUMMARY AND CONCLUSIONS

In this chapter we outlined strategies for coping with the strong emotions that arise on entry into a hoarded home and recommended methods for respectful handling of home visits. These include beginning the conversation about hoarding gradually by observing what is in the home without making judgments aloud or nonverbally and setting matter-of-fact goals for safety and meeting housing codes. Resistance to change is an inevitable part of hoarding problems that is best addressed by using motivational interviewing methods. We urge those dealing with nonvoluntary cases of hoarding to obtain specialized training and practice using these methods. Focusing on the importance of dealing with the problem and expressions of confidence in change can help clients see the possibility of change without digging in their heels to protect their possessions. Those who work with people who hoard should obtain personal supports that help release tension and keep perspective, as well as maintaining safety for clients. Although this is very challenging work, it is also very rewarding. There is little that makes one smile more than to see a person who was initially unwilling to let a worker in the door do a complete about face, opening the door wide and enjoying the small talk before the work begins. The ultimate improvement in the living situation that comes with patience and perseverance is worth the effort.

CHAPTER 3

Working with Service Delivery Systems

The Hoarding Task Force Model

Cases of hoarding that come to public attention often require intensive, lengthy, costly, and complex responses. Because multiple community, agency, familial, and individual resources are brought to bear on any single case of hoarding, those who encounter hoarding must respond strategically. A coordinated plan of intervention that maximizes resources across agencies is likely to achieve the best possible result with regard to reducing hoarding, benefitting the person who hoards and those affected by the problem, and long-term cost effectiveness. Information in this chapter derives from qualitative data collected on hoarding task force formation and operations in the United States (Bratiotis, 2009). The long-term impact of hoarding task force models, methods, and interventions remains untested and the policy implications are largely unexplored (see Chapter 13).

WHO BECOMES INVOLVED IN CARE FOR HOARDING?

Most communities are serviced by several professions and disciplines that are likely to encounter hoarding and bear at least some responsibility for responding to these cases. As noted in Chapter 1, these disciplines include, but are not limited to, housing, public health (including environmental health), mental health, protective services (for children, adults, and elders), aging services, legal (including civil and criminal justice and law enforcement), fire and police, medicine, and animal control. Although members of each of these professions may become involved for different reasons, the underlying intention is a united one—to ensure the health and safety of the individuals suffering from and affected by the hoarding problem.

Because hoarding can affect multiple areas of functioning and have a variety of associated problems, the laws, policies, and requirements that each discipline must uphold can include sanitation, safety, mental health, physical health, animal protection, and more. More often than not, several areas of a hoarder's life are compromised. This requires professionals to work together to ensure compliance with legal and ethical regulations toward the health and safety of the person who hoards and affected others. In addition to community, state, and federal agency involvement, often private sector services are needed to help resolve public cases of hoarding. For example, visiting nurses, occupational therapists, professional organizers, and professional cleaning companies may provide a portion of the intervention response.

Given the complex and multisystemic nature of hoarding cases and the demands on agency personnel time and fiscal resources, coordination of care is a critical component of intervention for hoarding. Agencies must share responsibility for various tasks, maximizing efficient division of labor to manage limited agency budgets. How the hoarding client perceives service providers can aid greatly in establishing and maintaining a positive intervention outcome. By their nature and function, disciplines such as nursing and social work are often (although not always, as in the case of protective services) viewed as friendly helpers. In contrast, others such as law enforcement and housing officials are frequently greeted with anxiety and dread as they seek to enforce health and safety regulations through sanctions. When carefully coordinated, these helping and enforcing roles can play off each other in a very useful manner as discussed in the chapters that follow.

The coordination of care often means that one or more disciplines serve as the "carrot" that supports and allies with the affected individual, whereas others play the role of "stick," enforcing laws and policies. This dual carrot/stick (sometimes referred to as "good guy/bad guy") arrangement provides needed encouragement while recognizing the seriousness of the situation that requires compliance that is difficult for the hoarding client. For example, if the Board of Health must issue a citation for a code violation in the home of an older adult hoarding client who is being seen regularly by a social worker, an initial conversation between the professionals before the citation is issued can ease the process. Accordingly, the social worker helps the client understand the citation and what is required to resolve the problem and also encourages and facilitates work in needed areas. Likely, the social worker (and any others who become involved) works to enhance the client's motivation and to cheerlead when progress is made. Likewise, the Board of Health helps the client meet the standards necessary for his or her continued health and safety by articulating appropriate and feasible expectations and instituting clear timelines and continued monitoring until the problem is resolved.

In addition to deciding what roles each discipline undertakes, thoughtful coordination of services allows cross-pollination of information and ideas, as well as collegial support and consultation to reduce staff burden and burnout. This is likely to lead to a comprehensive and accurate conceptualization of the client and the hoarding problem from multiple perspectives. Evaluating the person and the hoarding through various professional lenses is most likely to produce a successful response that takes into account the myriad challenges and opportunities in each case.

TASK FORCES AS A METHOD OF COORDINATING CARE

One method for coordinating agency responses to the multiple concerns in hoarding cases is through agency and community hoarding task forces. The first known task force in the United States originated in 1989 in Fairfax County, Virginia. Since that time, the number of hoarding task forces has grown exponentially as public recognition of the problem and its related social and community consequences have been acknowledged. As of 2010, at least 75 communities throughout the United States formed inter- and intra-organizational task forces to coordinate care. The mission, goals, and functions of the task forces are as varied as the communities in which they are located. The unifying purpose of all task forces is to provide a directed and managed response to hoarding cases that come to public attention. Whether in large metropolitan areas such as Orange County, California or in small towns and regions such as Northampton, Massachusetts and Wichita, Kansas, task forces provide public education about hoarding and coordinate dissemination of agency information, staff training, family support, and intervention efforts.

Task forces typically form as cross-agency collaborations; some smaller communities have chosen a model of intra-agency task forces. In communities such as Newton, Massachusetts, the town municipality prioritized hoarding as a problem that required a coordinated response from its police, fire, public health, social service, and inspectional divisions. Newton's hoarding task force is therefore comprised of staff from each of these departments and meets at least once a month. The mission of this cross-agency task force is to ensure that the various departments of the town government are working together to share resources and information to resolve their public hoarding cases.

ESTABLISHING A HOARDING TASK FORCE

Many communities throughout the United States already determined that there was significant benefit to organizing and operating multidisciplinary hoarding task forces. For those communities in the contemplation or early organizing phase, the following discussion may be useful with regard to ensuring that a new community task force will be purpose-driven and productive.

Communities considering developing a hoarding task force often benefit from an initial meeting in which all of the organizations and agency stakeholders who interface with the problem of hoarding are invited to attend. This initial meeting provides a forum to discuss current activities already operating in the community for hoarding and what gaps are evident in service delivery. This is also an opportunity to note which professions that actively engage in hoarding work are present and who is missing and should be included in future meetings. At this early stage, the task force chairperson(s) often comes forward and one community organization takes a leadership role on the task force.

Most U.S. task forces are led by one participating agency. A member who represents this lead agency usually chairs the task force. In some cases, the chairperson role is shared by two people representing two different agencies within the task force. Whether occupied by one or two people, some formalized leadership position is necessary to ensure that the task force is able to develop and accomplish goals. During the life of a task force, the chairperson role may remain constant, be transferred to a different agency, or may rotate among agencies. The typical responsibilities of task force chairpersons include coordinating and facilitating meetings, speaking to the media and outside organizations on behalf of the task force, disseminating information to task force participants, and overseeing task force committees.

Task forces typically have a regular meeting time. Some meet only three or four times annually whereas others meet monthly. In most cases, task force members agree that they will meet more often if an emergent situation arises.

As noted earlier, hoarding task forces are comprised of both public and private community agencies, including governmental, nongovernmental, nonprofit, and for-profit organizations. Although task force membership can include many professionals from a range of community organizations, attendance at most working meetings is typically limited to a core group of agencies/organizations. As one mid-size urban task force chairperson suggested, "We have about 15 people who represent 6 agencies that come to every meeting pretty regularly, there are another 30 or so on the mailing list, and at every meeting maybe we see one or two more of them." Task force chairpersons indicate that even though member organizations are not all involved at the same level, each plays a critical role in being aware of task force activities, supporting task force events, disseminating information, and providing resources for hoarding cases as the need arises.

The formation, operation, and sustainability of hoarding task forces vary considerably. Some task forces form for a specific purpose, such as hosting a hoarding conference or providing support groups for hoarders and their families. Others develop around specific goals and commit to a timeline for the achievement of those goals. Still other task forces are constituted because they have received funds for a specified period of time; these task forces often disband when funding is terminated. Although most task forces are not formally funded from a public or private granting agency, many arise and continue because the participating agencies provide a variety of in-kind contributions. These resources include personnel time devoted to task force projects and donation of goods and services, such as meeting space and printed materials (meeting minutes, handouts, brochures). Task force agencies also donate services such as dumpsters and clean-out services for people with hoarding who are working under the purview of the task force.

TASK FORCE BENEFITS

Communities with established hoarding task forces often take pride in the formation and operation of these voluntary bodies. Task force members report both individual agency and community benefits that result from task force operations. Members often experience enhanced professional networking from participation on the task force, as they learn who to call at what organization for various types of assistance with regard to hoarding clients, and also other types of clients. At an organizational level, task force participation can mean that the fiscal and personnel resources contributed by any one agency to a hoarding case is reduced by one-half to one-third because other agencies have agreed to share the intervention and case coordination responsibilities.

Hoarding task force members also report that education about hoarding is a significant benefit. Before their involvement, many task force members were unaware of the roles of other professionals, the perspectives of people who hoard and their family members, the community resources, and the latest evidence-based interventions for hoarding. As a result of participating on task forces, members, their organizations, and often the community at large are better educated about the problem of hoarding and the appropriate strategies for assisting with it.

Among other advantages noted by task force members, perhaps the most universally cited is the coordinated assistance given to people who hoard. Although not every task force directly delivers intervention, some coordinate services and others provide oversight to direct the hoarding intervention. In all of these cases, the coordinated systems of care keep the person who hoards at the center of the intervention, thereby limiting the number of confusing requests made by hoarding clients and/or by people or agencies with a stake in the hoarding problem. This encourages setting clear expectations that are more readily met by hoarding clients, enhancing the potential for sustained success in managing the hoarding problem.

TASK FORCE CHALLENGES

To date, hoarding task forces have been among the most effective intervention tools for public cases of hoarding. However, they are not without their challenges and obstacles. Few hoarding task forces have any dedicated staff whose primary responsibility is the task force. In fact, nearly all task forces operate with borrowed staff from agencies that attend meetings and participate actively in coordinated care responses. Some task forces have members whose agencies do not directly support their involvement but allow it as long as the employee's work performance on their primary agency duties is not compromised. In addition, an agency may agree to commit time to task force participation because of the personal interest and dedication of one or more staff members. However, when the committed staff member leaves the agency, the person replacing him or her may not share the same passion for working on hoarding problems. In such cases, that agency's participation on the task force typically declines or disappears altogether.

Another challenge mentioned earlier is funding. Some task forces receive local community foundation grants, whereas others have sought municipal (town, city) funding. Most task forces do not have dedicated funds to support their activities, and those funded initially from external grants usually disband when the funds are exhausted. In contrast, task forces that predate external funding are more likely to persist beyond the funding period.

Securing and maintaining leadership are additional challenges, particularly when the chairperson's regular employment duties do not include their work as task force chairperson. In such cases, the leader often feels strongly about the need for this work and remains deeply devoted to the role for several years. Gradually, however, this leader finds the duties and responsibility too much to manage alongside his or her regular agency roles. When a committed leader steps down, the change in leadership can be difficult for the task force, which may forego leadership for a limited period or spread the leadership role among members. In some cases the task force disbands entirely in the absence of a strong chairperson.

Although operating with altruistic intentions, task force members may nonetheless find themselves amid heated debates. Task force members may realize there are conflicting professional priorities about a course of intervention or the steps needed to be taken and in what order. For example, a fire official may insist that the building is structurally compromised and immediate action should be taken to condemn the property, whereas a protective service member concerned about the safety and permanence of the children living in the home is concerned that precipitous removal will jeopardize their welfare. In other situations, conflicting priorities may lie in a basic disagreement between the hoarding task force goals and the goals of the hoarding client.

The rights of the person with hoarding must remain the center-point of all coordinated task force responses. Well-intentioned task forces have found themselves in difficult situations wherein the desire to be responsive and supportive puts the task force and its participating member agencies in a compromising situation. For example, when one task force agency obtained a legal warrant to enter a hoarding home, it was the only agency listed on the warrant and therefore the only one with court permission to enter. Unfortunately, other task force agency staff members joined in and entered the home without permission, a misstep that occurred because task force members assumed that the warrant covered all of the agencies as part of the collective body. Task force member agencies should clearly understand the laws pertaining to warrants and their limitations in pursuing this course of action. Failure to use legal interventions appropriately can threaten the civil rights of the person who hoards and puts task force participants at risk for offending these laws. See Chapter 10 for a discussion of legal issues and their implications.

COORDINATING SYSTEMS OF CARE

Perhaps the greatest challenge to task forces is determining which member agency or agencies should respond, for how long, and at what point. This section recommends best practices based on information available from a study of task forces operating across the United States between 2008 and

2009 (Bratiotis, 2009). As noted earlier, intervention for public cases of hoarding requires considerable coordination among the agencies and personnel involved. The challenge of care coordination is evident in the following questions:

- How are public cases of hoarding identified?
- To whom is the referral made?
- How are cases triaged?
- Who determines the urgency of a case?
- What interventions are needed and who makes that determination?
- Who coordinates and manages the intervention activities?
- Who follows the case over time?
- At what point is the case determined to be successfully closed and/or no longer eligible for services?

Questions such as these are major topics of discussion among most task forces. Whether in rural areas, small communities, or large metropolitan communities, the current approach seems to be determination on a case-by-case basis. That is, no systemic overarching policy response currently exists (see Chapter 13 for policy recommendations). This is hardly surprising given the variation in community and agency structure, resources, and task force participation. Thus, community task forces must develop their unique coordinated care intervention for public cases of hoarding that fits their membership and resources. Below, we offer a model for coordinated care responses by hoarding task forces as a framework for communities to modify for their own specific needs.

HOARDING TASK FORCE INTERVENTION MODEL

The model depicted below is based on an understanding of the task force decisions and available resources from recent qualitative research (Bratiotis, 2009). Communities can adapt the proposed model to meet their regional needs, including regulations and laws as well as communication styles. The model is intended to help communities establish a systematic response that can be altered on a case-by-case basis as referrals are received.

Each level of care coordination requires decisions and community resources to intervene at multiple levels of the hoarding problem. These recommendations for systematic coordination of care may increase community recognition of hoarding needs and provide an effective way to manage these cases. Furthermore, the intervention model allows agency personnel to communicate the expected progression of care to the person who hoards and the family, helping them better understand and cooperate during the intervention process.

The intervention steps illustrated in Figure 3–1 begin with a community referral to the hoarding task force. This referral could originate from any concerned agency, individual (family member, neighbor, repair person), or self-referral from the person who hoards. The task force selects one agency to receive the referral (Level 1). To accomplish this, the contact information (phone number, e-mail, address) provided for the hoarding task force references only the referral agency. Alternatively, all task force agency members may direct every hoarding referral to the central receiving agency. This receiving agency can remain constant or rotate over time.

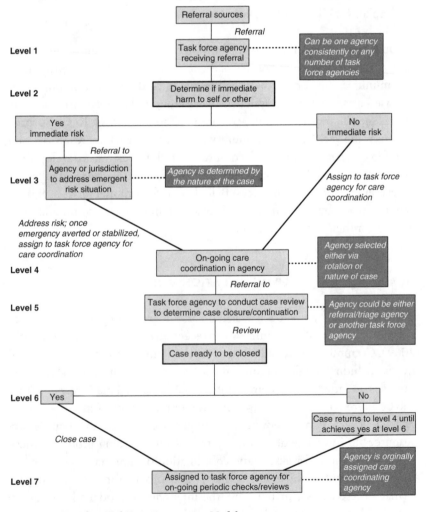

Figure 3.1: Hoarding Task Force Intervention Model.

Once the referral occurs, the receiving agency immediately conducts an initial screening for imminent harm to self or others (Level 2) and makes a determination regarding the level of care required, moving the referral process to the appropriate next level. If there is no immediate risk of harm to self or others, the referral becomes a case that is assigned to a particular task force agency for care coordination (Level 4). If risk of harm is present, a referral is made to the agency best suited to address the immediate risk (for example, the Board of Health for sanitation, the emergency room or crisis intervention team for suicidality) (Level 3). Once the risk is moderated or eliminated, the case is then assigned to a task force agency for care coordination (Level 4).

At Level 4, the selection of the agency to fulfill the case coordination role can be accomplished in various ways. This model proposes distributing cases across task force agencies that accept them on a regular, fixed rotation schedule or based on the nature of the case. If task forces prefer to use a rotation schedule, each agency takes a case in turn. For example, the Board of Health takes Case 1, the Fire Department takes Case 2, Family Social Services takes Case 3, the Board of Health takes Case 4, and so forth. The accepting agency then arranges for care with other agencies if additional services are needed. Alternatively, if the task force chooses to assign cases by the nature of the problems exhibited, some discretionary determination must occur regarding whether more than one agency should be involved. Rarely do cases of hoarding call for the intervention of only one community agency. For example, when the house structure is compromised and two small children are living in the home, a decision must be made whether Housing Inspection Services will accept the case due to structural damage or whether the Department of Social Services will accept the case because of the children living in the home. If this method of case distribution is chosen, some additional decision-making criteria must to be developed to direct cases to a primary coordinator of care.

Once hoarding cases are assigned to a task force agency (Level 4), they remain at this level of care. The coordinating agency requests needed services from the appropriate agencies to manage or eliminate the hoarding problem. A case remains at Level 4 until the coordinating task force agency determines that the case is eligible for closure or discontinuation (Level 5). The coordinating agency then turns the case over to a designated task force agency (for example, the initial referral agency or another agency selected to serve in this capacity) for a case review.

This final agency determines whether the case is ready to be closed (Level 6). If so, the case is officially closed and transferred back to the task force agency that provides the on-going care coordination (Level 7). Although the case can be officially closed at Level 6, it is likely that the care coordinating agency will need to monitor the case until a future time point (often 1 year) agreed on by the task force. If, after review, the agency determines that the case is not ready for closure, it returns to the originally assigned care coordinating agency (Level 4) for on-going coordination of services and intervention. The case stays at this level until it is again determined that it is time for review (Level 5), approval for closure is decided (Level 6), and on-going review and monitoring are needed for a specified period (Level 7).

SUMMARY AND CONCLUSIONS

Community service agencies are involved in many ways in responding to cases of hoarding. This chapter explored strategies for agency collaboration to coordinate care through inter- or intra-agency task forces. The task force approach has multiple strengths and some challenges, but provides an important avenue increasingly adopted by many communities to approach complex cases of hoarding, especially those that are nonvoluntary recipients of intervention. Although the hoarding task force intervention model is somewhat complex as it coordinates multiple levels of care, it offers a method of agency involvement and decision-making for managing the multiple needs of many hoarding clients. Unfortunately, at this time, no information is yet available to inform us about what models and methods work best over the long term for community task forces. The following case study illustrates the difficulty of multiple service providers making disparate requests of the person who hoards and argues for the need for coordinated care.

CASE STUDY: JANE

Jane was a divorced 52-year-old white woman who resided with her 16-year-old son and 12-year-old daughter. Jane and her children were victims of domestic violence perpetrated by Jane's then husband, the children's biological father. In addition to the physical violence, Jane's ex-husband also destroyed some possessions belonging to Jane and both children.

Jane lived in a three-bedroom home located in a town outside a large Northeastern city. The home is owned by her mother, and Jane pays her mother a tiny rent. Until about a year ago, Jane's children also lived with her at this residence, but she now lives alone in the home. Jane had a long-standing history of mental health problems including generalized anxiety disorder, depression, and posttraumatic stress disorder, in addition to hoarding disorder.

Jane's parents and brother found the condition of Jane's home unacceptable. They believed the clutter was so excessive that the home might be condemnable and reported Jane to the local Board of Health (BOH), whose staff conducted a health risk and safety assessment. The BOH determined that the home was within the range of being condemnable as it was in significant disarray and in need of substantial decluttering and repair. At the time of the assessment, the BOH also noted that Jane was mentally unstable. Her thinking seemed chaotic as she had difficulty presenting information coherently. She spoke faster than usual and she lacked focus, wandering from topic to topic. After the assessment by the BOH, Jane's mental condition began to deteriorate further. She was taken to a community hospital by her family and remained there for a 24-hour assessment. At this time, her brother also learned about a university-sponsored mental health treatment study for hoarding. Jane was persuaded by her family to enter the treatment study. Study staff members completed an assessment and placed Jane on a waiting list for the study; she began treatment approximately 3 months later.

After educating Jane about hoarding and its probable causes, and discussing her hoarding and other symptoms, her social work therapist began to help her organize her home. As is true of some people with hoarding disorder, Jane experienced several significant traumatic life events in the past. The strong emotions associated with these prior traumatic experiences reemerged as she began to sort the clutter in the home, which included clothing, kitchen items, books, old toys and games, and many other objects. She also worked to understand and master her trauma-related difficulties. Jane was successful in learning to sort and organize her possessions, but she was unable to discard any objects for most of her first year of treatment. Likewise, Jane also had a serious buying problem, using the positive emotions associated with acquiring to offset negative feelings linked to her past traumas and current life circumstances. In addition to providing a positive emotional experience, Jane's acquisition of free and purchased things provided her with feelings of safety and comfort.

During the time Jane was actively engaged in mental health treatment for her hoarding, her brother made a report to the local office of the Department of Social Services (DSS) regarding the safety of Jane's children. Without discussion and consultation with either the mental health treatment provider or the local BOH, DSS staff determined that Jane's children were at risk because they resided in a cluttered home environment. DSS removed the children and placed them in the temporary custody of Jane's brother and his wife. Shortly after Jane's children were removed, the BOH visited her for a second time to assess the home. The director of the BOH found it greatly improved, noting the organization, clear pathways, access to the furnace, and egresses. The BOH declared the home to be safe.

However, shortly after receiving this positive assessment by the BOH, DSS staff members called the local Fire Department to report their concerns about fire hazards and safety code violations. The Fire Department did not contact the BOH or the mental health provider to discuss the assessments already conducted and the interventions currently in place. The Fire Department determined that there were code violations (unrelated to Jane's hoarding problem) and stipulated that Jane had 30 days to bring the home into compliance with these codes. Although Jane did bring her home into compliance, DSS continued to find the home unsafe for her children, even after it passed inspection by the BOH and Fire Department.

Thus, during that first year after the family reported Jane to the BOH and convinced her to commence treatment for her hoarding, she experienced multiple challenges. She not only lost custody of her children, a portion of the roof of her house was damaged in a major storm, her basement flooded, she had a minor furnace fire, and she was involved in both divorce and custody court cases. Additionally, Jane was in a car accident that resulted in damage to her eye, which was repaired by surgery; she also suffered chronic back problems. Despite this slew of negative life events, Jane continued to make significant progress in decluttering her home.

DSS staff maintained their involvement with Jane as she continued her mental health treatment in a group intervention for hoarding to work on decluttering, resisting acquiring, and maintaining organization in her home. During Jane's second year of hoarding treatment, her children remained in the custody of DSS, living with her brother's family. Even after passing the Fire Department's and the BOH's assessment and completing the hoarding mental health treatment protocol, DSS determined that the home was still unfit for the children, citing excessive retention of toys and books that the children had outgrown. At present, Jane has continued active decluttering of her home and is maintaining substantial progress with discarding and organizing that leaves only a modest amount of clutter in the home. Sadly, Jane's children still have not been returned to their mother and home.

Case Discussion

Jane's experience with a variety of unconnected service providers demonstrates the need for a coordinated care intervention, such as hoarding task forces provide. An illustration of task force care systems that would be deployed to assist in this case is provided in Figure 3–2. The involvement of three separate safety regulating agencies—the Board of Health, Fire Department, and Department of Social Service—meant that Jane was being required to understand and comply with three different sets of standards and guidelines, some strict and others more lenient, without any educational and coordinating process. The lack of collaborative conversations among staff at the BOH, Fire Department, DSS, and the treating mental health clinician meant that there was no opportunity for these agencies to share valuable information, time, and personnel resources. Not only did this unnecessarily drain community agency resources, but it also compromised the client's understanding of what was required to resolve the problem.

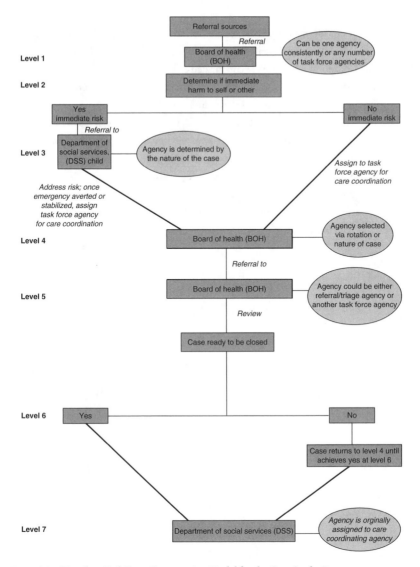

Figure 3.2: Hoarding Task Force Intervention Model for the Case Study: Jane.

The separate involvement of three agencies left Jane feeling entirely confused, unsupported, and even traumatized. She had difficulty understanding why different standards were being imposed by different agencies, and she had no single agency staff person to guide her through the process. Her mental health clinician tried to assist by contacting the various agencies as interventions were imposed, but was not able to promote collaboration among the agencies. Remarkably, Jane's tenacity and self-determination enabled her to achieve some gains with regard to correcting housing safety problems and learning organizational and eventually discarding skills, despite the lack of agency coordination. Unfortunately, the lack of coordinated care meant that Jane could not rely on any of the agency staff to provide a systematic approach to her hoarding problem.

Jane's experience might have been very different if her community had organized a task force that implemented an intervention model such as that presented in this chapter. The opportunities for sharing information and coordinating services could have reduced the number of home assessments, provided greater understanding of the nature and course of the hoarding problem, and, perhaps most importantly to Jane, a more expedient return of her children to their mother and home. Jane would have had a single point of agency contact to coordinate and monitor her involvement with the several agencies of the task force.

CHAPTER 4

Assessment of Severity and Risks to Self and Others

WITH CONTRIBUTIONS *BY SARAH L. DOWAL*

Hoarding is typically characterized as a private and personal difficulty. The chronic and worsening nature of the problem means that it can, however, quickly escalate to a condition that adversely affects the health and safety of the person who hoards as well as those who live in or near the home, including family and neighbors. As evident from previous chapters, this risk is often multidimensional and may require intervention from more than one professional provider. To determine the appropriate steps for an effective intervention, a careful assessment is needed. In this chapter we present the assessment methods that have been most commonly used to determine the nature and severity of hoarding symptoms and associated features. These include visual observation of the home, interviews with the person who hoards, and standardized self-report questionnaires. These can be used alone or in combination to provide a broad picture of the hoarding problem.

The assessment can be conducted by a range of human service professionals, including, but not limited to, those working in housing, mental health, public health, social work, nursing, professional organizing, fire, and safety. These professionals may be asked to respond to a referral or may be brought into the hoarding environment because of their expertise. Below we provide recommendations for conducting the general assessment and for the use of specific measurement instruments. Later chapters also contain assessment information pertinent to the professional expertise of the service provider.

A relatively standard assessment protocol can be implemented using the assessment instruments introduced in this chapter. Nonetheless, the subjective nature of hoarding is undeniable and both personal and professional factors will influence this process. For example, service providers' life experiences, as well as familial and cultural beliefs about tidiness and order, will affect their views of a cluttered environment. For professionals who grew up in a home that was kept very clean and well-ordered and who currently maintain a similar home, even a small amount of clutter may provoke strong negative reactions, potentially leading the evaluator to overestimate the severity of the hoarding situation. Thus, personal and family life experiences as well as culture and beliefs will inevitably color the judgment of even experienced professionals. In a similar vein, the culture, ethnicity, and mannerisms of the person who hoards will have an impact, positive and/or negative, on the observer.

In addition, professional differences influence not only how an assessment is conducted, but also the focus of that assessment. Whereas human service workers have significant concerns for the range of safety and health implications for people who hoard, certain professionals are likely to emphasize some risks over others. Thus, a housing inspector focuses first on accessibility, ease of egress, fire load, and working appliances. A nurse or occupational therapist will be concerned mainly about trip/fall hazards, the presence of airborne pathogens, and the ability to find and use medications effectively. All of these emphases reflect appropriate professional expertise and concern, and, in fact, the varied manifestations of hoarding call for multiple professional assessments. If appropriately negotiated, the variation in professional priorities in assessing hoarding problems is an asset.

A valuable part of hoarding assessment, then, is for all human service personnel working with a particular client to communicate their observations to each other. This helps develop a shared understanding of the person and the problem before designing an intervention. For example, a protective service social worker may observe family members interacting within the home, gather client self-report forms, and also give independent ratings of a hoarding client. Sharing this information with the housing property manager, to the extent allowed by law, is likely to be very useful in developing a coordinated plan of care. *It is critical that written consent be obtained as required by each provider's professional code of ethics before exchanging any protected personal information.*

Although each provider has specific goals for collecting needed information, several types of information may be useful to all of the professional groups involved. These include the severity of clutter and acquiring problems, significant threats to health and safety, building code violations, the presence of animals and their care, and interference in daily functioning.

PHYSICAL ASSESSMENT OF THE HOME

An informal physical assessment of a cluttered environment begins immediately upon entry into the space. The observer scans each room, attending to visual cues, as well as odor and other sensory cues while walking through the interior rooms and exterior spaces. Service providers may not be able to gain access to all spaces, but whenever it is feasible to do so, they should examine the standard rooms of the home—living and dining rooms, kitchen, bedroom(s), and bathroom—as well as additional spaces such as basement, attic, garage, storage areas, yard, and car. This provides a comprehensive picture of the living environment, the potential safety risks, and the overall scope of the problem in order to determine the types and extent of intervention. Assessors should be aware that the home dweller may also have other storage spaces such as a family member's home or one or more rental storage units in which other items, sometimes large amounts, may be kept.

HOARDING INTERVIEW

In addition to the physical observation of the home, the assessor will need to conduct a more formal interview to better understand the causes of the hoarding problem and important features that might affect intervention, and to identify likely avenues for and impediments to change. This interview assessment is best completed as a conversation with the person who hoards and with those living in the home if this is feasible. Chapter 2 provided some recommendations for how to talk to someone with a serious hoarding problem to avoid triggering strong negative reactions and avoidance of the very professionals who are trying to help. All of those skills will be needed during the hoarding interview. Ideally, a mental health professional (social worker, protective caseworker, counselor, psychiatric nurse) would conduct this interview, but other professionals with good skills in dealing with sensitive issues can also do so.

The assessment interview may require more than one visit to the office and/or to the home. An in-home interview is ideal as this allows the questioner to ask about immediate observations (for example, what things are kept and why, organizational systems or lack thereof). The following topics can be covered to the extent that this is possible:

- Onset and duration of the hoarding problem
- Home environment and its contents (especially squalid conditions such as molding food, rodent activity, animal excrement, and poor personal hygiene)
- Home dwellers' thoughts and feelings about the possessions
- Current acquiring (what is collected, when, and how)
- Reasons for saving items that are common in the home
- Strategies for organizing belongings
- Role of family, friends, and community members (in acquiring and removing items, complaints about the property, etc.)
- Immediate and long-term threats to health or safety
- Problems that have resulted from hoarding
- Previous interventions and/or attempts to clear the clutter and the outcomes
- Personal goals and values with regard to the current and future use of the home

We recommend that mental health professionals use the Hoarding Interview available in Steketee and Frost's (2007) clinical guide. We have included a modified version of this instrument in the Appendix suitable for use by professionals who may not have a mental health background.

STANDARDIZED ASSESSMENT INSTRUMENTS

Because assessing the nature and severity of hoarding and its consequences can be challenging, we recommend several standard instruments that have been developed and tested for reliability and validity by clinical researchers. Originally created to assess mental health aspects of the problem, these measures are now widely available and suitable for use across multiple human service disciplines. Several are available in the *Compulsive Hoarding and Acquiring* therapist guide and client workbook by Steketee and Frost (2007). We have included those that are most relevant for readers of this volume in the appendices.

Measures for Use by Both Providers and Clients

Several hoarding measures can be completed either by a service provider as an assessor rating or by the person who hoards as a self-report scale.

They include the Hoarding Rating Scale, the Clutter Image Rating, and the Activities of Daily Living for Hoarding. Each of these is described below with information about its usefulness, how to administer and score the measure, and the meaning of the scores. For all of these instruments, a comparison of the service provider's rating with the client's rating can shed light on the client's level of insight about the hoarding problem. For example, if both ratings are closely matched, insight is likely to be good, whereas substantial discrepancies (for example, provider ratings are substantially higher [more severe] than the client's) may signal poor insight and limited motivation for intervention. Such discrepancies might indicate the need to use motivational interviewing strategies before attempting substantial intervention on the clutter.

The **Hoarding Rating Scale** (HRS; Tolin, Frost, & Steketee, 2010) is a simple 5-item scale that assesses the severity of the main features of hoarding, including clutter, difficulty discarding, acquisition, distress, and functional impairment. The rater asks each question in turn and scores each symptom on a scale ranging from 0 (no problem) to 8 (extreme problem). Anchor points on the scale help to decide what rating to give, and experience with a range of cases of hoarding will help providers become more consistent and accurate. This measure takes only 5 to 10 minutes to complete and provides information about the clinical level of hoarding symptoms, as well as an overall severity rating. Tolin and colleagues (2010) studied more than 70 people with hoarding problems and compared them to people with other types of clinical diagnoses and with community samples. The raters in this study completed the HRS during a clinic interview and also in participants' homes. The items in this measure were internally consistent (closely correlated with each other) and the assessors' ratings were highly reliable across the home and clinic settings. In addition, the HRS scores clearly distinguished people who hoard (much higher scores) from those who did not, and the scores on this measure were strongly correlated with other well-known measures of hoarding behavior.

To qualify for a clinical rating of hoarding disorder, the client should score at least moderate (4 or above) on both clutter and difficulty discarding, as well as on either distress *or* functional impairment (only one of these needs to be moderate and often it is the impairment rating because many clients do not recognize the severity of their hoarding symptoms). Total scores on the HRS can range from 0 to 40, and most participants in research studies have average scores of about 24. Those with mild but significant hoarding might score as low as 16 and those with severe symptoms score above 30. The HRS is given in the Appendix.

The **Clutter Image Rating** (CIR; Frost, Steketee, Tolin, & Renaud, 2008) was developed to overcome problems associated with clients who overreport or underreport the severity of their hoarding symptoms. It is a pictorial measure that uses nine pictures for each of three main rooms in typical homes (kitchen, living room, and bedroom) to assess the severity of clutter. The pictures are numbered from 1 = no clutter to 9 = severe clutter (covering most of the space in the room). Professionals and clients can complete this measure by simply reviewing the nine standard photographs and selecting the picture that most closely matches the room in the home. Assessors and clients can rate additional rooms in the dwelling using the living room pictures to assess the amount of clutter. Clients who score 4 or more on any room are considered to have clinically significant clutter problems in that room. However, remember that this does not mean they would qualify for a diagnosis of hoarding as clinically significant hoarding requires not only moderate clutter but also difficulty discarding and impairment in functioning, which are best measured using other instruments (Hoarding Interview, HRS, and SI-R) recommended here.

Researchers examined the reliability and validity of the CIR in two separate studies (Frost et al., 2008). Their findings indicated very good reliability when the home was rated separately on two occasions a few weeks apart (test-retest reliability), and there was good convergence between the interviewer's and the client's ratings of the home (interrater reliability). In addition, CIR scores were strongly related to scores on other standard questionnaire and interview measures of hoarding (convergent validity) and were not very closely related to scales that measured other traits (discriminant validity). This instrument is very easy to use for the initial assessment of overall clutter severity and determining which rooms are most affected and will likely be targets for intervention. The CIR also helps gauge progress during intervention efforts. The CIR is available in the Appendix.

QUESTIONNAIRES FOR CLIENTS

In addition to the measures described above, two questionnaires that assess overall symptoms of hoarding and beliefs associated with possessions can be given to clients to complete. These are also standardized instruments, scientifically studied for reliability and validity.

The **Saving Inventory-Revised** (SI-R; Frost, Steketee, & Grisham, 2004) is a 23-item scale that includes three subscales to measure the essential symptoms of hoarding, including difficulty discarding, clutter, and acquiring. This self-report questionnaire is one of the most widely used measures of hoarding and is easy to for most clients to complete within 5–10 minutes, although some people who have problems with decision-making may agonize over what number to assign to each question and take longer.

When this happens, ask the client to answer quickly without thinking too much about the answer as their first reaction is usually the best choice.

The SI-R has been used extensively in research on people with clinically significant hoarding problems (e.g., Steketee, Frost, Tolin, Rasmussen, & Brown, 2010). It has shown good internal consistency (the items are related to each other) and good reliability over time. In addition, it clearly distinguished hoarding participants from nonhoarding comparison groups and was strongly correlated with other measures of hoarding and less related to nonhoarding measures of mood and other psychiatric symptoms.

The total SI-R score for most hoarding clients averages about 50 and scores of 40 or higher typically indicate clinically significant hoarding problems. With regard to the 9-item clutter subscale score, a score of 15 and above would likely indicate hoarding problems; 16 and above would be a clinical score for the 7-item difficulty discarding subscale, and 10 and above is a problematic score for the 7-item acquiring subscale. We have included the SI-R in the Appendix.

The **Saving Cognitions Inventory** (SCI; Steketee, Frost, & Kyrios, 2003) is a 24-item questionnaire that assesses beliefs clients experience regarding emotional attachment, need for control over possessions, responsibility for possessions, and concerns about memory. Examples of items are, "Throwing away this possession is like throwing away a part of me"; "No one has the right to touch my possessions"; "I am responsible for the well-being of this possession"; and "My memory is so bad I must leave this in sight or I'll forget about it." The rating scale ranges from 1 = not at all to 7 = very much. This scale is scored by summing the items within each of the four subscales and summing all items for a total score. Total scores of 85 and higher signal problematic beliefs associated with hoarding problems. Clinical hoarding scores on subscales are likely to be above the following numbers: 25 for emotional attachment, 18 for memory, 12 for control, and 18 for responsibility. In research studies of this measure, the subscales that were based on factor analyses were internally consistent and had good validity. This measure is most useful for mental health providers who plan to help clients change their beliefs about themselves and their possessions using cognitive and behavioral interventions. This instrument is available for clinical use in the therapist guide and client workbook by Steketee and Frost (2007).

OTHER MEASURES FOR ASSESSING HOARDING

Some professional groups may use discipline-specific assessment measures, focusing their assessment on the primary goals of their involvement with the person who hoards. For example, a housing inspector will use a housing-specific assessment instrument to determine the adequacy of pathways, access to exits, and fire load (see Chapter 6). Likewise, a professional organizer may use the Clutter Hoarding Scale (Chapter 12). Later chapters of this book reference specific assessment instruments that pertain to these specialized roles.

The **Activities of Daily Living for Hoarding** (ADL-H; reported in Grisham, Frost, Steketee, Kim, & Hood, 2006) captures the extent to which ordinary activities can be accomplished in the context of the hoarding problem, as well as the specific risks associated with the clutter and hoarding behavior. This measure inquires about how much the hoarding interferes with 16 ordinary activities such as bathing, dressing, and preparing meals. These items are scored by summing all items except those that are rated "not applicable" and dividing by the number of scored items to obtain an average score. A score in the 3 range is likely to indicate substantial problems with functioning due to clutter. In addition to these activities, seven questions pertain to the quality of living conditions (for example, presence of rotten food, insect infestation) and six items refer to safety and health concerns, such as fire hazards and unsanitary conditions. These two additional subscales are scored separately in the same way as the activity items.

This measure has not yet been studied to determine its reliability and validity in the context of hoarding and other instruments that assess hoarding severity. Its greatest value is in helping providers determine whether there are particular activities the client recognizes as seriously problematic. Providers can explore ways to fix the problems by addressing the hoarding concerns. Often, clients are more willing to commit to goals that will improve their ability to do things in their home that they want to do, rather than goals that focus on removing treasured items to clear space. A preliminary version of the ADL-H is provided in the Appendix.

The **Home Environment Inventory** (HEI; Rasmussen, Steketee, Brown, Frost, & Tolin, 2010) is a 15-item questionnaire that enables providers to rate the extent to which they observe squalid conditions in the home. The HEI is most useful when the assessor is concerned about squalid conditions. The measure includes questions about cleanliness in the home (for example, rotten food, dirty linens, containers and surfaces, insects, human/animal waste), as well as behaviors including doing the dishes and cleaning the bathroom. Items are scored from 0 = no presence of squalor to 3 = severe symptoms, and there are specific descriptors for each scale point to help make ratings consistent across raters. Although a formal scoring system has not been established, we recommend summing the scores across all items; scores may range from 0 to 45. Significant concern about squalor would arise when scores reach 20 or above.

The HEI was studied in almost 800 Internet research participants whose hoarding ranged from minimal to severe according to standard self-report measures, although the degree of hoarding symptoms could not be independently verified by an experienced professional. In this study, the HEI proved to be reliable and correlated well with measures of hoarding. It is interesting that it also correlated with negative mood, suggesting that squalid conditions might reflect some depression in hoarding clients. To date the HEI has been completed only by clients, but we recommend completion by an assessor as many clients will be reluctant to disclose squalid conditions in their homes. The 15-item HEI derived from preliminary testing is provided in the Appendix.

Finally, the **HOMES Multidisciplinary Risk Assessment** (HOMES; Bratiotis, 2009) is a new instrument developed to address the need for various service providers to have a common understanding of a range of problems associated with hoarding. This simple instrument is a check-list that can be used by anyone who encounters a hoarding situation, regardless of professional training or orientation. It is deliberately brief and makes minimal use of formal rating scales as it is designed to identify significant risks associated with hoarding across five domains: health, obstacles, mental health, endangerment, and structure and safety. The HOMES has not been empirically tested. It is available in the Appendix.

In the spirit of the HOMES assessment measure, the remaining chapters suggest how various professional groups understand, approach, assess, and intervene with the problem of hoarding. One thing is apparent: no one professional orientation or group is positioned to provide all the answers or even the best answers.

SUMMARY AND CONCLUSIONS

As evident from the above descriptions, there are multiple ways to assess the severity and features of hoarding problems. These include questionnaires and pictorial measures that can be self-rated or scored by an independent person such as a clinician or service provider who interviews the client and visits the home. Most useful for various service providers are pictorial measures such as the Clutter Image Rating and behavioral measures such as the Activities of Daily Living for Hoarding that document basic activities affected by the clutter problem. Other instruments with special value include the HOMES instrument designed for a wide range of observers to provide a broad overview using a relatively simple format for making the assessment. In most hoarding cases, it is important to choose an instrument that can be used repeatedly to assess the current status of the home and the person's capacity, and also to track improvement or deterioration over time.

CASE STUDY: JOHN

John was a single 50-year-old African-American man who resided alone in a two-bedroom apartment located in a large Northeastern city. The building is owned by a landlord who lives in the upstairs unit. John paid his rent with his social security income as he was unable to work for the past few years because of a physical disability. He suffered from chronic pain due to a long-standing joint condition diagnosed when he was 18 years old. His mental health history includes major depression in addition to hoarding disorder.

John grew up with several brothers and sisters. Although his family did not live in poverty, they had few material goods and he often wore hand-me-down clothing. Among his hoarding symptoms, John acquired clothing because he feared he might run out of something he needed and would be confined to his home due to his disability. He visited Goodwill or other thrift stores to purchase inexpensive clothing items and liked to feel well dressed and look "put together." John described certain clothing items as ties to the past when he was working and held on to them in the hopes he would be able to return to work. John's father was critical of him throughout his life and John expressed feelings of unworthiness. He rarely sought help from others due to these feelings and experienced anxiety and stress at the thought of someone entering his home. The clinician assigned to assess John's home was the first person to enter his home in the past 10 years.

John hoarded for most of his adult life, and acquired and lost multiple storage units due to his inability to pay the monthly fee. He recently experienced the loss of a long-standing relationship due to his partner's frustration with his hoarding behavior. Chronic pain and low mood have often limited his efforts to work on discarding.

Before the clinician's home visit, John completed the Clutter Image Rating (CIR) and Hoarding Rating Scale (HRS) as self-report forms. Following the visit, he and the clinician filled out his hoarding model (see Chapter 1) to help him articulate his thoughts and beliefs about possessions and to gain more insight into the sources of his hoarding problem. The day before the visit, the clinician checked in with John by phone to explain the home visit procedure and obtain a general rating of distress. John reported that he felt quite uncomfortable, 8 on a scale from 1 to 10, with 10 being the most discomfort he had ever felt. John reported feeling embarrassed about the state of his home and fearful that the clinician might force him to throw things away. The clinician was able to discuss these fears with John and his discomfort reduced to 5 by the end of the conversation. On the morning of the home visit, John's anxiety rating was 7 but fell to 4 after the clinician spent about 20 minutes in the home.

During the visit, the clinician observed the home and John's sorting and discarding behavior. On entering the home, it was difficult to get through the door because clutter blocked the entry way. Shades were drawn tightly to cover all windows, and piles of clutter covered the floor and most of the furniture surfaces. The clinician noticed mainly newspapers, other assorted papers, bottles, cans, and clothing. It was difficult to move around the home, and there was no clear pathway due to the piles of clothing and other items, although efforts at organization were evident in the presence of some large storage containers. Despite this, John often lost track of important papers or items. There was no evidence of squalid conditions at the time of the assessment. John's personal goal was to have his living room area clear in order to have family and friends visit his home in the future.

The clinician toured the entire apartment and assigned ratings using the pictures of the CIR instrument. The ratings were as follows: living room—7, kitchen—6, both bedrooms—7, and back storage area—7. John's car was mostly clear—2, and his closets were somewhat organized but overfull—5. In addition, the clinician used the HRS assessment tool, rating item #1 (difficulty using rooms due to clutter) as 7, at the severe end of the spectrum. On item #2, John had great difficulty getting rid of things that most people would not keep, again a rating of 7. Although John did not collect free items, he had a problem with acquiring significantly more than he needed, especially multiples of clothing or household items. Item #3 was rated 6 as he acquired things several times per week. As John experienced severe emotional distress due to his hoarding, item #4 was rated 7, and item #5, impairment including social and financial difficulties, was considered severe and also rated 7. Thus, the total score for the HRS was 34, placing him at the severe end of the spectrum.

John's self assessment on the CIR was slightly lower than the clinician's ratings. He gave the living room and bedrooms ratings of 6 and rated the kitchen 5, possibly because he felt he could still use these rooms. However, on the HRS, John gave most items ratings similar to the clinician's, with distress rated even a little higher at 8. The lack of discrepancy on these scales indicated reasonably good insight into the severity of his hoarding problem. After reviewing the standardized assessments, John and his clinician agreed that the goals of treatment were to (1) reduce acquiring so that additional items did not enter the home, (2) reduce clutter in the kitchen so it could be used for meal preparation, and (3) sort and discard possessions in the living room to create a safe and enjoyable living space.

During treatment, when working to throw away clothing, John's distress rating increased slightly as he feared he might need the clothing in the future. He also commented that he liked a shirt's texture or style and thought he might feel anxious in the future if he thought about wanting to wear it. At the same time, he indicated that he sometimes felt he was throwing away his future hope of returning to work. John was able to get rid of clothing that did not fit or that he did not especially like but had difficulty getting rid of items about which he was unsure.

Over the course of a mixture of group and individual treatment, John discarded several bags of clothing each week and established and maintained a schedule of chores and cleaning activities. At the end of treatment, John's assessments indicated reduced anxiety and distress surrounding discarding (HRS question #2 lowering from 7 to 5). John also reduced his acquiring (HRS question #3 from 6 to 4). After 6 months of treatment, the clinician's CIR ratings showed improvement in certain areas of the home (4 for kitchen and 6 for living room); however, John's self-report CIR did not show the same progress. This may be a reflection of John's beginning to view his clutter differently as treatment progressed; he originally rated the areas slightly lower than the clinician.

The HRS ratings also decreased from an overall score of 34 to a score of 27. Specifically, John showed greatest improvement on the HRS related to curbing acquiring (question # 3). As he began involving himself in social activities such as a weekly dance group, his symptoms of depression improved. John's insight and motivation to work on the clutter continued as he gained understanding of how the problem developed and began to realize that his continuous devaluing of himself was a major contributor to his acquiring and hoarding. That is, he often felt unworthy of having friends or potential partners and in some respects the state of his home protected him from letting anyone into his life. John also began to notice the cyclical affect his hoarding symptoms had on his depression. His depression contributed to his difficulty starting a discarding session, and in turn, the failure to accomplish the planned task increased his depression, creating a vicious cycle.

John was able to discard items each week by donating them to local charities and by recycling items, as well as significantly reduce his acquiring. He continues to receive treatment to remove more clothing, and also receives treatment for depression and pain management. John still struggles with organization and periods of depression, but he to maintains the areas that he cleared of clutter. Areas needing further work included both bedrooms (where CIR ratings remained at 7) and John's difficulty in discarding certain types of items, specifically clothing—which causes John greater anxiety. John made progress through treatment and the ratings provided significant insight into progress achieved and areas of further work.

Case Discussion

In confronting his hoarding problem, John first gained control over his excessive acquiring, limiting his trips to stores and questioning his motivation for purchasing items, including asking himself whether he needed an item before buying it. John felt the clinician's home visits and homework assignments helped keep him on track, so that rather than just saying that he was "doing this for himself," he began to believe it. As his CIR and HRS ratings improved and the clutter diminished, John was able to see real progress, which inspired him to continue working toward his goal.

CHAPTER 5
Hoarding and Mental Health Services

By now it should be clear that hoarding is a complex problem that manifests as clutter, difficulty discarding, excessive buying and acquiring, and negative and positive mood states that accompany these symptoms. These can lead to substantial impairment, but not always to distress, except among those around the hoarder. This syndrome, combined with the high frequency of comorbid mental health problems, regularly brings people who hoard to the attention of mental health professionals. This may occur indirectly as other professionals encounter hoarding and refer their clients for mental health services, or it can occur directly as hoarding sufferers voluntarily seek treatment. Regardless, the mental health provider often plays an important role in coordinating services and/or triaging cases to appropriate care for both the hoarding and comorbid problems. This requires extra effort to communicate accurately and helpfully with a variety of human service professionals, especially when clients are not seeking help voluntarily. Chapter 3 provided guidance for how to manage this process through task forces whenever these exist or can be formed.

Given their limited insight and motivation to reduce clutter, it is not surprising that many people who hoard seek treatment for other concurrent difficulties rather than for their hoarding problem. Tolin and colleagues found that 12% to 25% of clinic patients seeking treatment for various anxiety disorders (especially generalized anxiety and obsessive-compulsive disorder) reported significant hoarding problems (Tolin et al., 2011). Interestingly, the hoarding symptoms appeared to be related to their level of anxious and depressed mood and to impairment in functioning. These patients did not report the hoarding problem until they were specifically asked about these symptoms.

The most common co-occurring mental health conditions in people who hoard are major depressive disorder (MDD, more than 50%) and anxiety disorders—most commonly social phobia (about 30%) and generalized anxiety disorder (GAD, also about 30%) and to a lesser extent obsessive compulsive disorder (OCD, 17%) (Frost, Steketee, Tolin, & Brown, 2006). Attention deficit problems occurred in nearly 30% of hoarding participants in research studies and hyperactivity was evident in over 15% (Frost et al., 2010; see also Sheppard, Chavira, Azzam, & Grados, 2010). These problems add to the challenge of treating hoarding and may require additional clinical therapeutic efforts. In the relatively rare case of posttraumatic stress disorder (PTSD), a serious barrier to intervention occurs when the hoarding behavior is directly connected to the traumatic event.

Psychotic conditions or dementia may also be present in some hoarding cases. Our clinical experience suggests that these are probably rare among hoarding clients who receive mental health services, even among older adults. However, those working in protective service settings such as nursing homes are likely to encounter hoarding in this context (Andersen, Raffin-Bouchal, & Marcy-Edwards, 2008; Marx & Cohen-Mansfield, 2003). Likewise, a number of clients present with personality disorders (PD) or features (especially dependent, obsessive compulsive [OCPD] and paranoid personalities) that can complicate the relationship to the clinician and add additional challenges during the intervention process. Additional features that appear to be common among hoarding clients are perfectionism and rigidity, sometimes occurring in the context of OCPD. The case described below illustrates some of the struggles mental health clinicians encounter when treating hoarding.

HOARDING AND OCD

Hoarding has long been considered a subtype of OCD, but increasing research evidence suggests that these conditions are not as similar as once thought. As we noted, hoarding behavior occurs in a variety of Axis I disorders, including serious mental illness (e.g., schizophrenia, bipolar disorder, organic mental disorders, dementia), as well as behavior and mood disorders such as anorexia nervosa and depression (reviewed by Saxena, 2008a). Only about 17% of hoarding research participants reported other OCD symptoms such as washing, checking, repeating, and ordering rituals. This is a surprisingly small percentage if hoarding was a subtype of OCD, as the majority of people with one type of OCD symptoms also report another type (Abramowitz, Franklin, Schwartz, & Furr, 2003). An important difference between hoarding and OCD is evident in the extent to which the symptoms provoke discomfort and are viewed as repugnant. People who hoard appear just as likely to embrace their behaviors ("my stuff is important; I need it") as to find them problematic. People with OCD usually recognize that their obsessions and compulsions are unreasonable and impairing, whereas those who hoard are less likely to have insight, for example, saying, "I like it this way" and "I'm not causing anyone any harm" (Steketee & Frost, 2003; Tolin, Fitch, Frost, & Steketee, 2010).

Although not definitive in determining the relationship of hoarding and OCD, it is noteworthy that studies of OCD subtypes found consistently that hoarding usually stands alone as a distinct subgroup. It is sometimes associated with symmetry obsessions and ordering rituals (see the review by Calamari et al., 2004). In our experience, it is common to find that people who hoard also have strong perfectionist beliefs and behaviors, such as rigid efforts to keep things just so or to attempt to read a newspaper cover to cover regardless of the importance and currency of the information. Other types of OCD symptoms such as excessive checking, washing, or repeating rituals were not strongly associated with hoarding (e.g., Abramowitz, Wheaton, & Storch, 2008; Frost et al., 2000). Interestingly, the hoarding features of difficulty discarding and excessive acquiring were found to be closely related to OCD, whereas the hallmark feature of clutter was not (Frost, Steketee, & Grisham, 2004). An overlapping feature on which most clinicians and researchers agree is the excessive doubting and reassurance seeking that occurs when trying to decide whether to discard an item or complete a ritual (Rasmussen & Eisen, 1992).

Recent neurobiological and genetic research also provides compelling evidence that hoarding and OCD are different conditions, although the behaviors may overlap (Pertusa et al., 2008, 2010). For example, neuroimaging studies found different patterns of neural activity among those with hoarding compared to those with OCD (Mataix-Cols et al., 2004; Saxena et al., 2004). When researchers studied functional magnetic resonance imaging (fMRI) patterns during an actual decision-making task in which participants decided whether to shred a document, people with hoarding showed patterns similar to those of OCD participants who did not have hoarding problems (Tolin, Kiehl, Worhunsky, Book, & Maltby, 2008). Several genetic studies indicated different inheritance patterns for OCD and hoarding (see review by Pertusa et al., 2010a). Another difference between hoarding and OCD emerges in treatment outcome research in which hoarding symptoms have typically predicted worse outcome following medication and cognitive behavior therapy methods that usually work well for OCD symptoms (Abramowitz et al., 2003; Steketee & Frost, 2003, 2007). In fact, having hoarding symptoms has been a marker for treatment dropout and failure.

Overall, research suggests that hoarding and OCD may involve different biological, cognitive, and/or behavioral mechanisms. These are likely to require more specialized treatments, psychosocial and psychopharmacological, that target the causes of clutter, difficulty discarding and acquiring problems, especially as these latter symptoms more closely resemble addictions than anxiety disorders. Recent research (Tolin et al., 2007; Steketee, Frost, Tolin, Rasmussen, & Brown, 2010) indicates reasonably good success with a cognitive-behavioral therapy that utilizes a multimodal strategy for the multiple elements of hoarding. This treatment is described briefly below and in considerable detail in Steketee and Frost's (2007) therapist guide for hoarding.

PARTICIPANTS IN MENTAL HEALTH SERVICE DELIVERY SYSTEMS

In this chapter, we restrict our discussion to the several types of professionals who are *licensed* or *certified* to provide mental health services in the private and public sectors. The licensing and certification requirements and labels differ state by state, but in general the following professions are qualified to deliver these services:

- *Bachelor's level social workers (BSW)* usually licensed as Licensed Social Workers (LSW). They often serve as case managers, protective services workers, or advocates in social service agencies.
- *Masters-level social workers (MSW)* usually licensed as Licensed Clinical Social Workers (LCSW) or Licensed Independent Clinical Social Workers (LICSW). They often provide mental health therapy and related services (e.g., family interventions) in social service agencies, hospitals or in private practice settings.
- *Psychiatric nurses (RN* degree plus a masters' degree in nursing or MSN), usually licensed at the RN level. They are qualified to provide mental health assessment and intervention and often help triage patients to appropriate services.
- *Psychiatrists (MD)* complete a residency and board certification in psychiatry. They typically provide diagnosis, assessment, psychotropic medication, and sometimes psychotherapy.
- *Clinical psychologists (PhD or PsyD)* can be licensed as psychologists to provide psychotherapy and related mental health services (including psychological testing) in a wide variety of settings, including private practice.
- *Counseling psychologists (EdD)* are trained in Schools of Education to provide mental health services in educational settings (school

psychology). They can be licensed as psychologists and provide testing and direct psychotherapy in various agency, hospital, or private practice settings.

- *Mental health counselors* (Licensed Mental Health Counselors [LMHC] or Licensed Professional Counselors [LPC]) have a masters degree in counseling and are qualified to provide psychotherapy and related mental health services.
- *Marriage and family therapists* (MFTs) have a masters' degree in one of the mental health fields listed above (psychiatric nursing, social work, psychology, education) and receive training and certification in providing family therapy and family treatment.

Although hoarding can and does come to the attention of any of these professionals, social workers are most likely to encounter hoarding because of their large numbers and their delivery of services in the community and often in the home. As we noted above, many mental health practitioners may be seeing clients/patients with serious hoarding problems without knowing this because the client has not mentioned the clutter or other hoarding symptoms. It seems likely that many of these clients have sought treatment for depression or forms of anxiety disorders (especially generalized anxiety or social phobia) and do not report their hoarding problem because it provokes shame and embarrassment or perhaps because they are not interested in reducing their clutter and acquiring problems. Because hoarding is often missed in clinical contexts, we recommend that clinicians completing an initial mental health assessment include brief questions about clutter in the home, excessive buying, and difficulty getting rid of things (for example, items from the Hoarding Rating Scale described in Chapter 4 and provided in the Appendix).

Staff members in community agencies that provide direct services to clients are most likely to encounter hoarding as a primary or secondary problem. These agencies often employ social workers who provide protective services to adults and geriatric clients with a variety of needs. Among this clientele are people whose hoarding puts them at risk for fire, falls, health problems, and other concerns we have noted previously. For example, an adult child might contact a geriatric social worker because a parent has a serious hoarding problem. A common problem with these referrals is determining how to gain access to the home to evaluate the level of risk and impairment.

The state Department of Mental Health (DMH) may also be called on to authorize and provide mental health services to hoarding clients who are identified as needing assistance. Typically, DMH is state-mandated to provide mental health care to residents who are determined to have disabling and chronic mental health conditions (most commonly depression, bipolar disorder, and schizophrenia) and lack the capacity to identify and use other private or public resources. For example, the Massachusetts DMH sets the standards for the operation of mental health facilities and community residential programs and provides clinical, rehabilitative, and supportive services for adults, adolescents, and children with serious mental illness. According to the mission statement, the Department

"assures and provides access to services and supports to meet the mental health needs of individuals of all ages, enabling them to live, work and participate in their communities. The Department establishes standards to ensure effective and culturally competent care to promote recovery. The Department sets policy, promotes self-determination, protects human rights and supports mental health training and research. This critical mission is accomplished by working in partnership with other state agencies, individuals, families, providers and communities." www.mass.gov/dmh

Because DMH is federally funded but state administered, the types of services provided vary from state to state. Delivered via regional offices, the services typically include housing, case management, vocational rehabilitation, social rehabilitation (e.g., clubhouses), and in-home services such as homemakers or personal care assistance. The latter in-home services are often the most relevant for hoarding clients who meet the state's bar for serious mental illness.

ASSESSING HOARDING SYMPTOMS AND SEVERITY

In Chapter 4 we described several client questionnaires and clinician measures of hoarding and related features. Several of these will be especially useful to mental health clinicians because they capture the severity of specific features of hoarding, including clutter, difficulty discarding, excessive acquiring, and beliefs about possessions. These include the Saving Inventory–Revised (SI-R) to assess the main symptoms of hoarding, the Saving Cognitions Inventory (SCI) to assess beliefs about possessions, the pictorial Clutter Image Rating (CIR), and the Activities of Daily Living (ADL) scale which measures the extent to which clutter and related hoarding behaviors interfere with daily functioning.

We particularly recommend that both clinicians and clients complete the Hoarding Rating Scale (HRS) to determine the extent of difference between these ratings. This is a helpful way to determine the client's recognition of the severity of the problem. A discrepancy in ratings in which the clinician's ratings are substantially higher than the client's suggests low insight and limited capacity for self-motivated treatment. Under such circumstances, mental health clinicians will want to have a thoughtful discussion of the client's goals and values that will form the backdrop for each treatment step, as well as use motivational enhancement techniques outlined by Miller and Rollnick (2002) to increase motivation.

ASSESSING COMORBID MENTAL HEALTH PROBLEMS

As noted above, unfortunately, clinical hoarding often comes with substantial comorbid mental and physical health problems (see Chapter 11 for health-related aspects of hoarding). Because of the extensive comorbidity, clinicians are often faced with the need to determine the primary problem that merits immediate attention and what secondary conditions may need concurrent or later intervention or perhaps none at all. This requires a good working knowledge of *DSM-IV-TR* diagnoses (APA, 2000) that most commonly co-occur with hoarding. These include major depression, generalized anxiety, social phobia, OCD, ADHD, psychosis, and dementia. For clinicians who believe they need to brush up on this content, a review of the *DSM-IV* or courses on psychopathology will be useful. In assessing clients' mental health comorbidity, we recommend first identifying comorbid mental health problems and then asking about the onset of these problems during their lives and the degree to which the problem is causing distress and disrupting their ability to function. This line of questioning will help determine which conditions are long standing and may have predated the onset of hoarding, as well as those that are most impairing. Both of these can be used to decide what diagnosis is primary and should be treated first.

Consider, for example, a man 45 years old who sought group treatment to deal with hoarding that prevented him from inviting others to his home. His demeanor strongly suggested depression—a listless presentation, sleeping a lot, low mood, and few activities outside the home. On further assessment, it appeared that he had suffered from low-grade depression throughout his life with occasional serious bouts in which he sometimes had suicidal ideation, although with no plans or attempts to kill himself. In contrast, the hoarding problem was fairly recent, mainly in the past 3 years. Questions about his social life indicated that he was uncomfortable in many social situations and had few lunch companions or friends at his workplace. The group leader asked a series of questions to better understand the extent of his social discomfort and his depressed mood and behavior and their connection to his hoarding symptoms. It soon became clear that an important reason for not sorting and putting his things away at home was his low mood and lack of interest in making his home attractive. "Why bother?" he said. "Nobody comes here anyway. I look at the video tapes and just can't make myself straighten up the mess." In contrast, he did not have a problem sorting and organizing in his office at work where he reported that he was concerned that others would think badly of him if he left his workspace a mess. It soon became clear that his hoarding behavior was not improving after a few sessions and that his depressed mood was interfering. The clinician referred him for a formal medication consult and evaluation for cognitive therapy, both of which are evidence-based treatments for depression. The clinician also suggested that as his depressed mood improved, he might consider being evaluated for group treatment for social phobia as his anxiety in social situations and concern about how others evaluated him appeared to be the main source of his lack of social contact.

When hoarding is the primary problem, assessment of comorbid conditions helps identify additional problems that can affect the client's response to treatment for the hoarding behavior. For example, clients with attention difficulties are unlikely to be able to stay focused on any task, including sorting and organizing their things or making decisions about what to remove. Frequent short assignments and rotating across tasks may be most helpful for them. Anxious clients who worry easily may benefit from stress reduction strategies to help them manage their discomfort. Some of these clients will benefit from having background music playing and/or having another person around while they are working, even if they don't talk or work together. Clients who exhibit evidence of memory impairment are unlikely to make much progress without another person, the clinician or a coach of some sort, guiding the work. Neuropsychological testing may be indicated to determine cognitive capacity and identify intervention strategies that are appropriate. In general, when concurrent mental health problems interfere, clinicians will need to review clinical knowledge about these problems and use problem-solving techniques to identify potential solutions that will reduce acquiring and facilitate removing items that contribute to the clutter.

INTERVENTION

Many hoarding clients, regardless of their point of entry into human service systems, require mental health treatment to address their hoarding symptoms and/or other concurrent mental health problems. We have detailed how to implement cognitive and behavioral treatment (CBT) interventions for hoarding in the Steketee and Frost (2007) therapist guide and will not repeat that information here, except for a brief description of the therapy methods. This section will instead focus mainly on strategies for encouraging clients to engage in CBT methods, as well as medications, case management, and medical management when necessary.

Treatment Format

CBT for hoarding consists of 26 individual sessions scheduled once weekly in the clinician's office, with every fourth session conducted in the home. The last few sessions are less frequent, usually every other week. Most office sessions last about an hour, but home sessions are usually 2 hours long and can be longer if clients can tolerate the sustained effort. Unfortunately, client scheduling problems and ambivalence about working on clutter often extend treatment longer than planned as they miss and reschedule their appointments. In the most recent study of 36 people who engaged in CBT, the average duration of the 26-session treatment was about 50 weeks, ranging from 30 to 75 weeks (Steketee et al., 2010a). Highly motivated clients whose lives were not complicated by severe functioning difficulties or other health and mental health problems were able to finish therapy in 7 to 8 months.

We have also studied CBT for hoarding using group therapy models (Muroff et al., 2009). Group therapy has the advantage of using social interaction to encourage motivation to complete homework and reduces the social isolation so common among people with hoarding problems. However, some clients with serious social anxiety and/or personality problems that make social interaction difficult or contentious should not be included in group methods. Although the outcomes from these groups are not quite as good as from individual treatment, a number of clients have benefitted substantially in our 16- and 20-week groups (Muroff, Bratiotis, & Steketee, 2010). The best outcomes occurred in our most systematic groups in which assessments of progress were collected by an independent assessor who called clients on the phone or saw them in person after they attended group.

Treatment Methods

Briefly, CBT for hoarding begins with clinician and self-report assessment of hoarding symptoms and severity. Therapists educate clients about hoarding from a mental and behavioral health perspective. This enables

clients to put their symptoms in context. Clinicians then work collaboratively with clients to develop a case formulation (an individualized cognitive-behavioral model) that clearly describes the patterns of behavior,
thinking, and emotions for each client's hoarding problem. This is followed
by treatment planning to determine where to start in therapy (for example,
on excessive acquiring or on organizing skills).

Therapists use motivation enhancement strategies (Miller & Rollnick,
2002) whenever they judge that motivation is lagging. For example, when
clients miss sessions, arrive late, or fail to complete a homework assign-
ment, clinicians intercede with queries about why this is happening
without challenging clients to change their behavior. Learning to use motivational interviewing methods requires training because some strategies
are counterintuitive (for example, the devil's advocate strategy) but work
very well to help change ambivalence and reluctant behaviors. We strongly
recommend that clinicians learn these methods to help reluctant hoarding
clients. Chapter 2 provided recommendations for ways to talk with clients,
and Steketee and Frost's (2007) therapist guide presents a fuller discussion
of motivational methods. Miller and Rollnick's books and video trainings
on this topic are helpful learning tools and clinicians can often find professional education workshops on these methods.

During CBT sessions, clinicians apply several intervention techniques to
reduce disorganized clutter, compulsive acquiring, and difficulty discarding. Some strategies focus on training skills to improve organizing, decision
making, and problem solving, as most clients have deficits in these areas.
A central part of the therapy involves exposure to sorting piles of possessions to train organizing skills and to reduce discomfort with this process.
Additionally, exposure to acquiring situations (favorite discount stores,
yard sales, free offers, trash sites) is needed to reduce urges to acquire and
enable clients to gain control over these impulses without adding to their
hoarding problem. In both of these exposure contexts, mental health clinicians employ cognitive therapy methods following Aaron T. Beck's work
to help clients correct unrealistic beliefs about reasons for acquiring or
keeping items.

To facilitate direct exposure and application of cognitive therapy methods, about 25% of sessions are conducted in clients' homes or at sites of
excessive acquiring. In addition, some clients may need one or more "marathon" sessions of several hours each (we have done 3- to 6-hour sessions) in
which the clinician and several other team members travel to the client's
home to help with sorting, organizing, and discarding. This is most likely to
be needed in cases of extreme clutter and when the client has limited physical ability to remove clutter. These sessions are scheduled only with the

client's full agreement. Such intensive sessions typically occur after session 18 when clients have learned skills and can comfortably direct team members in advance about what items can be discarded, recycled, put aside to sell, and so forth. All discarding and nonacquiring decisions are determined by the clients themselves based on the rules they establish, and when a decision is not clear to the team, the client is asked to render a judgment.

These techniques are applied flexibly based on the initial assessment and treatment plan. Skills training, cognitive therapy, and exposure to acquiring, sorting, and discarding are often interwoven as clients make progress in some areas and gain skills and confidence. Therapists and clients together agree on homework tasks between sessions; typically clients contract to engage in some hoarding-related treatment activity several times a week until the next session. After clients make sufficient progress to consider ending therapy, the final few sessions focus on methods to prevent relapse. At this time, clients learn to manage future stressors and temptations without reverting to hoarding behaviors.

Mental health clinicians, especially clinical social workers, psychologists, and psychiatric nurses, will bear the main responsibility for delivering CBT to hoarding clients, but all human service professionals who encounter hoarding will need to identify appropriate referrals for mental health services. The temptation for most people who encounter hoarding is to want to jump right in to clear the clutter. *Resisting this urge is important*, especially for clinicians, as people who hoard must learn new skills to combat their urges to acquire, their disorganization, and their difficulty discarding, which generate the clutter. These become the focus of mental health treatment.

Unfortunately, at this time there are no alternative magic bullets for treating hoarding. Researchers have tested medications such as serotonergic reuptake inhibitors that are usually effective for treating depression and anxiety symptoms. In most studies these drugs have not been robustly effective in reducing hoarding symptoms, although there are some exceptions. For example, Saxena et al. (2007) found that paroxetine was as helpful for hoarding patients as for OCD patients. Although at present there are no specific medications recommended for hoarding per se, in light of the complex comorbidity that commonly accompanies hoarding, consultation with a psychiatrist regarding medication options may be helpful. For example, people with severe attention-deficit hyperactivity disorder (ADHD) that makes it hard for them to organize and clear clutter may benefit from stimulants. Psychiatrists may prescribe antipsychotic medications (usually in low doses) for people who are not overtly psychotic but who may be able to better organize their thoughts and process information more effectively with the medication.

As a general rule, mental health clinicians need training to deliver effective CBT methods for hoarding. Consultation and regular supervision are especially helpful for the first few cases until the clinician is confident in delivering the several therapy components (skills training in organizing, decision making, and problem solving; cognitive therapy; motivational interviewing; exposure to nonacquiring and discarding; relapse prevention). Although we and our colleagues in other clinical/academic settings provide frequent workshops in these methods around the country, access to training is still very limited.

When working with hoarding clients, we recommend seeking consultation and supervision, especially group supervision to help ease the frustration of working with ambivalent clients who are challenged in a variety of ways. We also recommend that clinicians who plan to provide CBT for hoarding identify and refer their clients to a second provider who can serve as a case manager or therapist for comorbid conditions that are so common among people who hoard. When two providers are working together on a hoarding case, we strongly recommend that they schedule regular check-ins with each other (with written permission of the client) to make sure their approaches are compatible and clearly understood by the client. In addition, understanding what additional human services are available locally to support the therapy process will be helpful. These include housing (Chapter 6), public health (Chapter 7), and protective services (Chapter 8), as well as legal (Chapter 10) and medical (Chapter 11) resources. The services of a professional organizer (Chapter 12) may be useful, especially if home visits are difficult geographically and the client has no one who can serve as a coach or assistant while learning skills and working on clutter.

TIPS AND STRATEGIES

The following recommendations derive from our clinical and research experience in providing clinical mental health treatment for those with serious hoarding problems:

- Take time to make an accurate diagnosis and to determine the contributions of hoarding, OCD, depression, ADHD, and bipolar disorder to the symptom picture.
- Utilize hoarding-specific assessment tools to assist in diagnosis and determining severity.

- Whenever feasible, coordinate intervention with other human service professionals who can assist with the specialized problems in each case.
- Learn evidence-based specialized cognitive and behavioral strategies for hoarding.
- Learn and use motivational enhancement strategies whenever clients display ambivalence about treatment.
- Obtain consultation and support to ensure that the substantial challenges associated with treating serious hoarding do not overwhelm the mental health service provider.

CASE STUDY: SHARON

Sharon was a 52-year-old divorced white woman living alone in the home in which she grew up. She lived away from home in another city for several years and then returned home when she was 37 to care for her ailing parents. Her parents died 10 years before she began treatment for her hoarding problem. In her home, she lived among her parents' furniture and personal effects as well as her abundant possessions. Although she lived only a short distance from two of her three siblings, Sharon saw them only once or twice a year. She worked full time as a senior administrative assistant in a large dental practice and also part-time at her local library on weekends. Her many talents include playing several musical instruments she owns and keeps in her living room and writing poetry. She was active in Narcotics Anonymous (NA) and was also busy outside the home most evenings attending NA meetings, performing, and taking classes. Her closest friends were her NA sponsor and a friend from a former job, and she also had many acquaintances. She herself sponsored people in NA.

At the time she was evaluated for individual treatment, Sharon received a primary diagnosis of hoarding at a severe level. She also had additional diagnoses of generalized anxiety disorder (GAD) and major depressive disorder (MDD), both at lower severity than her hoarding. She reported problems with binge eating some years before but this was not a current problem and was therefore not addressed during treatment.

Sharon was not taking any medication. Her overall hoarding severity was considered moderately severe based on an evaluation of the clutter, difficulty discarding, and problems with acquiring. On the pictorial Clutter Image Rating scale (see Chapter 4), she scored in the 5–7 range for her living room, kitchen and bedroom, again indicating moderately severe clutter. These rooms were passable, but with some difficulty, and could not be easily used for their intended purpose (cooking, sitting, entertaining). Interestingly, Sharon tended to rate her clutter as less severe than did her clinician, suggesting some difficulty with insight. Sharon also had a problem with buying more than she could afford (for example, office supplies such as notebooks and pencils) and also acquiring free items like flyers and newspapers.

Sharon's home was full of random piles of important and unimportant items, but she did not try to sort these and thus did not engage in a common practice of "churning" the piles as many clients do. She saved mainly for sentimental reasons and because she thought things would be useful; occasionally she reported saving because an object was just attractive to her.

As evident from her pretreatment diagnostic assessment, Sharon was also depressed. On a measure of depression, she endorsed feelings of hopelessness about the future, she had difficulty concentrating and sleeping, and she appeared slowed down during her assessment. Sharon also suffered from general anxiety about a wide variety of situations, including some obsessive thinking. For example, despite being a valued employee, if she did not perform a task well on a particular day, Sharon ruminated about being fired even though she knew this was very unlikely. Among these mental health vulnerabilities, she also reported that her parents espoused values of frugality and responsibility, and that her father also saved excessively; she felt these contributed to her hoarding problems. She had additional constraints in finding time to work on sorting because she held two jobs and also attended NA support group meetings and took occasional classes in the arts. With regard to cognitive functioning, Sharon had pronounced problems with distractibility and considerable difficulty categorizing everyday household objects. She was drawn to bright primary colors and for this reason often bought two or three versions of items in different colors.

With regard to her beliefs and the meanings she assigned to possessions, she acquired and saved things mainly because they seemed useful and offered her opportunities she did not want to miss. For example, over the years, Sharon bought several different tools to help her with her finances (e.g., books on budgeting, financial notepads, holders for sorting bills, etc.). Although she did not actually use any of these tools, she continued to save these items because they might be useful one day. She also held perfectionist beliefs and felt responsible for objects, sometimes stating, "I need to find a home for this." She had strong urges to control her things, allowing no one to touch her possessions, even her therapist. She kept newspapers and magazines because she thought they would help her remember important information. Safety and comfort were particularly important in her thinking and she stated, "My home is like a fortress." In fact, after her home was burglarized, her saving and clutter increased because she thought it might slow down a thief who was trying to get into her home. She reported a childhood trauma in the form of a brutal beating that she felt contributed to her sense of comfort from possessions because they didn't hurt her.

Sharon's acquiring derived from strong positive emotions she experienced when seeing items in a store; she reported pleasure, excitement, satisfaction, and pride of ownership on these occasions, only to be followed by negative feelings of shame and regret after leaving the store, even within the store parking lot. This led to considerable accumulation of debt as well as clutter. In fact, she connected these feelings to her former drug habits, articulating the parallel of the initial high from drug use and from buying unnecessary items and then let down and regret following her behavior. She also reported that whenever she experienced loneliness, rage, or anxiety or ruminated about past injustices, this increased the likelihood that she would acquire.

When the clinician asked about Sharon's treatment goals, she identified the following:

- Be able to play my musical instruments (drums, guitars) in the living room
- Have friends and family over to visit
- Have a safe kitchen where I can work on the counter and table
- Be able to take a bath
- Discard "noninheritance" belongings of my parents (e.g., my mother's leg brace, my father's old books)
- Enjoy more breathing space, beauty, and order

Sharon's treatment began with training in sorting items she brought to her therapist's office and later at home. This helped her identify some problems that exacerbated hoarding, such as avoidance of decision making. Sharon began by sorting mail during therapy sessions into simple categories of "keep," and "discard." Her difficulty making decisions, together with negative feelings associated with finances, led to difficulty paying bills and avoidance of opening mail. During the course of this work, Sharon reported anxiety, helplessness, and even rage about her past financial struggles. She connected her financial problems to her previous physically abusive relationship. In sorting her clothes and other items at home she exhibited some unique strength. She was not excessively attached to many things and could therefore discard them relatively easily once she stopped avoiding making a decision. The therapist worked on Sharon's organizing skills by helping her develop her own organizing principles. These included "putting like with like" and "finding a home for everything in the home."

The logistics of decluttering began with breaking down big tasks into smaller goals, for example, sorting objects and removing clutter from one corner of a room rather than the whole room. Sharon first completed an overall sort by moving easily accessible items from one room to another to clear more space. For example, by moving a lamp and other objects from the living room to the bedroom, she created more space to sort and rearrange the living room. During early exposures to sorting and discarding, the therapist used cognitive therapy tools to identify and challenge problematic beliefs. This included Socratic questioning to pose logical questions about the decisions Sharon was making, taking another perspective to bring in alternative points of view when she seemed stuck on an idea, and suspending her "internal critic" to enable her to move forward with an idea. During this work, Sharon also recorded automatic thoughts about acquiring to help her contain negative thinking that was interfering with her work.

The therapist also used motivational interviewing strategies to help Sharon verbalize her ambivalence whenever this erupted and prevented her from taking logical next steps. "Change talk" (statements indicating Sharon might want to reduce acquiring or clutter) was reinforced by expressing empathy for her struggle and helping her recall her stated therapy goals to see if these matched her planning around clutter (developing discrepancy). The clinician also supported her sense of self-efficacy by helping her recall other successes that suggested she would be able to make the changes she desired. Sharon engaged in active sorting and discarding in her home (for example, her deceased parents' effects) and at the office (for example, by paying bills) and also completed a nonacquiring trip to a favorite store where she practiced not buying an item on sale that caught her eye. Sharon's therapist provided moral support with regular home visits that also served as social events in which Sharon received her therapist as a visitor in her home. After 26 sessions of therapy, Sharon showed measurable improvement in the clutter in her home with a 2-point drop in the Clutter Image Ratings to ratings of 3–5. By this posttreatment point, Sharon's ratings were nearly identical to her therapist's, indicating more agreement between them and more insight on Sharon's part. In addition, her buying and acquiring free things decreased considerably so this problem was now minimal.

Interestingly, her over-involvement with outside activities was more of an impediment to progress than her comorbid depression and generalized anxiety. During treatment she quit her job at the library and kept one evening a week free from classes and NA to work on the clutter. Her mood gradually improved as she made progress; she became more hopeful and had more energy to work at home. Sharon continued work with another clinician for mood and anxiety problems on a twice monthly basis and these problems gradually remitted. She also continued to receive home visits for hoarding every 3 months for 2–3 years and these showed that she completed as much decluttering during this time as during the more weekly 26-session treatment. Sharon met all of her stated goals, although 2 years passed before she was able to invite friends and family to her home.

Case Discussion

Sharon's case illustrates good progress achieved on organizing and decision-making skills and reduction of acquiring and clutter in her home with the help of a social work clinician. This therapy has been used successfully for approximately 70% of clients who were rated by their clinicians as "much" or "very much" improved on their hoarding symptoms (Steketee et al., 2010a). As Sharon's case indicates, full improvement from hoarding symptoms often takes more than 26 sessions, often requiring a year or more. This suggests that longer intervention is needed in most cases and additional support from other human service personnel is likely to be useful. Sharon was a highly motivated client who had overcome other difficulties, such as substance abuse, and was ready to tackle her hoarding disorder. Other clients who are ambivalent about seeking help may need more time spent addressing motivational problems and thus may have a slower start than those who are further along the continuum of insight and motivation.

The assistance of those who wield the "stick" (e.g., public health officers, housing inspectors, protective services, or the courts as described in Chapters 3 and 7–10) can be a helpful adjunctive intervention when used cautiously to impel very ambivalent clients to seek mental health treatment. However, the mental health clinician's role must be to convert such involuntary clients to voluntary ones who set their own therapy goals and take pride in working toward and accomplishing them.

Sharon was fortunate in being able to find a skilled clinician to assist. Unfortunately, within both public and private mental health systems, few clinicians are trained in these methods of psychotherapy intervention. She also was not taking medications, perhaps because of her earlier struggle with addictions, although these might have been helpful in managing her negative mood or in improving her concentration and attention. Overall, Sharon's experience was a positive one that required limited involvement of other human service professionals, in part because she had already worked successfully with professionals on her addiction problem. However, our experience suggests that many clients have concurrent problems that require the attention of other service staff, if only to enable the mental health professional to concentrate on the hoarding problem.

CHAPTER 6

Hoarding and Housing

WITH CONTRIBUTIONS *BY JESSE EDSELL-VETTER*

Hoarding often affects housing settings, and this chapter is intended as a guide for those who provide services in such situations. This includes landlords, property managers, inspectors (e.g., Board of Health, Fire Department), housing associations, and neighbors of people who hoard, as well as subsidized housing providers (SHPs) who manage federal Housing Choice Vouchers (formerly Section 8) and state vouchers, and agencies contracted through the Department of Housing and Urban Development (HUD). Many of these groups provide an entry point for hoarding intervention. For example, the neighbor who notices an odor emanating from the apartment next door calls the Board of Health, which triggers an inspection and possible further intervention. The landlord whose tenant repeatedly refuses him access to the home to complete repairs might recruit the Board of Health or engage the legal system to access the home (and possibly ultimately to evict the tenant). Property managers, housing associations, and SHPs become aware of hoarding problems through routine home inspections. Some agencies are equipped to both uncover hoarding problems and provide intervention, whereas most SHPs will refer these cases to other human service providers. Housing associations may employ both inspectors and service coordinators who can work in tandem to assess the hoarding problem, negotiate decluttering goals with the person who hoards, and monitor progress toward those goals.

This chapter provides several illustrations of common problems caused by hoarding that run afoul of various housing codes. However, laws differ from region to region within the United States, as does the organization of services. In addition, professional titles also differ. For example, a Public Health Officer in one state may be called an Environmental Health Officer in another. Unfortunately, these considerations limit the extent to which information in this chapter can be generalized from one region to another. Another important factor with regard to housing is whether the individual who hoards owns or rents his or her property and, if the latter, whether the rental is private market rental or subsidized housing.

EFFECTS OF HOARDING ON HOUSING

As it increases in severity, hoarding and the associated clutter can have very serious housing consequences, sometimes putting the building itself at risk, as well as the people living in or near the home and the building owner. Various types of housing risks are outlined below.

Risks for Occupants

Hoarding possessions can lead directly to health and safety risks for the occupant(s) of the home. Dwellers may suffer physical injury from falling over possessions, falling down stairs, or having possessions fall on them. Every year, newspapers around the country report injuries and even death from falls and avalanches of possessions piled too high. This may be particularly risky for elderly or disabled occupants, small children, and especially those living in earthquake-prone areas. Dwellers may also develop health problems or illness from mold, insect infestations, and the accumulation of pathogens from unsanitary conditions. Common examples include asthma, respiratory infections, and other serious infections from insect or rodent infestations. For example, house mice can transmit the lymphocytic choriomeningitis virus to humans via their droppings and urine. This virus can cause meningitis or encephalitis (Centers for Disease Control, 2007). Dwellers can be poisoned by eating unsafe food such as canned or fresh food that has passed its date of use.

Hoarding commonly impedes the provision of emergency medical services. This can be complicated by occupants' feelings of shame and fear of calling authorities even when safety and life are at risk. In one case familiar to us, the hoarding occupants called 911 to report a medical emergency (a heart attack) and then exited the apartment, locking the door behind them to wait on the front steps for the Emergency Response Team to arrive. In another case, a wife delayed calling for emergency medical assistance when her husband fell in their cluttered basement and was unable to get up. So great was her fear that the house would be condemned that she let him remain there for 2 days before finally requesting help. The clutter itself can impede provision of emergency services as entrances and pathways are obstructed, slowing emergency medical responders and sometimes preventing them from entering the home. This can and has led to medical complications or, in some cases, death.

Of grave concern is that occupants may be burned or die in a fire caused by hoarding. This is especially worrisome when flammable items are placed near stoves, heating elements, heating systems, and water heaters, or when electrical outlets are outdated, overloaded, or not repaired. In such cases, occupants who would otherwise be able to escape in time from an uncluttered home cannot exit and/or emergency fire fighters cannot reach them in time. This sad situation occurred in a town outlying one Northeastern city when an 80-year-old occupant was trapped in a second-floor bedroom as the fire raged through mountains of debris collected over many years. Windows and doors were inaccessible and the man perished as fire fighters could neither reach him nor control the fire in a timely fashion.

A recent study of fires in hoarding homes in Melbourne, Australia provided some very helpful information about this problem. The majority of fires resulted from cooking fires (39%) with the remainder caused by heaters, open flames or lamps (22%), electrical problems (22%), and smoking (12%) (Harris, 2010). These homes were 63% owner occupied, 23% public housing, and 14% private rental; 77% of those who hoarded in fire-damaged homes were men, consistent with epidemiological data that most people who hoard are men (although more women seek help). Most (75%) of those whose homes burned were 50 years old or older, and about half of these were over age 65 years. Interestingly, the financial loss to the owner for a fire in a hoarding home was much greater than for a nonhoarding home: $100,000 versus $12,500. This was at least partly because 90% of fires in nonhoarding homes were contained to the room of origin, whereas this was true of only 40% of fires in hoarding homes. Furthermore, fewer than half as many hoarding homes had operating smoke alarms. The average cost to the fire department for a hoarding fire was more than 15 times higher: $34,000 versus $2,100 for a nonhoarding home, mainly because of the large number of staff, fire trucks, and time required to put out fires in hoarding homes. Most alarming was that fires in hoarded homes accounted for 25% of all preventable fire fatalities in the past 10 years. Also of interest was the finding that fires occurred in moderately cluttered as well as severely cluttered homes as assessed on the Clutter Image Rating (see Appendix), suggesting that moderate clutter still represented a serious fire hazard (Harris, 2010).

Apart from fire hazards, all too often hoarding leaves home occupants without vital services such as plumbing, electricity, and heating, sometimes for months and years at a time. Accumulated possessions often block electrical wiring, plumbing, and heating systems, preventing access to these systems for repair. Furthermore, excessive acquiring may induce such financial strain that occupants cannot afford to pay their utility bills. When elders or children are living in the home, these risky situations are likely to constitute neglect that requires protective services (see Chapter 12). In some cases, home dwellers who were afraid that repair service people would report them to the authorities went without heat during cold winters, using stoves and ovens to keep warm. Obviously this further increased the likelihood of a serious fire.

A person's housing stability is also affected by hoarding. Renters risk eviction because of lease violations. An unsafe or unsanitary rental property usually constitutes a violation of fire, sanitation, and/or public health codes and a breach of the lease agreement. Landlords who are willing to overlook lease violations still may be subject to external pressure from authorities—usually the local Fire Department or Board of Health—to bring the building into compliance with relevant codes. Building owners can risk having their property condemned due to their tenant's hoarding. Similarly, when the person who hoards is the property owner, he or she has primary responsibility for maintaining the home in compliance with these codes. Although privacy rights (see below) make it more difficult to identify and initiate legal proceedings, the owner risks having the home condemned if violations are not addressed. Furthermore, neighbors concerned about property values may complain to the city or town that a hoarded home is unsightly. Once a home has been inspected by the local Fire Department or Board of Health, property owners generally have a short period of time (30 days is typical) to bring the home into compliance with the relevant code(s) or at least to show a "good faith" effort to address the problem. These authorities have the legal right to condemn property judged to be unsafe, thereby forcing the occupants to move, potentially having to lose or store their possessions (see Table 6–1). At the same time, individuals whose hoarding is considered a disability must receive reasonable accommodation under the Fair Housing Law (see Chapter 10 for more about this law).

As apparent from the above comments, hoarding may result in short- and long-term homelessness (Mataix-Cols et al., 2010). Of course, homelessness does not resolve the hoarding problem, as evicted people are likely to collect and retain many possessions while living in a shelter or other temporary housing. This creates additional risks in the temporary housing context. Furthermore, while securing permanent housing is a primary goal for these people, human service professionals will need to assist them with additional services to address the hoarding problem itself over the long term.

Table 6.1. COMMON VIOLATIONS DUE TO HOARDING OF
THE MASSACHUSETTS HOUSING CODE

Violation	Example
Obstruction of any exit, passageway, or common area caused by any object, including garbage or trash, that prevents egress in case of emergency	Boxes or bags of items or furniture piled against an exit to the home preventing the door from being used
Obstruction of light	Furniture or other possessions placed or stacked in front of windows
Shutoff and/or failure to restore electricity, gas, or water	Failure to arrange routine maintenance or repair of utilities, leading to system breakdowns due to hoarding
Any defect that renders the kitchen sink, the stove or oven, the bathroom washbasin, the shower, or the bathtub inoperable	Failure to maintain or repair plumbing or appliances; sink/bathtub rendered unusable due to possessions placed inside
Failure to maintain a sewage disposal system	Failure to maintain or repair plumbing; this may be accompanied by hoarding of human waste
Accumulation of garbage, rubbish, filth, or other causes of sickness that may provide a food source or harborage for rodents, insects, or other pests or otherwise contribute to accidents or to the creation and spread of disease	Hoarding of garbage that directly attracts pests; accumulated possessions, such as paper and books, provide a home for pests

The list is drawn from 105 CMR 410.000 "Minimum Standards of Fitness for Human Habitation" (the Massachusetts State Sanitary Code, Chapter II).

Risks for Neighbors

The negative consequences of hoarding can spread to nearby neighbors who share the same building or whose homes are adjacent. These neighbors are at risk of fire and infestations from insects and rodents. Fires that begin in the homes of those who hoard are more difficult to extinguish, making them more likely to become serious and to spread to adjacent homes (Harris, 2010). Similarly, infestations that begin in such homes are more difficult to detect and control than those occurring in homes with fewer possessions. Thus, pests have more opportunity to multiply and spread to neighboring dwellings. Of course, the consequences of these types of problems for neighbors include health problems, loss of property or property value, and injury, illness, or even death.

Risks for Building Owners and Their Property

Hoarding may put the integrity and safety of the building at risk. Structural problems can develop when tenants hoard heavy items, such as books and magazines or appliances, because the weight of the possessions exceeds the load limits of the building construction materials. For example, we know of one client living in a wooden building who hoarded dozens of wooden and plastic crates filled with hardcover books stacked many feet high and sometimes two rows deep along several walls of her home. Both a builder and a housing inspector judged that the books posed a danger to the integrity of the building. In other cases, insect and rodent infestations may spread from one part of the building to another, weakening the structure, especially in the case of termite infestations that cannot easily be detected or corrected. Likewise, as we noted, utility systems such as plumbing, electricity, and heating are more likely to break down when they cannot easily be accessed for maintenance and repair. Flooding caused by pipes in disrepair or fires caused by electrical wiring or heating systems in disrepair can damage buildings or destroy them outright. When flooding due to clutter comes from the sewer, the building occupants are at risk of illness.

Even moderately serious hoarding problems can put a property owner's investment at risk. Hoarding induces substantial monetary costs that undermine the owner's livelihood. Among these costs are structural repairs, pest management, clean out of possessions and cleaning services (e.g., to contend with unsanitary conditions or after a flood or fire caused by hoarding), as well as loss of rental income during repairs and from prospective tenants who become aware of a hoarding problem in the building and decide against renting. Property owners may also incur significant costs through legal proceedings to exert pressure on tenants to resolve the hoarding problem or to terminate a lease and evict a tenant. Unfortunately, owners who seek to recoup lost assets from their insurance company may be unsuccessful if negligence is alleged. An important nonmonetary cost to property owners in contending with hoarding is the emotional cost they incur in coping with lost income or property or protracted legal proceedings.

PRIVACY AND PRIVATE OWNERSHIP

The potentially serious consequences of hoarding must be weighed against individual privacy rights that undergird the U.S. legal system. In general, the owner(s) of a property is/are the individual(s) who holds the deed for the property. The owner(s) may also be the occupant(s) of the property (i.e., individuals and families living in homes they own). In other cases, the occupant (or tenant) rents the property, usually through a lease with a landlord. Such rentals may be contracted through the private market or through a public subsidy (see Schwartz, 2010, for a guide to different types of rental and subsidized housing). Low-income families and people who are elderly or disabled can rent apartments below market rates through a public housing agency in their area (more information can be found at http://www.hud.gov/offices/pih/programs/ph/programs.cfm and http://portal.hud.gov/portal/page/portal/HUD/topics/rental_assistance/phprog). In addition, low-income individuals and families can access subsidized housing through a housing voucher, such as a Housing Choice Voucher (see http://www.hud.gov/offices/pih/programs/hcv/about/fact_sheet.cfm) or a state housing voucher (for more information on rental assistance by the state see http://portal.hud.gov/portal/page/portal/HUD/topics/rental_assistance/local).

Each geographic area across the United States has public health and fire codes that can differ substantially depending on the region of the country. In some states landlords have the primary responsibility for maintaining the property in compliance with the public health code, whereas in other regions (such as Los Angeles County, California) tenants have this responsibility. Cities and towns have the right to write their own codes or to adapt the international code, which is amended annually (International Code Council, 2009). Property owners have an obligation to learn the code for their area and to maintain their property in compliance with the code.

Although property ownership per se cannot be removed due to hoarding, properties can be condemned and even demolished if they are deemed hazardous or unfit for human habitation. At the same time, private ownership of property brings with it certain rights not available to renters. In general, private property is protected, limiting the access of certain authorities. In Massachusetts, property owners can rightfully refuse a property inspection by a Board of Health inspector unless a warrant is issued through the courts. The scope of such warrants may also be limited. For example, a complaint by neighbors about the accumulation of possessions in the yard might result in a warrant to inspect the exterior of the property, but that does not extend to the interior of the home unless there is due cause and this is specified in the warrant. Therefore, someone who has entered the home and can report visual evidence of risk (e.g., family member, friend, repair person, emergency responder, or a home services provider, such as a visiting nurse) must lodge a separate complaint. Because laws vary by state, it is important to verify the legal requirements for obtaining entry before undertaking such proceedings.

In contrast to what occurs in private ownership, hoarding and its consequences may be easier to detect and resolve in private rentals and subsidized housing. Landlords and property managers have the right to enter tenants' homes. Indeed, when housing is subsidized by federal, state, or city governments, regular inspection of the home is a condition of residence and eligibility for renewal of a housing subsidy. (Note, however, that specific lease agreements and housing inspection codes differ across subsidized housing programs.) Landlords and property managers are positioned to exert pressure on their tenants who hoard to resolve the problem and to monitor improvement. When this pressure is not sufficient (for example, when a tenant bars access to the home) the legal system can be recruited to exert additional pressure. For more information on hoarding and the legal system, see Chapter 10.

SELF-DETERMINATION

Apart from privacy rights, the adverse effects of hoarding must also be weighed against the right of self-determination as an ethical principle within human service settings. Within the guidelines of the law, individuals have the right to live as they choose. For example, if there is no concern about structural damage, it is neither dangerous nor illegal to own a large number of books. If libraries and the homes of wealthy book collectors are not generally considered a fire hazard, it seems unreasonable to designate the home of a person who hoards a fire hazard simply because there are many books (assuming, of course, that the books are not stacked on radiators or so heavy as to a present structural danger, etc.). Similarly, it is not a sanitation or safety hazard if a woman chooses to routinely hang her laundry over the bathtub, preferring to use the bathroom sink to bathe. People differ widely in the interest and attention they give to housekeeping, whether or not they hoard. Some individuals clean often and keep their homes neat, whereas others dust and clean rarely, leaving clothing and household items strewn throughout their homes. People also differ in the number of items they choose to keep on various surfaces, such as kitchen counters and tables. A cluttered kitchen counter may seem to have too little space to prepare food (a violation of the health code). However, the occupant may have adapted effectively to the environment and still be able to regularly prepare food on the cluttered counter.

While hoarding is often a significant problem for many people, it is important to preserve personal rights amidst differing preferences and standards for how to live. Landlords, building managers, and inspectors will have values and standards for how a home should look. Awareness of these internal rules and judgments is critical since interpretation of public laws should be independent of personal expectations. Most professionals are well aware of this critical distinction, but it bears repeating that our judgments are often clouded by our own cultural, familial, and personal expectations. A home need not meet our standards to be judged acceptable by legal standards. Nonetheless, it is important to determine actual violations of relevant codes. To this end, we recommend that visual inspection of homes be accompanied by appropriate questioning to clarify whether the conditions of the home truly constitute code violations or whether they simply reflect the personal preferences of the occupant.

ASSESSING HOARDING SEVERITY

As indicated in Chapter 4, objective measures of the severity of the hoarding problem are needed to conduct a thorough assessment of the risks and needs in the residence. The presence of an elder, adult with a disability, child, or animals may warrant a higher severity rating because of the special risk to these vulnerable populations. Repeated assessments provide a record to judge change or lack thereof. When hoarding problems require court action, measures that document the problem and efforts to resolve it are especially important. Measures that are particularly useful for housing concerns are the Clutter Image Rating (CIR), the Activities of Daily Living–Hoarding (ADL-H), and the Home Environment Index (HEI). These tools can be used by service providers as well as landlords. Two additional measures specific to hoarding and housing are the Hoarding Referral Sheet—Inspectors, developed by Jesse Edsell-Vetter of the Metropolitan Housing Partnership in Boston, MA and the Clutter-Hoarding Scale developed by the Institute for Challenging Disorganization (see Chapter 12). Housing inspectors will also have their own assessment form to determine whether housing code violations have occurred. Before we review the measures suggested here, a cautionary note is needed.

Accurate ratings on these measures depend on objective assessment. Those responsible for evaluating housing situations may be tempted to exaggerate severity ratings. We caution raters to avoid a rush to judgment when housing violations are evident as it is easy to notice a problem and generalize this to ratings of other contexts. However, to use one example, a filthy kitchen awash in debris does not necessarily mean that the bathroom and other living spaces merit a similarly high severity rating. We recommend that housing professionals learn to recognize the range of hoarding severity both across and within homes. This can be accomplished by accompanying a more seasoned inspector to a handful of homes with hoarding and by becoming familiar with the Clutter Image Rating, which depicts clutter severity visually, reducing the role of personal judgment. Assessors' goals are to make objective ratings of the observed situation without placing blame. Doing so helps clients feel better understood and also enables them to make improvements that will be evident on the rating scales. Such indicators of progress can motivate clients to continue their efforts.

The *Clutter Image Rating* (see Appendix) can be completed by both the inspector and the occupant if he or she is willing to do so, thereby inviting the dweller to become part of the solution and permitting a comparison of ratings. For example, if the inspector rates a room at the level of 6 (out of 9), whereas the client rates the room at 3, the inspector can point out these differences of viewpoint and describe how the inspector's ratings support the determination of a code or lease violation. The *Activities of Daily Living–Hoarding* (see Appendix) may be useful in providing supplementary information on the behavioral consequences of hoarding. The *Home Environment Inventory* (see Appendix) enables professionals to rate any squalid conditions in the home and is useful when nonhousing professionals such as home health aides or visiting nurses are providing detailed information to legal authorities.

The *Inspections Hoarding Referral Tool* (Metropolitan Boston Housing Partnership, Boston, MA, 2007) allows housing inspectors to draw the clutter present in each major room of the home. It also tracks whether the entry and exit to the room are blocked and provides a space for the inspector to add a verbal description of each room. This instrument is available in the Appendix. The ICD Clutter-Hoarding Scale (NSGCD, 2003, see Appendix) for professional organizers is described in Chapter 11. It can also be used by inspectors to measure the level of clutter in the home as well as structural concerns, the presence of pets and rodents, impediments to typical household functions, and sanitation and cleanliness.

Together, these measures take 20–30 minutes to complete and can be repeated periodically to track the client's progress on resolving the hoarding and housing problems. Of course, housing inspectors will also need to make a determination regarding the client's overall progress on resolving code violations. When assessments suggest that other social services might be needed, inspectors can ask for a consultation with a human service professional. For example, concern about dwellers' mental health or about protection of children and elders living at home should generate a call to the relevant local agency to determine the appropriate next steps. As noted in Chapter 3, community task forces can be helpful in facilitating this process.

USE OF INSPECTIONS TO PROMOTE CHANGE

In settings in which annual inspections are part of the housing agreement or in cases in which a landlord suspects there may be a hoarding problem, inspections can serve as a tool for communicating about the problem and motivating change. Repeated inspections provide an opportunity to monitor the change process. As the home improves, inspections can become less frequent (e.g., perhaps initially biweekly or monthly and with improvement quarterly or every 6 months). Reducing the frequency might also motivate more decluttering work for hoarding occupants who are anxious to limit the number of visitors who come to the home.

IMPEDIMENTS TO INSPECTIONS

As discussed in Chapter 2, individuals with hoarding often experience intense anxiety at the prospect of a home inspection. Many have barred even close family members and friends from their home because of shame and embarrassment and it is not surprising that they exhibit self-protective behaviors toward the person conducting the inspection. They may try to avoid the inspection and argue or refuse to communicate during or after the inspection. Chapter 2 provides recommendations on how to talk to people who hoard. Here we add additional suggestions for housing personnel. To help build a relationship with a reluctant occupant, we recommend direct statements and questions asked in a civil matter-of-fact manner. Communication that respects the occupant, even when the inspector disagrees strongly with things the client says or does, helps facilitate discussion and eventually actions that bring the home into compliance with the lease or housing codes. In short, an effort to understand why people who hoard react as they do, together with a commitment to communicate respectfully with them, will better enable housing professionals to do their work.

TIPS AND STRATEGIES

- Explain the inspection process. If the occupant does not already know you, introduce yourself and show relevant identification. Spend a few minutes informing the occupant about what to expect during the inspection process (e.g., visiting every room, including the basement and attic). If possible, give the occupant a written list of the areas that must be inspected and criteria to ensure that the home is in compliance with the relevant law.
- Give the occupant as much control during the inspection as possible. For example, within the limitations of standard inspection procedures, ask if the occupant has a preference for where to begin or ask him or her to guide the way.

- Ask the occupant permission before opening doors to rooms, closets, or cupboards. If the occupant hesitates or says no, explain the reason for your request. If the dweller still refuses, consider returning to the area later or during another visit. Continued denial of access may require a warrant to view that area of the home. Even with a warrant, indicate that you do not wish to upset the occupant or that you can see that this is difficult for the occupant before proceeding to inspect the area.

- Meet with the occupant outside the home if possible to discuss concerns about the home and an intervention plan. The home visit can provoke strong feelings that make it difficult for the person to process information about issues such as the timetable for decluttering.

- A visit outside the home at a later date provides a second opportunity for the occupant to ask questions and understand the process. This second visit affords an opportunity to develop the relationship further, clarify concerns, and plan methods and timelines for decluttering the home.

- Use objective language when reporting the inspection findings. For example, "The area around the sink was filthy" is better stated in behavioral terms such as "Scraps of food lay around the sink." Keep in mind the following question: "How would I respond if this were my home being described in this report?"

- Acknowledge strong feelings and use calm but firm language. Even when the inspection is conducted respectfully and the report is objectively written, occupants may still become upset or angry. You can suggest that the occupant seek consultation with someone they know (e.g., social worker, primary care provider, minister) for help in coping with strong feelings.

SUPPORT FOR INDIVIDUALS AND AGENCIES IN HOARDING CASES

As highlighted throughout this book, cases of hoarding routinely require disproportionate amounts of time and effort to resolve and take a toll on human service providers. Despite their best efforts to build a relationship with occupants and to behave in a respectful and friendly manner, those who work with hoarding and housing can still receive strong negative reactions. As suggested, close agency or departmental colleagues can be helpful listeners after visits with difficulty hoarding clients. Frustrated landlords may also need to find understanding and support among agency staff members who are willing to listen; again, task force members are an excellent source of support. Of course, support for human service providers should respect client privacy and confidentiality.

CASE STUDY: JUDY

Judy was a 55-year-old single white woman living alone in a large Northeastern city in a 1½-bedroom apartment in a multilevel home. She was a recovering addict and alcoholic who had multiple relapses. Judy was trained as a nurse but she has not been able to work for 8 years. She lived on disability income and had subsidized housing through a Housing Choice Voucher administered through a subsidized housing program. She was therefore required to submit to annual inspections to ensure that her home was in compliance with requirements for maintaining her voucher. When she initially obtained her housing voucher, she was assigned a regular housing inspector through the SHP and passed her inspections. She was assigned a new inspector just prior to the start of the case and he found a number of housing code violations in her home.

Some of the following situations in Judy's home were out of compliance at the inspection: (1) items stored on radiators; (2) both bedrooms impassable or nearly so; (3) no pathway from the main bedroom door to the bed, so Judy had to climb over her possessions to get into bed; (4) clothing hung on the doors to both bedrooms so the doors could not be moved and only a small passage remained; (5) a pile of newspapers filled the space between the couch and the coffee table preventing access to the couch and posing a risk for falling; (6) too many cords and wires in places that posed a risk for tripping; (7) the kitchen sprayer hose was missing and no cap covered the hole; (8) a shelf installed in Judy's hallway blocked a closet door; (9) the roof had structural damage and needed repair; and (10) one of the exterior door locks was broken. When her home was assessed using the Clutter Image Rating scale, her living room was rated 5 (of a maximum score of 9), her kitchen 3, and her bedrooms 5.

Judy was fortunate that the SHP administering her housing voucher had a specialized hoarding team that had been formed to work with hoarding cases because they were costly and time consuming to staff. The team's work was funded by grants and donations to the SHP. Judy freely admitted to having a hoarding problem, reporting that she had "never not been a hoarder." She was referred to the hoarding team. Using the inspection report, the team created a plan with Judy's input and negotiated a reasonable accommodation agreement based on her disability (see Chapter 10 for information about reasonable accommodation). Under the agreement, Judy was granted a 3-month extension for reaching goals in her unit.

A caseworker from the hoarding team was assigned to work with Judy after her initial meeting with the team. He met with her every 1–2 weeks in her home and helped her to understand the relative urgency of each concern on her inspection report. He also clarified the concerns that were her responsibility (e.g., placement of clothes and papers) and those that were her landlord's responsibility (e.g., the roof repair work, the exterior door lock). The intervention plan had specific benchmarks for each area of the home (e.g., clearing away books and papers from the windows, clearing clothes hanging from doors to permit the closing and opening of the doors in the home). At Judy's direction, the caseworker helped with hands-on work sorting and moving items to support her in meeting the benchmarks in time for her inspection. He also gave Judy information about treatment options and encouraged her to seek help from a trained mental health professional to overcome this problem.

Judy entered a 4-month cognitive and behavioral treatment (CBT) group program for hoarding shortly after she began working with her SHP caseworker. When this treatment group ended, Judy began individual CBT with one of the group therapists. She met with the therapist weekly in the office and monthly in her apartment to apply the skills she learned toward goals she set. Given her other mental health difficulties, Judy also worked concurrently with a substance abuse counselor, another psychotherapist for personal concerns, and a psychiatrist for medication management. During her CBT treatment for hoarding, Judy also worked on some of her symptoms of posttraumatic stress disorder that appeared in the context of her decluttering work. Judy was repeatedly sexually and physically abused from early childhood until well into her adult years. She came to understand that decluttering her home provoked anxiety and feelings of being unsafe that stemmed from these experiences. With the support of her hoarding therapist, she was able to tolerate the considerable distress of having her landlord enter her home to make repairs. Judy's therapist and SHP caseworker communicated regularly to coordinate the declutter work.

Three months after her initial inspection, Judy's unit was inspected and found to be in compliance with the most critical concerns. She was given additional time to make more changes in her unit, and she and her SHP caseworker revised her plan to reflect the new priorities given her successful inspection. Because Judy was eligible for the services of an occupational therapist (OT—paid for by Medicaid), her therapist discussed this service with her. Shortly after her second inspection, Judy began weekly work with an OT trained in declutter work in the home. Judy, her hoarding therapist, and her OT outlined week-by-week goals for the home. Working with her OT allowed Judy to declutter her home more quickly and effectively. Judy's use of OT services allowed her SHP caseworker to reduce his home visits to once every 4–6 weeks. He continued to communicate with Judy's therapist about her progress and upcoming inspection priorities.

Judy continued work with her SHP caseworker for 9 months after the second inspection. During that time, she discarded several pieces of furniture (chairs, shelves, etc.), recycled her newspapers, and curtailed her acquiring of new newspapers (she now subscribes to one weekly newspaper, which she reads and recycles within a few days). She categorized her winter clothes, donated unwanted clothing, stored clothes she kept in a closet, and sorted and organized the clothes in her bedroom. As a result, her clothes no longer impeded access to the window, movement within the room, or opening her bedroom door. She also sorted and discarded items previously stored in boxes, thereby creating more living space. She removed items from the kitchen counter and decorated the cleared space with chosen items she enjoyed. At the end of their work together, Judy's SHP worker rated her living room 2.5, her kitchen at 2, and her bedroom at 3.5, all in the minimal to mild range. Overall, the clutter in her living space was very much improved.

Case Discussion

This case illustrates a successful intervention with a hoarding client whose home failed to meet several inspection criteria. Although Judy considered herself a life-long hoarder, the hoarding did not emerge as a serious problem for many years. The first and second inspectors who visited Judy's home had different impressions of the home. It is unclear whether this was because the home did not initially have code violations or because the first inspector had a more lax interpretation of the code relative to the second inspector. Once the home was found to be out of compliance, a coordinated plan of care was put in place to support Judy in making the necessary changes. Judy's initial declutter plan prioritized code violations over personal goals for the home and specified a timeline for completion of the goals. After she passed her second inspection, the initial plan was revised to include goals that would substantially reduce the overall clutter in the unit.

Had Judy not been motivated to seek treatment, her SHP caseworker (or other human service provider) would have needed to explore her reluctance to acknowledge her difficulties to help her prioritize her goal to retain her housing voucher. Overall, the declutter work was accomplished through initial and ongoing help from her SHP caseworker to guide her through the inspection process, as well as training and in-home work with the CBT clinician and ultimately with the OT who worked extensively in the home. In addition, Judy's other mental health problems were addressed through work with additional providers (a psychologist, a psychiatrist, and an addictions counselor) to help her to manage these difficulties. Had Judy not had these providers, her CBT clinician (or another human service provider) would have discussed this with her. Although Judy had an unusually large number of human service professionals working with her (SHP caseworker, CBT clinician, substance counselor, psychotherapists, psychiatrist, OT), her CBT clinician helped coordinate their efforts (with her written consent to contact the other clinicians) to ensure that care efforts were not confusing to her or working at cross purposes. Although not all hoarding cases will require as many human service providers, multiple service providers are often needed to avoid derailing decluttering efforts that maintain stable housing, even if only periodically.

CHAPTER 7

Hoarding and Public Health and Safety

WITH CONTRIBUTIONS *BY PAUL HALFMANN*

As evident from previous chapters, how a person with hoarding comes to the attention of human service professionals differs greatly by situation. This chapter is directed at public health officers, fire and police officers, and emergency medical staff who encounter hoarding. Typically, public health and safety officers become involved when a family member, concerned friend, or neighbor perceives a threat and contacts the fire or public health department. Sometimes, boards of health, sanitation departments, and/or inspectional services may be notified by another agency that becomes aware of a seriously hoarded home. Unfortunately, the first notification of hoarding can arrive through a call about a fire or a medical emergency in which emergency medical technicians (EMTs) are unable to get appropriate equipment into the home. Regardless of the point of entry, public health and safety officials play a critical role in the identification, assessment, and intervention for hoarding.

FIRST RESPONDER AND SAFETY PROFESSIONALS

By the nature of their professions, police officers, fire officials, and emergency medical technicians enter people's homes—most often in emergency situations. The reason for the call may have nothing to do with hoarding. The first responder arrives to intervene in situations that range from criminal activity to public health and medical emergencies. While in the home, the first responder often scans the environment for health and safety concerns that can reflect the consequences of hoarding (for example, unsanitary kitchen conditions). In this regard, first responder professionals play important roles in the early identification of serious problems due to hoarding. Accordingly, it is essential that these professionals know how to assess the severity of the situation and whom to contact for follow-up and intervention.

Police or fire officials can be called to a home specifically because of hoarding-related concerns. In these instances, a concerned neighbor or family member may have called one of these first responder agencies asking for an investigation and intervention. A timely response by these public servants can prevent the serious and even dire consequences of hoarding. In addition to police and fire professionals, public health officers (sometimes called environmental health officers) and sanitation officials may be called to assess and resolve hoarding problems. Working in tandem with building code officials, public health officers address conditions in the home or on the property such as strong odors, infestations of insects or rodents, standing water, structural load, or building dilapidation. A call requesting the presence of a public health official often indicates that a hoarding situation has progressed from a minor private concern to a serious public community concern.

ASSESSING HOARDING-RELATED PUBLIC HEALTH AND SAFETY CONCERNS

Assessing the nature and severity of the public health and safety risk related to hoarding is sometimes complex and often difficult. As discussed in Chapter 2, people who hoard may have limited insight about their problem and its adverse effects, leading them to deny that any problem exists or that the specific health and safety complaints are accurate, even in the face of contradictory evidence. For example, when confronted by a public health official with concerns that buckets outside the home were collecting standing water and creating an area for mosquitoes and other insects to breed, one woman indicated that bugs were not a problem and that she needed to recycle the rain water for watering her indoor plants in order to avoid being wasteful. In other situations, the person with hoarding may recognize the problem and its consequences but be unwilling to accept assistance or intervention. A common refrain in such situations is, "I know I need to clean that up and I was just about to, but. . .," followed by an excuse that seems unlikely. Perhaps the most common of these refers to assertions that a cleanup was in the works but some unfortunate accident (or health problem or failure on the part of someone assisting) intervened.

Further complicating assessment of hoarding environments is the challenge of gaining access to privately owned homes. A person who hoards in a home they own has greater control over the circumstances under which public health and safety professionals are permitted to enter. As noted in Chapter 6, those who rent their homes, and especially those living in public housing, may have less personal control over entry by officials such as building inspectors. Nonetheless, public health officials are mandated to address health concerns in both public and private contexts from a regulatory perspective.

When a health official calls, gaining entry to the home can be thwarted because the dweller is apparently at home but refuses to answer the door, or the occupant answers the door but refuses to permit the officer to enter. Public health and safety officials who are repeatedly turned away can seek a warrant for entry from the court system. As will be discussed in Chapter 10, obtaining such a warrant is sometimes the only way to enter some hoarded homes, presuming there is sufficient evidence of a probable health or safety risk. However, seeking a warrant to enter the home should be a strategy of last resort, with less restrictive and litigious measures tried first, if at all possible. Often, other human service professionals such social workers can help health officers gain entry into a hoarded home through an already established relationship with the person who hoards. In this case, the professional with the prior relationship will need to engage the occupant in a frank conversation about the professional's personal concerns about the occupant's safety. This must be compelling to the hoarding dweller for him or her to decide to allow assistance, despite fears of loss of control over his or her possessions and the home itself.

For example, a social worker already working with a client may say, "I've come to understand how valuable your possessions are to you and that it's difficult for you to think about discarding many of them. We can work together so you can keep the things that mean the most even though you know you must reduce the overall amount in order to be in compliance with the request of the Health Department. I know you want to avoid paying the fines that are being threatened, so let's make a plan to work together."

Once inside, public health and sanitation officials are guided in their assessment by state laws, regulations, and codes that define unsafe situations created by hoarding. So too, fire personnel and law enforcement officers are bound by laws that require them to take specific action in the presence of situations that threaten personal and community health and safety. Some examples of these situations include the following:

- blocked egresses—the front and/or back doors do not easily open
- insect or rodent infestations—rats, squirrels, or other rodents; ants, fleas, termites, or other insects
- rotting food
- mold

- nonworking appliances—refrigerators, ovens, heating units, hot water units
- excessive fire load—too much combustible material in a given space
- flammable materials near a fire source—papers on top of radiators or hot air vents, curtains near baseboard heaters, materials piled near furnace, magazines or newspapers piled next to a working fireplace
- inoperable sanitation facilities—broken toilets, nonworking showers, sinks plugged, nonworking faucets
- lack of potable water

Although codes and regulations guide the assessment process, much of the determination of the severity of the situation is subjectively judged by the professional. This assessment may be influenced by factors such as the assessor's general experience, familiarity with cases of hoarding, knowledge of or training in hoarding-specific assessment measures (see Chapter 4), and participation in a multidisciplinary team as described in Chapter 3. As discussed in Chapter 6 on housing regulations, it will be most helpful for a new official to be accompanied by a more experienced one who has seen a variety of hoarded homes and has a sense of the continuum of conditions in order to reliably judge their severity.

Once the assessment is complete, public health and safety professionals are charged with helping the person who hoards understand the specific legal or code violations. After explaining clearly the threats to safety and health, the professional determines the actions needed to rectify the situation and return to code compliance. The professional then provides detailed information about each element of the home that needs to be addressed, actions the dweller must take to rectify the problem areas, and a timeline for completion. As a reminder from Chapter 3, dividing larger tasks into smaller, more manageable ones and setting realistic, measurable goals with appropriate deadlines will help the hoarding client achieve compliance. Delivering these requests both verbally and in writing is also helpful. It is critical that the professional requesting change and improvement return to the home, as scheduled, to reassess the situation and provide feedback about any progress. People who hoard often struggle with limited intrinsic motivation to address the problem, and human service professionals can help by providing structure and follow-up.

In the most extreme cases, home environments plagued with severe or multiple public health and/or safety concerns may be assessed as too dangerous for occupancy, leading to temporary or permanent resident eviction and/or property condemnation. Assessments leading to these severe consequences are difficult for all parties involved. However, public officials are required to prioritize the health and safety of people within the community above all else. Again, working with the legal system can provide needed leverage for implementing change (see Chapter 10). Since these difficult and undesirable orders and actions can cause significant distress for the persons living in the home, it is often helpful to involve other human service professionals as appropriate—for example, elder service, mental health, or health workers. Involving them early in the process can mitigate the severity of the effects of eviction.

PUBLIC HEALTH AND SAFETY INTERVENTIONS FOR HOARDING

The intervention roles and activities of public health and safety officials in cases of hoarding differ greatly depending on the type of code violations and the plans for achieving compliance with statutes. Individual agency protocol, and to some extent the professionals themselves, determine the human service professional's participation in the hoarding intervention. Some officials complete the initial inspection, detail the violations in a report, and in some cases, conduct a follow-up assessment within a few weeks to verify compliance. Other officials remain involved for the longer term. For example, a police officer called to the home of an older adult who fell may only assess the situation, write a brief report, and refer the person to another agency. Alternatively, a public health official called to the home may conduct a more thorough assessment, work with the person to establish a plan, and return several times to monitor progress. Longer involvement is obviously more likely to produce better initial compliance and sustained change, but the duration of contact with hoarding clients is likely to vary depending on the agency expectations of the officer.

Health and safety officials employ a range of hoarding intervention activities—from removal of biohazard waste to authorizing plumbing repairs. Because the nature of these professions requires officials to enforce legal codes and regulations, most often they rely on other human service providers to help the individual comply with regulations, providing occasional support during this process. Sometimes, however, the officer works directly with the person who hoards, showing him or her how to make appropriate decisions to discard, recognizing which areas of the home require immediate attention, and identifying potential community resources, such a dumpster service. Regardless of the professional's ability to assist more directly in this fashion, ongoing monitoring is an important role and is critical to ensuring initial compliance with the requested changes, as well as long-term commitment to health and safety modifications.

Many challenges confront health and safety officials who are able to intervene directly with hoarding clients. As noted in earlier chapters, people are often embarrassed by and ashamed of the state of their home and avoidant of possible negative judgments from officials. Many also fear the sanctions imposed by health and safety professionals. Most of all, people who hoard fear that their possessions will be discarded or mistreated. These strong fears can make it difficult for professionals to develop a good working relationship with someone who hoards. Furthermore, sustaining motivation to address the violations and comply with requirements can be difficult, as motivation waxes and wanes with fluctuating emotions (fear, guilt, pleasure in handling possessions), insight about the problem, the perceived importance of compliance, and the person's confidence that he or she can make the required changes (Miller & Rollnick, 2002). Other mental and physical illnesses can also reduce the person's capacity to address the hoarding problem efficiently and effectively. Successful intervention requires the health and safety officer to consider each context and personal limitations carefully before requesting specific changes.

Collaborative efforts with other professional disciplines can be especially helpful in this regard, and are much easier to access when health and safety officials already play active roles in community hoarding collaborations or task forces. Teaming up with professionals representing housing, animal control, protective services, and mental health agencies often advances compliance with codes and regulations. Below are some specific recommendations to guide these interventions.

TIPS AND STRATEGIES

- Be proactive. Too many health officials delay action, especially when properties are owner-occupied, because hoarding cases are complicated. The situation is very unlikely to improve on its own, and taking action sooner may *decrease* the complications.
- Directly reference the regulations when explaining violations and writing orders. Specific citations in the regulations provide a foundation for prioritizing tasks and help establish time frames for correction.
- Prioritize what needs to be fixed based on the severity of the hazard, not the ease of the task. The health officials' responsibility is to protect the health and safety of the hoarding occupant as well as other occupants in the building.
- Keep detailed notes, assessments, and/or pictures to document progress. You may need to explain progress or lack thereof in court where a picture of the unit is "worth a thousand words" to inform the judge.

- Stay on track. Reinspect within the established time frame. Allotting more time to avoid enforcement will only weaken your authority with the hoarding occupant and weaken your case should you end up in court. Let the court arbitrate continuances.
- Make referrals to additional agencies for enforcement. Health officials do not have to limit code enforcement only to their respective regulations.
- Explain the limitations of your authority to any referring organizations before you enter the home. Other agencies do not necessarily understand health and safety limits and may have requested your involvement based on your perceived authority.
- Keep other involved agencies apprised of your expectations, progress, and planned actions. Avoid surprise by letting them know your intentions *before* you act.
- When it seems appropriate, refer people with hoarding problems to other human service professionals who can help, such as mental health providers and tenant agencies.
- Work collaboratively with other human service professionals involved in the case to motivate change. For example, you may need to take the role of "bad guy" who enforces regulations, while the other professional assumes the "good guy" stance to provide support and strategies to help the client make progress. Sometimes these roles might be switched; for example, when a child welfare agency is involved, it may take the bad guy role while you assist as a good guy to ensure code compliance so children can remain in or be returned to the home.

CASE STUDY: STEVEN

Steven was a 53-year-old man of Italian descent who owned a small two-bedroom home in a rural area of a Northeastern state. Steven was recently widowed and lived alone at the time of engagement with hoarding personnel. He is described by neighbors as reclusive, especially since his wife's death two years ago. Currently unemployed, Steven spends most days at home, going out only to do banking and grocery shopping once a week. The curtains to his home are always drawn and his doors and windows remained closed. Steven had three broken-down cars in his front yard, along with multiple bins, buckets, baskets, and tubs filled with rainwater. Two lawn mowers and a boat can be found in the rear of Steven's property. His yard is unkempt and the weeds are overtaking the lawn and driveway. Steven does not answer his front door and his answering machine takes all his phone calls.

Steven recently came to the attention of the town's public health officials when a neighbor complained about the appearance of Steven's front yard and the odd odor emanating from his property. On receiving the report from the neighbor, the public health officer, Joe, made a visit to Steven's home. Joe found the property much as described by the neighbor, although he did not notice the reported odor. As he approached the front door, Joe observed that the curtains were pressed against the windows and that the front porch was cluttered with old furniture, books, and garden tools. After knocking and ringing the bell repeatedly with no answer, Joe left his business card at the door and departed.

Several days later, Steven called Joe at the Department of Public Health. "My name is Steven and you were at my house last Thursday. You left a card in the door and I want to know what you want with me." Joe explained that he'd come to visit Steven at his home after receiving a complaint about the appearance of Steven's yard—including the multiple cars, lawn mower, and boat. Steven angrily reported that he owned his home and the ½ acre surrounding it and that what he kept on the property was his business. Joe said that he agreed but had a responsibility to ensure that the community was safe and enjoyable for everyone. Joe asked if he could visit Steven at his house the next day. Steven responded, "Fine, but I'll meet you outside, you're not coming into my house."

On arriving at Steven's house the following day, Joe again did not detect any problematic odor. Steven hesitantly answered the door and joined Joe on the porch. Joe explained to Steven that according to town statutes, automobiles and other machinery could not be kept in the front yard, and if they were stored in the back yard, they had to be in a shed or covered with a tarp. He added that violations of town statutes could lead to a fine but explained that if Steven made a good faith effort to work on the violations, he would avoid being fined.

Joe asked Steven to first work on removing the items from the front of the house. "If you do that first, then we'll worry about the backyard." Although unhappy with the infringement on his personal rights, Steven eventually acknowledged that maybe he could straighten things up a bit. Joe asked Steven specific questions to understand how Steven would both afford to and arrange for the removal or moving of items. When Steven gave a noncommittal and general answer, Joe asked if he needed financial or manpower assistance. Steven said he thought he could get it done with the help of a friend and he "didn't need a handout from anyone to do it, either."

Joe arranged to return to Steven's house in 3 weeks. Specifically they agreed that Steven would have the buckets, tubs, and bins removed and the lawn mowed and the yard cleaned up, especially removing the overgrown weeds. Steven said he wasn't sure he wanted to get rid of all three cars but knew he could take one to the junk yard. Joe reminded him that eventually all three cars had to go or be appropriately stored, but that taking one to the junk yard along with the other commitments would be a good start during this first 3-week period. Joe assured Steven that he was there to work with him rather than punish him and that he would do whatever he could to help both Steven and the community. Steven continued to make progress, albeit slowly. Joe was able to support Steven by suggesting specific, small tasks that needed to be completed within a specified timeframe.

Case Discussion

In this case, as the public health official, Joe both assessed the property and became involved in the intervention process. Rather than being put off by Steven's initial resistance and defensive stance, Joe persisted and found an interim step (meeting on the porch rather than insisting on meeting in the home) that this uncomfortable man could tolerate. He helped Steven establish a timeline that met the public health goals and was also feasible, recognizing that Steven needed assistance breaking down large tasks into manageable and achievable goals. Joe offered additional support to help Steven accomplish the required tasks and always offered to help him remove unwanted items. In doing so, he balanced firmness regarding the regulations with friendly noncritical or punitive overtures to help. Additionally, Joe provided continued monitoring in the same style that affirmed Steven's efforts and that ensured that Steven could comply without receiving a fine.

CHAPTER 8

Hoarding and Protective Services

The adverse effects of hoarding can pose significant threats to the safety of individuals and their family members. Although safety is important for everyone, certain groups of people are specially protected by law from abuse or neglect. In particular, children, adults with disabilities, and older adults are protected classes of people. In the United States, two federal statutes cover laws regarding child abuse and protection of elders and disabled adults (see Chapter 10 on legal issues). The specific ages of the protected classes, what constitutes abuse or neglect, and the reporting guidelines and protocols vary from state to state. Thus, the content of this chapter provides general information about the relationship between hoarding and protective service agencies, focusing first on child protection and then on elderly or disabled adult protection. However, knowing the details of the laws in the state in which you work is important for informed practice. Even the names and types of agencies that provide protective services differ by state. In general, information about local protective service agencies can be found in the phone book under "child abuse" or "elder abuse." Also, searching the Internet using these terms in conjunction with the name of the state will typically yield the agency name and contact information desired.

CHILD PROTECTION AND HOARDING

The main concerns about hoarding in homes in which children are living pertain to potential threats to the physical and emotional safety as well as the appropriate development of the children. When protective services is called to investigate suspected abuse or neglect of children in hoarded homes, particular attention is paid to the following:

- Determining who hoards. Knowing whether it is a parent or child, grandparent, or other family member living in the home or a combination of family members is critical to assessing the risk for abuse or neglect. The impact of the clutter on children in the home may vary greatly based on the role of the hoarding person in the family system. Appropriate assessment and determination of intervention depend on understanding the source of the problem. For example, clutter brought by a live-in aunt may be much more easily addressed than hoarding by a single mother.
- Assessing whether and how the manifestations of hoarding—accumulated clutter, difficulty discarding, and acquisition—put the children at risk for neglect or abuse. These determinations are not easily made and require considerations such as the age of the child, the locations of the clutter, and the length and severity of exposure to particular situations. For example, a 5-year-old and a 15-year-old girl or boy will have different needs for space. Likewise, recent clutter caused by inheriting items following the death of a family member does not produce the same restrictions as longstanding clutter that interferes with cooking, cleaning, play space, and visits from friends.
- Understanding how a hoarding problem interferes with the age-appropriate development of children in the home. Developmental milestones such as walking and important activities such as completing homework and peer socialization may be impeded or prevented as a direct result of a hoarding problem.

Child protective service professionals are charged with interpreting child welfare statues as they relate to the symptoms of hoarding, which include clutter, disorganization, and possible lack of cleanliness of the home. In making this interpretation, protective services is called on to assess the level of risk and, if needed, to develop a plan with the family for intervention and continued monitoring as necessary. Because these determinations often involve difficult decisions, child protection workers, case managers, student interns, and other staff may benefit from regular supervision and consultation with colleagues experienced in addressing hoarding.

The protective service assessment typically involves at least one visit to the home, and multiple visits may be necessary. All child protection service staff will utilize their own agency's interviewing and inspection protocols to determine whether child abuse and/or neglect is present. However, interpretation of these assessments must be made with an understanding of the history, duration, and source of the hoarding, as well as when and how home spaces are used. The protective service worker should communicate directly with any other human service professionals involved with the family (for example, mental health clinicians, health workers) to obtain a cross-disciplinary perspective on the problem and its impact on the immediate family and others living in the home.

During the initial stages of involvement with families struggling with hoarding, the protective service worker is likely to encounter some denial of the severity or persistence of the problem and resistance toward professional assessment and intervention. Not surprisingly, the person who hoards and other members of the family are often ashamed and embarrassed by the problem and its effects. In the case of protective service investigations, they are also especially concerned about having children taken away or being accused of neglecting or harming their children or dependent adults in the household. Almost by definition people who are being investigated by protective services are nonvoluntary clients. Blaming them or using techniques that provoke even more feelings of shame will inevitably provoke more intense denial and refusal to cooperate with the investigation. Certainly this approach will not excite motivation to reduce acquiring or clutter.

As discussed in Chapter 2, motivational enhancement strategies will be most helpful in promoting at least some admission of the problem. We recommend a matter-of-fact approach that focuses on simple descriptions of the obvious without judgments. For example, "The floor and furniture in the living room are covered in papers, clothing, and other items at this time" is a statement of fact. When delivered without a negative emotional overtone, it can be followed with further questions about how long the floor has been covered and where the child usually plays with his or her toys. Further questions might focus on how the mother would like to use this room in the next few months and a cautious inquiry about her goals for her child in the coming months. This encourages positive statements about desired improvements rather than defensive assertions that the hoarding is not so bad or does not affect her daughter's behavior.

Once the responsible adult has expressed some motivation for change, no matter how small, intervention efforts can proceed, although still cautiously to avoid triggering denial and avoidance. Often protective service workers play a critical role in identifying others who can provide additional services needed to help with the hoarding problem. These might include mental health clinicians, occupational therapists, public health officials, professional organizers, and family members. Although protective service workers will not provide all the needed services themselves, they can broker and coordinate the services that maximize benefit without overwhelming the client.

Because child protection cases often involve the courts, especially when agencies seek temporary or permanent custody of children to ensure their safety, another important role played by the protective service professional is that of advocate and liaison to the court. Especially helpful is information about the participation of the person who hoards in the intervention efforts and about progress made over time. Further information about hoarding and the legal system can be found in Chapter 10.

TIPS AND STRATEGIES FOR CHILD PROTECTIVE SERVICE PROFESSIONALS

- Build a relationship of trust and mutuality with the family, making it clear that the goal is to help rather than to cause harm to the family.
- Notice whether the hoarding behavior is having an adverse effect on the social, emotional, biological, psychological, and educational development of the child. Be careful not to jump to conclusions but to objectively assess if and how the clutter and home environment might limit a child's development.
- Consider whether clutter may cause potential harm to children in the home with regard to falling and crush hazards from tall piles or clutter on the stairs, fire hazards, and health hazards (dust, mold, infestations, etc.).
- Focus on the safety and health of the children and the stability of the home environment, rather than the illness or pathology of the parent or adult care-giver.
- Determine who will be primarily in the enforcer role and who will take a helping role. Work closely with other human service professionals to motivate and maintain a process of change.

CASE STUDY OF HOARDING AND CHILD PROTECTION: LISA

Lisa was an unemployed 38-year-old black American mother of three boys aged 17, 9, and 1. She lived with her three sons and boyfriend in a small two-bedroom apartment in the inner city of a major metropolitan community. Her rent subsidy through the federal Section 8 housing program required an annual housing inspection per the terms of her lease. During the most recent inspection, the inspector noted that Lisa's home was significantly cluttered with piles of unwashed laundry, multiple bags of garbage, cat feces and litter throughout the house, dirty diapers, and spoiled food that were attracting fruit flies and other insects. At the time of the inspection Lisa's sons slept together in one bed in the second bedroom of the apartment. The mattress had no sheets and only a small quilt in the center of the bed. In the corner of the boys' bedroom was a pile of toys, food wrappers, containers, and clothing. During the inspection Lisa's middle son was searching in this pile and when asked what he was looking for, he said, "I can't find the other shoe. Someone help me."

When the inspector inquired about the condition of her home, Lisa said she was overwhelmed by the responsibilities of raising her children. She reported feeling depressed most days and admitted to having difficulty getting out of bed. Lisa often asked her two oldest sons to assist her with the care of their 1-year-old brother, including feeding, diaper changes, and "keeping him quiet." Lisa admitted that things in the home had "gotten away from me" and that her 17-year-old son did most things around the house. She said, "He's a good boy and does what I ask. He even left school so he could help take care of his brothers. My other son, Tyron, he does the dishes for me sometimes and laundry when we have the money."

After talking with Lisa to understand the condition of her home and current stressors, the housing inspector informed Lisa that he was concerned for the health and safety of her children. The inspector specifically noted that the sleeping arrangements and presence of insects and cat feces throughout the home were of significant concern. Additionally, he discussed with Lisa her depressed mood and apparent difficulty caring for her children. The inspector informed Lisa that he would need to make a report to child protective services.

On receipt of the housing inspector's report, the state Department of Child Welfare (DCW) assigned a child protective service worker to the case. This staff member contacted Lisa to arrange a time for an initial visit to the home. Lisa initially resisted and asked about her rights to privacy and if she was required to let the protective service worker into her home. After a lengthy and challenging initial conversation wherein the DCW worker assured Lisa of her rights and helped her understand the resources and assistance she was able to offer, they established a first meeting time.

When the protective service worker arrived at Lisa's home on the scheduled date and appointed time, she found no one home. The shades on the windows were drawn and after repeated attempts to ring the bell, knock on the door, and call Lisa by phone, the protective service worker left her card at the door and returned to the office.

Two days later, the protective service worker went by Lisa's house to see if Lisa might be at home. In her protective service capacity, the professional is obligated by law to make an initial home visit within a specified time of receiving the initial report. Lisa's 9-year-old son answered the door wearing his pajama bottoms and said, "Hi. Who are you?" At that moment, Lisa called for her son to shut the door and not to answer it without an adult. The protective service worker called into the home and announced her presence. Lisa's boyfriend came to the door saying that Lisa wasn't feeling well and couldn't see anyone today.

After an initial exchange in which the protective service professional convinced the boyfriend that she needed to meet with Lisa, she entered the home and found Lisa in a house coat lying on the couch watching TV. Lisa turned off the TV, sat up, and yelled to her 9-year-old son to come and take care of the baby. The protective service professional explained that she had come by on the appointed day for the scheduled session and was sorry that she was unable to meet with Lisa. She confirmed that Lisa found her business card at the door, but Lisa offered no explanation for being unavailable on that day.

The protective service worker began by indicating that she received a report that indicated concern for the health and safety of Lisa's children due to the clutter and disarray of the home. Lisa interrupted to say that she knew the housing inspector made the report and that she was angry at him for "not minding his own business." The protective service worker assured Lisa that she was there to help her become the best mom she could be and to see if Lisa would benefit from any services to help her with feeling overwhelmed regarding her house and children. Although Lisa was initially guarded and refused any offers for assistance or services, the protective service worker continued to offer support, empathizing and inquiring further about the current conditions of the home. After some while spent talking about her children, housework, lack of employment, and financial instability, Lisa finally asked the question that was worrying her: "Are you going to take away my kids now?"

The protective service professional indicated that she was very interested in helping Lisa improve her quality of life so that she could be a better mom to her children and that she wanted very much to help Lisa and her children remain together, but more healthfully and safely. Lisa began to look relieved and even relaxed into the back of the couch. The protective service worker ended the session by scheduling a time to come back the following week to create a plan for their work together. As she left, the protective service professional asked Lisa to think of the top three things that would be most helpful to her and her children. She said that they would begin next time by talking about them.

Case Discussion

This case indicates how a family in which the mother hoards can become connected with child protective services. It shows a helpful partnering between the caseworker and the mother, although the question of "what happens next?" is left unanswered. One challenge is making an initial successful connection with the family, as most families are understandably resistant to having a protective service worker come to ask them questions. The inspector and the case worker noted the specific problems that posed health and safety risks as an important point of entry for addressing hoarding problems.

More work will be essential to determine whether and in what ways these problems affect the children's development. The caseworker's offer to provide help to this overwhelmed mother is obviously an important point of connection, especially as it appears that the mother will need a mental health clinician's assistance in reducing her serious depression.

DISABLED AND ELDER PROTECTION AND HOARDING

People with physical and cognitive disabilities and older adults are two additional classes of people with special protections under state and federal laws. The definition of an adult with a disability is determined by federal law and can be found by consulting the website for Americans with Disabilities, www.ada.gov. This information can help determine if someone qualifies for protective services according to the definition of a protected class. The definition of older adult, however, is far more variable. As is true with the laws defining what constitutes abuse or neglect in children, the laws regarding abuse and neglect of people with disabilities and older adults are determined at the state level. Service agencies charged with protecting these classes of citizens can be contacted for information about state-specific laws and regulations that define the populations and what constitutes abuse or neglect.

When hoarding occurs in these homes, protective service professionals may be called on to provide assessment and intervention to protect the individuals and minimize the risks that can accompany hoarding. In particular, trip and fall hazards (especially cluttered stairs; tall piles that can fall on top of a person; pathways that prevent navigation using a cane, walker, or wheelchair), access to all home exits for use by emergency medical staff if needed, availability of healthy food, and medical concerns (such as dust and allergens in the case of cardiopulmonary disease, the ability to find medications amid clutter, space for adequate bathing in the case of skin care needs) are among the pressing concerns. A special problem occurs when two cohabitating older adults are both hoarding. In this type of *folie a deux*, both older adults contribute to the accumulation of clutter and actively protect their hoarding behavior by denying the problem to outsiders and resisting offers of help. This situation can be especially challenging and may require the intervention of more than one protective service worker and, most likely, collaboration with other human service professionals.

The role of the protective service worker in cases of hoarding by people with disabilities and older adults is similar to that of the child protective service worker. However, intervention for disabled persons and elders is entirely voluntary unless there is an issue of competency or the person is already under the care of a guardian. By contrast, in cases of suspected abuse or neglect of children, involvement of the child welfare agency is mandated. Assessing the risk to the protected person is of paramount importance with regard to risks related to clutter (e.g., falling, items toppling on someone), as well as cleanliness and the presence of squalor in the home. Determination of the client's role in the hoarding behavior is essential. In some cases, the older or disabled adult living independently may be actively hoarding and therefore putting themselves at risk, whereas in other cases, the disabled or older adult is at risk by virtue of living with others who are hoarding. Sometimes both are true, for example, in a home in which an older parent who hoards is living with an adult child who is also hoarding. These determinations are made through careful, systematic assessment to determine how items are accumulated and who makes the decisions about their removal.

Hoarding assessment for older and disabled adults occurs through visits to the home, as these clients are often unable to attend an office visit, in contrast to child protective service visits, which may occur more readily at the agency setting. During the home visits, a hoarding interview and standardized measures of hoarding (see Chapter 4) can be used to determine who in the home is responsible for the hoarding problem, the levels of severity, and the daily living activities that are impaired.

Protective service workers who intervene in these cases are mandated to identify imminent risks to health and safety that need immediate attention and create a plan for expeditious resolution of these situations. As noted in Chapter 6 on housing (see also Tompkins & Hartl, 2009), an important strategy is to focus on immediate threats and develop a plan that ensures safety without necessarily insisting on major changes to the environment at the outset. Certainly, a major cleanout would not be appropriate if safety concerns can be resolved with less radical changes in the environment. Once these serious threats are resolved, the protective service worker develops a plan for on-going monitoring. This is especially important for elderly and disabled clients as their functional capacity is likely to decline more rapidly as they age.

A useful strategy for working with older adults and those with cognitive impairments is to create small behavioral goals that are measurable and achievable within a specified period of time. Workers should allow more time for clients with limited capacity to accomplish goals, to help them become confident of their ability to make changes. As each small goal is achieved, the professional works with hoarding clients to establish the next one, learning from and building on earlier successes. Regular home check-ins, follow-up on homework assignments, and recognition of achievement of goals are gateways to continued progress and sustained motivation.

The relationship component of work with older and disabled adults is a critical factor for exciting and maintaining the motivation to address the hoarding problem (Ayers, Saxena, Golshan, & Wetherell, 2009; Bratiotis & Flowers, 2010). When establishing this relationship initially, protective service workers can focus on the goals of self-efficacy and self-determination. Helping people who hoard understand how their problem interferes with the lifestyle they desire can be a powerful motivator, especially with regard to the ability to live independently. Additionally, when human service professionals ask about specific objects and are willing to listen to the tale behind memorabilia from past experiences and life events, this communicates sensitivity to the meaning of possessions for the client. Attention to personal treasures can greatly assist older adults in establishing and maintaining the trust necessary for continued work on the hoarding problem.

As protective service professionals work with older and disabled adults, it is important that they assess and monitor functionality and any decline in cognitive or behavioral capacities. For example, age and disability may actually increase hoarding problems and create barriers to resolving hoarding as the person can no longer move a heavy trash bag or a box of discarded magazines out of the home. Such limitations will require special assistance from outside providers. Furthermore, additional human service resources such as occupational and physical therapists, mental health clinicians, professional organizers, and visiting nurses can provide needed supports (see Chapters 5, 11, and 12 for information about hoarding intervention by individuals in these roles).

Another role for the protective service professional is that of advocate and liaison, especially in situations involving the legal system. In some cases, matters of guardianship arise in cases of hoarding—especially when a person's cognitive abilities appear to be compromised. When someone with impaired judgment has a hoarding problem, concerns about finances, acquisition, clutter, and squalor can lead to court orders pursuant to protection. In these cases, protective service staff will need to interface with professionals from other disciplines to provide comprehensive support services to the hoarding client (see Chapter 10 for more information about hoarding and the legal system).

TIPS AND STRATEGIES FOR ADULT PROTECTIVE SERVICE PROFESSIONALS

- Begin by building a relationship of trust and mutuality with the older or disabled adult. This requires time spent in conversation about the past as well as the current context, including listening to stories about possessions.

- Approach intervention from a harm-reduction perspective to ensure compliance with codes and regulations rather than attempting an overall clean-up.
- Recognize that progress may be slow.
- Enlist additional help, especially for tasks that require physical exertion, to address serious clutter.
- Use the client's motivation to decide where (location, types of objects) to begin working on the clutter.
- Establish an ongoing visitation plan to help monitor older and disabled clients who are likely to lose capacity gradually over time.

CASE STUDY OF HOARDING IN OLDER ADULTS: IDA

The elder protective service professional knocked loudly on the door to the one bedroom assisted living unit. A frail, small-framed, and thin woman greeted her with a smile and said loudly, "Hello, I'm Ida. Are you Jane? Come in, be careful not to trip on anything, there's a pile here and there, but I'm used to it." In her role as an older adult protective service professional, Jane was visiting Ida to conduct an initial assessment after her department received a report from Ida's concerned pastor.

Ida is a 79-year-old woman who lives alone in an assisted living facility on the outskirts of a small town. A member of her local congregation, she suffered from diabetes and rheumatoid arthritis and has begun to show signs of forgetting things, including the names of her children and grandchildren. Her pastor recently visited Ida in her home and was shocked to find it in terrible condition. The floors of Ida's very cluttered home are covered with newspaper, spilled food, clothing, and bags, as well as countertops and furniture piled nearly a foot high. Ida can't take a shower because she uses the tub to store extra canned food, paper products, and clothing. She acknowledges that she no longer sleeps in her bed because it takes too long to clear it off each night and she feels too tired. Because Ida's refrigerator is no longer working properly, she kept small containers of milk and yogurt and some leftovers from meals in a cooler in her living room.

After initial introductions and an offer of tea, Jane thanked Ida for welcoming her into her home and indicated that the elder protective service office had received a concerned call regarding the condition of Ida's home. Jane asked if Ida would show her around the apartment so she could better understand the concern and talk with Ida about her home and her belongings. Ida responded, "It's nice to have someone here. I don't get out much anymore and I don't have too many people to entertain. Are you sure you wouldn't like some tea?" Ida showed Jane around the apartment and offered explanations for the clutter—reasons why she didn't need to sleep in her bed and that she was happy taking a sponge bath out of the sink. "I'm perfectly fine here, Jane. As you can see, there's nothing for you to worry about." Ida did acknowledge living with chronic pain and having difficulty managing her medications, but she denied any concerns about her home or its condition.

Jane recognized Ida's rationalizations and limited awareness about her clutter and hoarding, behavior that occurs commonly among older adults. Instead of arguing with Ida and refuting her claims about the home environment, Jane decided to use managing medications as a way to schedule another visit with Ida. Jane was able to delay addressing the home clutter with Ida because it did not pose an imminent risk to Ida's health and safety, though there were some areas of concern.

During the next few visits, Jane worked with Ida to set up a pill-box and prescription refill system that included delivery to the home. Ida expressed her gratitude: "You've been very helpful to me Jane and I appreciate it." Jane then used the relationship she'd established with Ida to again broach the subject of the clutter, asking if Ida would like some help doing dishes or laundry. Ida reluctantly acknowledged that tasks such as that had been getting harder and that she probably could use some help. Thus began a relationship that gradually focused more and more on hoarding problems.

Case Discussion

In this case, the visiting professional began by building a trusting relationship with this older and increasingly disabled woman. Recognizing the client's limited insight, the worker approached the situation from a harm-reduction perspective rather than pressing her to remove possessions and used the client's motivation to resolve medication problems as a place to start. As the client felt more comfortable, she began to accept help for tasks that were difficult for her. Over time, this client will need continued monitoring as her capacity will undoubtedly decline further.

CHAPTER 9
Hoarding of Animals

WITH CONTRIBUTIONS *BY JESSE EDSELL-VETTER AND GARY PATRONEK*

A nimal hoarding cases are often complex and involve professionals who serve the interests of animals, as well as a wide range of human service providers who focus on the human owner(s). On the animal side, legal statutes that protect animals from cruelty provoke the engagement of animal protection workers, municipal animal control officers, and lawyers and judges in the legal system. Other professionals who become involved include veterinary medical providers who determine which animals can be saved and which ones are beyond medical care and must be euthanized, animal shelter workers who care for hoarded animals taken in a raid, and animal behaviorists who may be called to evaluate the animals for adoption. On the human side, animal hoarding may call for the involvement of public health officials who evaluate the home, as well as child, adult, or elder protective services for the hoarder and/or others living in the home. In addition, the service of mental health professionals is often needed to assess mental health status and, if appropriate, provide treatment. This chapter is intended for all of these individuals and organizations that encounter cases of animal hoarding.

Relatively little is known about animal hoarding compared to hoarding of objects, but recent published work provides some guidelines for professionals trying to manage this challenging problem in the public and private domain. This chapter contains information about possible reasons for animals hoarding, as well as guidance for assessment and intervention.

The Hoarding of Animals Research Consortium (HARC) was formed in the late 1990s by experienced veterinarian Dr. Gary Patronek and colleagues at the Massachusetts Society for the Prevention of Cruelty to Animals and Angell Memorial Hospital located in Boston, MA. HARC aimed to address the need for research on animal hoarding, which was almost non-existent prior to that time. This multidisciplinary group has included researchers from mental health (clinical psychology, social work, psychiatry), sociology, and veterinary medicine, as well as social work clinicians and administrators and staff from the animal protection field. In 2006, HARC members published a landmark report titled *Animal Hoarding: Structuring Interdisciplinary Responses to Help People, Animals and Communities at Risk* (Patronek, Loar, & Nathanson, 2006). We strongly recommend that professionals dealing with cases of animal hoarding in the community read this detailed document known as the "Angell Report," which can be found at the following url: www.tufts.edu/vet/cfa/hoarding/pubs/AngellReport.pdf. More recently, Patronek and Nathanson (2009) reviewed much of the available information on animal hoarding and articulated theoretical conceptualizations and recommended intervention strategies based on research and clinical experience.

DEFINITION OF ANIMAL HOARDING

Animal hoarding is defined by the presence of large numbers of animals kept in homes and as having the following four main characteristics (Patronek 1999; Patronek, Loar, & Nathanson, 2006, p. 1):

- "Failure to provide minimal standards of sanitation, space, nutrition, and veterinary care for the animals
- Inability to recognize the effects of this failure on the welfare of the animals, human members of the household, and the environment
- Obsessive attempts to accumulate or maintain a collection of animals in the face of progressively deteriorating conditions
- Denial or minimization of problems and living conditions for people and animals."

This definition matches fairly closely the laws of most states requiring that animal owners/caretakers must provide adequate food and clean water, shelter, a clean sanitary environment, and adequate veterinary care. It is not surprising that in many if not most cases, the animal hoarder has little insight into the problem, often denying that the animals have any health problems despite obvious evidence to the contrary. Note that the number of animals alone does not determine whether a hoarding problem is present, as some breeders and trainers own many animals but provide sufficient care and suffer no apparent limitation in their personal functioning (Patronek, 1999).

Thousands of cases of animal hoarding are reported yearly across the United States, with hundreds of thousands of animals involved (Angell Report). The most egregious cases with scores of animals that are ill, dying, or already dead make the headlines in local newspapers, but most cases are less severe, although they meet the above definition of animal hoarding. Still, there is concern that animal hoarding and the intended or unwitting cruelty that accompanies it is increasing as one online national database suggests (Patronek & Nathanson, 2009).

Case Description

An example is a 65-year-old woman who lived in a one-bedroom apartment on the second floor of a small apartment building in a large metropolitan area with her 27 cats. These cats came to her in various ways—she collected a few neighborhood strays because she felt sorry for those that seemed to have no home. As the animals mated, she kept the newborn cats. Although she neutered several of the animals, as she continued to collect an occasional cat from neighbors who knew she liked animals, some breeding among her animals occurred before she could afford to neuter them.

She had a relationship with a local vet who provides veterinary care at a reduced cost, but as her animal population grew, she was no longer able to afford even low cost care for all the cats that needed it. She tried to feed them as best she could, but gradually the number of animals overtook her budget for food. She soon learned to identify places that would give away food or sell it cheaply. But this was more and more time consuming as her cat population doubled and then tripled. Initially, she brought in boxes and kitty litter for the cats, but this was also too expensive. She tried to keep up with discarding the refuse, but not surprisingly, her apartment smelled of cat urine and feces. Although the powerful unpleasant odor was very obvious to her neighbors, she herself did not seem to notice it.

CHARACTERISTICS OF PEOPLE WHO HOARD ANIMALS

Most animal hoarders are middle aged or older and 75% or more are women, usually unmarried and somewhat socially isolated from family and friends (Steketee et al., 2010; Hoarding of Animals Research Consortium, 2002). These characteristics seem similar to those of people who hoard objects, but unfortunately few systematic studies of animal collectors are available at this time. Cats are the most often collected animal, followed by dogs (Patronek & Nathanson, 2009; Steketee et al., 2010). Other collected animals include birds, horses, sheep, goats, rabbits, rodents, reptiles, and even wild animals. Most of these animals are adopted from other people or from rescue organizations and animal shelters, although some are bred at home or purchased (Steketee et al., 2010). The average number of animals ranges from 30 to 40, with some hoarders amassing hundreds of animals (Hoarding of Animals Research Consortium, 2002). Patronek (1999) found dead animals in almost 60% of animal hoarding homes he studied. In most cases, animal hoarding is reported to legal authorities by neighbors, social workers, or other service personnel who file complaints (Patronek, 1999).

Perhaps for obvious reasons, as in the case mentioned above, squalid conditions are common in animal hoarding homes, undoubtedly far more so than for object hoarding. About 60% of homes had animal feces and urine covering the floor (Patronek, 1999). Often some of the household utilities, such as toilet, shower, sink, stove, and refrigerator, are no longer working, thus increasing the unsanitary conditions (Hoarding of Animals Research Consortium, 2002). This can generate a serious public health concern from exposure to disease for the home dwellers and for neighbors in the immediate community. In the case of animal hoarding, a by-product of unsanitary animal conditions is ammonia, which can cause eye and breathing problems even at modest concentrations. Thus, whereas personnel who clear and clean homes with hoarded objects may choose to wear protective respiratory gear, such gear is indispensable for professionals who are working in homes with animal hoarding (Hoarding of Animals Research Consortium, 2002).

News reports on animal hoarding expose the serious public health concerns that arise in these cases, but also provide misinformation. An analysis of more than 100 newspaper reports on animal hoarding indicated that writings tended to sensationalize the problem with characterizations likely to confuse readers and draw feelings of revulsion, sympathy, indignation, and amusement (Arluke et al., 2002). For example, people who hoard are often depicted as animal addicts who love their pets to death, and some homes have been described as a "little shop of horrors" (Andrews, 1999). In addition, press reports are biased in reporting only extreme cases with dire consequences. Media portrayals can have unwanted effects that may exacerbate the problem, evident in some sympathetic readers' monetary donations to the person who is hoarding. Professionals at public agencies may avoid addressing problems they believe will overwhelm their resources, postponing resolution and potentially increasing the severity of outcomes for the animals and owners.

An essential first step for determining how to help those who hoard animals is an understanding of their mental health characteristics and attitudes toward animals and themselves. Several explanations of animal hoarding have been offered. Initially, the behavior was likened to an addiction to having more animals (Hoarding of Animals Research Consortium, 2000). Another early explanation was that those who hoard animals have dementia, as they often show signs of delusional thinking (for example, thinking that animals possess special powers and abilities to communicate; Hoarding of Animals Research Consortium, 2000). However, clinical experience suggests that these are unlikely explanations. For example, few individuals who hoard animals have been found to be mentally incompetent. Nevertheless, a variety of behaviors suggest that significant mental health problems may account for some hoarding. Support for this comes from the striking lack of awareness many animal hoarders exhibit regarding their poor treatment of the animals and inadequate functioning of their homes (Hoarding of Animals Research Consortium, 2000).

Another recent explanation of animal hoarding is that it is due to significant problems with attachment to other people (Nathanson, 2009). Many people who hoard animals are socially isolated. In addition, some of them may have difficulty grieving a loss—perhaps because the loss was complicated or traumatic (e.g., a parent who was killed). In particular, people who save their dead animals' corpses might do so because of grief and denial, but other explanations for such behavior are also possible. For example, the person may be hiding their animal hoarding behavior from authorities. Attachment problems and grief responses could also lead sufferers to acquire unwanted or homeless animals with which they identify. Clinical experience and recent research give some support to the explanation that excessive attachment to animals sometimes replaces inadequate human relationships (see Hoarding of Animals Research Consortium, 2002; Patronek & Nathanson, 2009; Steketee et al., 2010). This is bolstered by case studies in which abuse, neglect, and trauma characterized some animal hoarders, and many appeared to adopt a parental role toward their animals, expressing their desire for the unconditional love that their animals display (e.g., Hoarding of Animals Research Consortium, 2000).

A third explanation of animal hoarding is that it comes from strong feelings of responsibility, a sort of savior role. A number of people who hoard animals describe such feelings and urges to save all animals (Arluke, 1998). Accordingly, amassing many animals could be an effort to save them from danger and death. As indicated in Chapter 1, one feature of hoarding is beliefs about having responsibility for objects. For those who hoard animals, beliefs about responsibility for animals may be a causal factor (although the source of this belief might be explained by other factors noted above). In fact, researchers from the Hoarding of Animals Research Consortium (2000, 2002) have suggested that animal hoarders often believe they are the only ones who care about and can provide for their animals. Accordingly, some people who hoard animals allege that in collecting animals, they are maintaining private "no-kill" animal shelters, rescues, or sanctuaries (Patronek & Hoarding of Animals Research Consortium, 2001).

Steketee, Frost, and the Hoarding of Animals Research Consortium (2010) study of animal hoarders suggested a three-part model for hoarding that combines features suggested above. The model begins with a failure to develop strong attachments to people early in life, at the same time that stressful and sometimes chaotic life events were occurring. This combination might reduce the person's ability as an adult to interact effectively with people and to cope with adverse situations. Those with easy access to animals may come to rely on them for emotional comfort and to confer human characteristics onto their animals, viewing them as the providers of unconditional love and support that was lacking from human sources. This model certainly requires further confirmation from research studies. Also, the neurobiology of animal hoarding has not been studied at this time, and thus possible similarities to other mental health conditions are not clear. On a cautionary note, it is likely that the majority of people with strong attachments to animals do not become animal hoarders and that most traumatized children do not develop animal (or even object) hoarding problems. Furthermore, our information about animal hoarding that guides this model is gathered retrospectively rather than prospectively. Still, this model merits further study and may prove a useful guide for resolving animal hoarding behavior as proposed later in this chapter.

The Angell Report (Patronek et al., 2006, pp. 19–20) offers criteria for three types of animal collectors with regard to the context of their hoarding. These remain speculative, as they are based on the impressions of 14 contributors to the report, and the categorizations may be overly simplistic as it is likely that more than one motivation for animal hoarding can occur within a single individual. The categories are as follows:

- *Overwhelmed caregivers* are thought to be the most common type. They begin their pet owning career by providing adequate and often very good care for passively acquired animals. They are often socially isolated and become strongly attached to their animals, which they consider family members. However, over time the caregiver gradually loses the capacity to care for and control the animals. The sheer number of animals puts economic pressure on the caregiver. They may also have trouble coping with their own social and/or medical challenges, leading to impaired personal and/or family functioning.

- *Rescuers* actively acquire animals and feel a strong mission to save them from mistreatment or death. They may work in no-kill shelters or other animal care settings, perhaps with others who share similar values. These individuals also begin with sufficient resources but gradually the number of animals overwhelms their ability to provide adequate food, shelter, and care. Despite this, they are unable to restrict the number of animals, relinquish animals to others for care, or work with authorities to correct the problem.
- *Exploiters*, who are believed to be rare, are thought to acquire animals to serve their own needs (e.g., staging dog fights) and lack empathy for animals or people, suggesting some sociopathic personality characteristics. Their denial is extreme and they can be manipulative, self-concerned, sometimes overtly charming and articulate, but entirely lacking in guilt about the animals' conditions. These are among the most difficult to pursue as they can successfully evade the law for years.

As evident from these descriptions, the intervention strategies for addressing the problem should probably be quite different across these groups. Some ideas for intervention tailored to the type of animal hoarding are offered below.

DETECTION AND LEGAL ENFORCEMENT OF ANIMAL HOARDING

In most cases, animal hoarders are reported to authorities by neighbors or by service workers (e.g., a utility repair person or housing inspector). After a home visit by the appropriate authorities, formal complaints are filed by public servants (public health, sanitation, housing code, police or fire safety, Department of Agriculture officers) and/or human service workers (animal protection, child/adult/elder protection, and mental health staff) (Patronek, 1999). A wide variety of animal care agencies across the country can be called on to assist in animal hoarding cases. These include the local humane society or the state Society for the Prevention of Cruelty to Animals (SPCA) agents who may also be sworn police officers. When the home is publically owned (public housing), the relevant housing authority can authorize entry by investigators (e.g., fire, police, aging, child protection).

However, when the property is privately owned, obtaining a warrant to examine the property may be difficult unless there is clear evidence outside the home of a legal violation that would enable law enforcement authorities or public health and fire officers to request a warrant to enter the home. Such evidence often appears in the form of a feces-strewn yard or piled garbage that is attracting rats and other rodents or standing water that is attracting insects. Both represent a community health risk for which a warrant to enter the home might be secured from a court judge. On a cautionary note, as noted in Chapter 3 regarding object hoarding, a warrant for one agency (e.g., public health) does not automatically permit a staff member from another agency (e.g., housing or zoning authority) to enter the home. Thus, if possible, the first warrant for entry should include all agencies that may need access to the home to manage the problem (see Chapter 10 for more information about hoarding and the legal system).

As the Angell Report proposes, a multidisciplinary team approach is undoubtedly the best method for enabling communities to cope effectively with the problem of animal hoarding (Patronek et al., 2006). A number of communities have developed animal hoarding protocols in the context of general hoarding task forces as outlined in Chapter 3. Collaboration among several agencies in which individual professionals know each other is extremely helpful in obtaining the necessary warrant(s) and engaging the animal hoarder's cooperation. As for hoarding of objects, human service professionals at the bachelors or masters level are most likely to become involved when they encounter animal hoarding cases in the context of their work in child, adult, or elder protection agencies, in housing organizations, and in mental health services. Their role in investigating and understanding the problem must be anchored by knowledge of legal regulations, probably much more so than in the case of clients who hoard only objects.

Due to state animal cruelty laws, nearly all investigations of significant cases of animal hoarding begin at the legal level, with social work and other human service professionals assisting to assess the mental health and social capacities of the animal hoarder(s). In this regard, animal hoarding is treated differently from object hoarding because of laws about cruelty to animals. Once discovered, the animals are usually taken away from the person, and limited effort is made to protect personal autonomy as is typical for people who hoard objects. Thus, human services staff who become involved may need to help balance animal protection efforts with the protection of owners in these cases. Below we outline some of the recommended steps derived from the practice experience of animal hoarding experts and from task force groups.

Assessing animal hoarding cases is often more complex than assessing object hoarding because of the multiple factors involved. That is, assessment must encompass the animals' welfare, the state of the home, and the status of the people who are hoarding. Depending on how each community assigns this task, the assessment of animal care and safety generally falls to regional SPCAs, humane societies, or animal control officers. Standard assessment protocols shared across communities are undoubtedly helpful in this field, but require adaptation to the laws of each state. One useful instrument is the Tufts Animal Care and Condition (TACC) scale (Patronek, 2004), reprinted in the Appendix. This simple two-page instrument is a concise way to summarize animal care for a population of animals. Of course, the decision to prosecute should be made based on a range of factors that go beyond the condition of the animals and/or the home. This requires assessment of the mental and physical health of the animal owner/caretaker, a previous history of animal collecting and animal cruelty, community environmental risk (public health laws may apply), and the health and safety of others living in the home (child/adult protection laws apply, see Chapter 8). Of course, even when formal assessment methods are employed, legal statutes must be interpreted in light of the specific context for each charge of animal cruelty based on the factors noted above.

Authorities and human service personnel are confronted regularly with denial of the problem and resistance to authority, presenting a real challenge for both assessment and intervention. Usually, by the time of discovery, severe animal hoarders have passed the point at which they recognize the problem. Likely they have been refusing for some time to admit their difficulty in caring for their animals to themselves and to family members, neighbors, and friends. This denial may stem from an inability to admit their mistakes and shortcomings because of very strong beliefs in their caretaker role ("I love animals and they love me" from the overwhelmed caregiver), in their mission to save animals ("I save animals who need me" from the rescuer), or in their right to do as they please ("I'm a great person; I'm perfect" from the narcissistic exploiter). With reference to self-neglecting elders who come to the attention of adult protection workers, Nathanson (2009) suggested that another reason for denying animal hoarding problems may be the elder's belief that if he or she finds the living conditions satisfactory, this must also be true for the animals.

Once entrenched, such beliefs interfere with insight and motivation to change and contribute to strong resistance to differing views and to efforts to change. However, with sensitivity to the hoarders' beliefs and to the human–animal bonds at work, human service workers and animal protection officers may be able to engage the individual who hoards in a dialogue that facilitates disclosure and assessment of the person's situation and capacity. This is no small task, given the powerful urge to avoid the loss of the animals by refuting the allegations and avoiding legal prosecution. A carrot and stick approach may help as professionals charged with legal responsibilities focus only on those (using neutral language to convey concerns and regulations), whereas nonregulatory professionals (e.g., mental health) engage the person in a discussion of their feelings about the experience, their love for animals, and their history of experiences with animals. As the person warms to these topics, nonthreatening explorations of problems in managing the household and animals can facilitate an admission of problems and needs that leads to reasonable solutions for future planning.

INTERVENTIONS FOR ANIMALS

The outcomes of prosecutions for animal hoarding were examined in a study of 56 cases identified through media reports (Berry, Patronek, & Lockwood, 2005). The findings indicated considerable disparity in the disposition of hoarding cases and in communications among agencies in different regions of the country. Most of these media cases focused mainly on animal outcomes and did not provide follow-up data for the owners with regard to psychological evaluations and counseling. One concern is that lenient treatment of the animal collectors in exchange for authorities taking custody of the animals will lead to recidivism as hoarders simply continue their problematic behavior. Of course, this is not surprising, if little effort was made to alter basic beliefs and behaviors in this group. As the Angell Report suggests, clear identification of those who hoard animals and periodic monitoring of animal care as part of the sentence could help resolve these legal cases more quickly and reduce animal suffering.

Animal hoarding cases often place enormous strain on the resources of animal care facilities and community resources. As the Angell Report notes, for even one case of animal hoarding, a team of animal control officers and shelter workers must typically work hours and even days to find and triage the hoarded animals. In some cases, animal recovery requires specialized assistance from firefighters or police officers, especially in severe cases in which there are high concentrations of noxious fumes, dangerous structures, and fire hazards. Additional costs include public health and housing inspections, property clean-up or demolition, as well as administrative and court costs. Loar and colleagues are currently developing an on-line method for calculating such costs (Nathanson, 2010, personal communication).

In addition to these expenses are the costs associated with the health and welfare of the animals themselves. In some cases in which the health of the animals is severely compromised, they must be euthanized immediately and their bodies removed with appropriate care. For many animals, however, extensive veterinary care is required over long periods of time to restore the animals' health. When large numbers of animals are involved, the costs for veterinary care, food, and housing can be substantial and overwhelm usual budgets.

Professionals will need to determine whether any pets should be allowed to remain in the home and, if so, how many and which ones. This decision requires the input of the animal care team as well as those evaluating the psychological and behavioral capacity of the owner to provide appropriate care and supervision of the animal(s). Thus, this requires a decision after consultation across relevant agency staff members and may involve the decision of a judge. Working with the person who hoards to develop a plan for placement or adoption can mitigate the emotional anguish over the removal of animals. If the owner is allowed to keep some animals, it is essential to establish a time frame for monitoring animal safety and progress in maintaining a suitable home environment. This task might be assigned to animal care agency staff with veterinary knowledge and/or to protective services staff as appropriate, but it does require a home visit to verify that standards are met. We are not aware of measures for assessing such improvement at this time, and therefore this decision would be a judgment call based on interpretation of legal statutes.

INTERVENTIONS FOR PEOPLE WHO HOARD ANIMALS

Human service professionals working with people who hoard animals need to understand the person's relationship to their animals to help develop essential rapport and communication. This lays the groundwork for a cooperative response to service planning and case management (Nathanson, 2009). Similarly, it is critical that workers learn the applicable local and state standards for human and animal habitation to best understand what required changes are necessary to protect the animals, as discussed above.

Appropriate interventions for people who hoard animals depend on the characteristics and history of the owner and the severity of the hoarding situation. For example, in some cases, pets were appropriately cared for over many years until the person lost his or her capacity to control the numbers of animals and to manage their care. More likely, however, such individuals will require substantial assistance to remain in the existing home (presuming it is habitable) and will be unable to manage more than one or two neutered animals in the home. In some cases, an assisted living situation that provides oversight with everyday activities may be required; however, animals are rarely allowed in such settings.

When the person who hoards animals appears to have mild to moderate mental health problems (e.g., depression, anxiety disorders), court mandates might require social workers or other mental health clinicians to conduct a thorough diagnostic assessment (see Chapter 5) to identify current symptoms and help determine appropriate care. For example, when the person expresses a strong need for attachment because of a poor early family attachment history and social isolation, it may be advisable to allow one or two animals in the home with periodic oversight to ensure adequate care. This might be recommended in conjunction with regular court-mandated mental health services to provide support for animal care and identify ways to increase appropriate social activities and decrease other mental health problems. The retention of at least one animal might be especially important for someone suffering from depression with suicidal ideation, especially as the removal of animals constitutes a traumatic loss requiring substantial adjustment.

More serious mental health concerns such as severe personality disorders or psychosis accompanied by full denial of the problem are more likely to require complete removal of animals and mandated mental health services to ensure adequate self and home care. Adequate treatment that includes medications, psychotherapy, and support from family or others may improve the person's mental health so that limited and monitored animal ownership can be reinstated. Thorough assessment is critical in determining the most appropriate and humane course of action for both the owner and the animals in these situations.

TIPS AND STRATEGIES FOR ANIMAL HOARDING INTERVENTION

- Learn the criteria for animal hoarding and share them with others working on the case.
- Identify and meet with the authority responsible for humane animal law enforcement in the community (e.g., SPCA, humane society, animal control officer, or police).
- Clarify expectations of the animal agency with respect to custody, veterinary care, and disposition of the animals.
- Decide how to address the media to ensure client confidentiality is maintained.

- Interview the hoarder about his or her relationship to the animals and about any other immediate problems (e.g., housing, financial, health) to be sure you understand the full extent of the problem.
- Observe the dwelling carefully to obtain details about the following:
  - the animal population (types of animals, ages, neuter status, location in home, confinement status, ownership status, source of animals)
  - the condition and safety features of the home.
- Summarize the animal's health. If possible, use a screening tool such as the TACC (see Appendix).
- Obtain information about state and municipal legal requirements for animal care and review these with the person who is hoarding.
- Engage needed human service resources (e.g., health, mental health, housing and neighborhood code enforcement, police, fire, child/adult/aging protective services, disability services, public assistance) to facilitate collaborative multidisciplinary efforts for crisis intervention and case management.
- Be sure that those who are clearing and cleaning the home use appropriate protective gear, particularly respiratory masks and gloves.

CASE STUDY: JENNIFER

Jennifer was a 31-year-old, single mother living in a two-bedroom apartment in a small urban town. She came to the attention of a staff member in a metropolitan housing organization after an inspection of her home that is required to maintain her Section 8 voucher. She suffered from depression and bipolar disorder and reported a significant history of trauma and a previous problem with substance abuse. Her daughter was in the custody of state child protective services because of emotional and behavioral problems until Jennifer is able to develop better self-care skills. At the time of intake, Jennifer's only income derived from occasional financial contributions from her boyfriend, who she described as emotionally abusive, exploitative, and controlling. Her severe untreated depression left Jennifer unable to work. Possibly because of her low mood, she has not applied for disability benefits and therefore receives only a small subsidy in the form of a voucher for her housing.

During the inspection of Jennifer's apartment, the inspector noticed a strong smell of urine coming from the exterior window air conditioning unit. Inside the apartment, he found one dog and 35 cats, as well as animal feces and urine covering most surfaces; the single litter box had not been cleaned in some time. An overturned bag of cat food was spilling from a cabinet in the kitchen. Cats were found in the cabinets and had penetrated the lower portion of the kitchen wall, exposing nails in the floor underneath the carpet. Jennifer's bedroom was similar to the kitchen and living rooms—her sheets and other bed linens were covered with dog and cat urine; the odor was so strong that the inspector worried about his health because of the ammonia fumes. He felt obliged to ask Jennifer to open a window during the inspection. Surprisingly, the bedroom that Jennifer's daughter would have occupied had she been living in the home was clean and well organized, completely free of any animal presence.

After completing the inspection, the inspector followed his agency's protocol, notifying Jennifer of the specific violations he found and advising her that he was making a referral to help her obtain the resources and support necessary to bring the unit back into compliance. He also told her that the town's animal control department might be contacted and explained that someone from his agency would tell her if this step was necessary. The housing inspector then contacted the housing agency's Hoarding and Sanitation Initiative to request immediate help for Jennifer's situation.

Following the inspection, two case managers from the agency who were trained to assist with hoarding problems contacted Jennifer and arranged to visit her the following day. During this visit, the case managers interviewed Jennifer and also assessed the physical conditions of the home. They identified Jennifer as an overwhelmed animal owner who had started with three cats but found that she was unable to manage the animal care as they bred and the number of cats increased. Interestingly, the presence of the cats served as a deterrent to Jennifer's abusive boyfriend who had minimized his visits to the home as the conditions deteriorated. In addition, the caseworkers learned that Jennifer had become a mother at the age of 14 and had received little familial or social support after her daughter was born.

Using the information from their interview, the case managers worked with Jennifer to develop a stepped service plan. With Jennifer's knowledge, they contacted the SPCA to obtain assistance in removing some of the animals. However, the SPCA initially screened the case out of their jurisdiction as not sufficiently severe to warrant their involvement. The case managers then called the town fire department and spoke with the fire chief who knew of the animal hoarding but was unsure how to proceed. Following the conversation, he too made a referral to the SPCA. This dual referral led to a visit by the animal officer who worked with Jennifer to select animals to remove in order to allow her to retain her Section 8 housing voucher. She chose 20 cats that were removed during the first visit and in a subsequent visit an additional 14 cats were removed. This left Jennifer with two animals she chose to keep—a cat and the dog. At this time the SPCA officer also arranged veterinary care for all of the animals, including the two remaining in the apartment.

After the animals were taken away, the case managers worked with Jennifer on proper care for her remaining animals and ensured that these animals were neutered. They also helped her gain access to appropriate mental health treatment for her depression and bipolar symptoms. The case managers coordinated with the local child protection agency to assist Jennifer in applying for disability benefits to provide sufficient income so that she would not need to rely on her boyfriend for financial assistance. At this time, the case managers were also able to arrange for a reasonable accommodation based on Jennifer's disability (see Chapter 10 for more about reasonable accommodation). As part of this accommodation the housing inspection department increased the amount of time Jennifer had to address the sanitation concerns. Finally, the property owner agreed to pay for the cost of sanitizing or replacing the carpet in the unit.

To ensure continued compliance with health and safety codes, the housing agency's Hoarding and Sanitation Initiative implemented a monitoring component that began as soon as the resident's apartment passed inspection. Jennifer met periodically with a case manager to support her in continuing her mental health treatment and maintaining her apartment appropriately. Six months after passing inspection, Jennifer continued to keep her unit in good condition and was regularly attending mental health and substance abuse treatment. Furthermore, her daughter was scheduled to return to the apartment in the coming months.

Case Discussion

A diagram of the services accessed in Jennifer's case is provided in Figure 9–1. Her animal hoarding was moderate in severity, as some cases can be very severe with many more animals as well as dead and dying animals. Her case was typical in that it encompassed multiple other problems, including housing damage and sanitation problems, as well as mental health, financial, and child and family problems. This necessitated careful assessment of the family problems. The inspector also noted the odor emanating from the home, and although he did not employ the animal assessment methods mentioned above, it is clear that the animal hoarding had led to serious health and sanitation concerns.

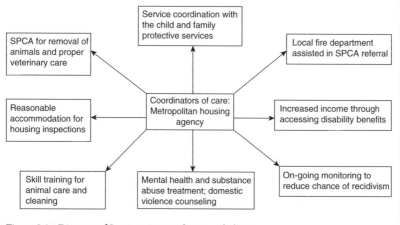

Figure 9.1: Diagram of Services Accessed in Jennifer's Case.

With several identified problems, it is not surprising that multiple agencies were needed to achieve the positive outcome evident here. In Jennifer's case, the case management team from the housing agency provided coordination for the several human service agencies involved. These housing managers were well trained in understanding hoarding problems and had considerable experience accessing services for tenants under their purview. It is clear that good relationships with various agency staff helped facilitate access to needed services, a goal that is typical of hoarding interventions conducted by community hoarding task forces.

The ongoing involvement of a case manager and other treatment providers appeared to help Jennifer meet the goals set by the housing agency for maintaining her home. These professionals had more leverage to achieve compliance than in some animal hoarding cases, perhaps because Jennifer wanted to secure the return of her child. Nonetheless, it seems likely that without the support of the case manager, she would have relapsed, a common occurrence among those with animal hoarding problems.

CHAPTER 10

Hoarding and the Legal System

This chapter is intended to guide those working within the legal system or in liaison with legal staff. This includes judges, public defenders and prosecutors, private attorneys, state and municipal police officers, court-appointed housing specialists, staff at legal service agencies, paralegal staff, and *guardians ad litem*. Other human service professionals, such as housing inspectors and those working in child, adult, elder, and animal protective services, may find this chapter helpful insofar as their hoarding clients become involved with the legal system.

As noted in Chapter 1, hoarding is often associated with limited insight into the problem. Although it is often immediately obvious to others when the person has accumulated more possessions than is safe or comfortable, this is often not apparent to the person who hoards. In addition, these individuals often do not perceive their attachment to a wide range of possessions, fears about discarding possessions, and regular acquisition of unneeded items as exaggerated. Unfortunately, the unintended consequences of hoarding can be devastating, resulting in potentially deadly housing fires and pest-borne illnesses (Chapter 6), neglect or abuse of children, the elderly, and the disabled, including impediments to normal development and health (Chapter 8), and animal abuse evident in starving and maltreated animals (Chapter 9). The severity of these consequences calls for action, but as indicated in earlier chapters, intervention is often not a simple matter as the limited awareness of the hoarding problem limits motivation to correct the situation. In such cases, the legal system is an important avenue for protecting the people and animals affected by hoarding and motivating individuals to make necessary changes.

The legal system becomes involved with hoarding cases when the consequences may lead to civil or criminal charges. For example, as a condition of leasing a home, many states require that the home be kept free of excessive possessions and that trash must be kept safely and disposed of promptly. Thus, as hoarding moves from mild to moderate, it can be judged to be a violation of the lease. The landlord may then bring this civil matter to the courts by seeking to evict the tenant. In another example, federal and state statutes protect children, the disabled, and elderly adults; moderate to severe hoarding by an individual with whom they live may be judged to constitute abuse or neglect of these vulnerable populations. In such cases, protective agencies can file civil or criminal charges against the home dweller. In cases of animal hoarding, criminal charges can be brought in federal court for conditions that constitute abuse and neglect of animals.

Cases involving hoarding are heard in a variety of courts depending on the nature of the complaint and the consequences involved. Civil housing cases are heard in counties with housing courts or in district courts when the county has no housing court. Hoarding cases involving neglect or abuse of elders and disabled adults are heard in probate or family court, and cases pertinent to child abuse or neglect are heard in these courts or in juvenile court. Criminal charges related to abuse or neglect of vulnerable people or animals are heard in district court.

The legal system can play a key role in effecting change in cases of hoarding. One role is to grant permission to authorities to enter a home and/or remove individuals and animals from harm. In many states, certain authorities, such as public health officials, must appear before a judge to request a warrant that gives them the right to enter a home and conduct an inspection. Child, adult and animal protective service professionals often appear before a judge for permission to remove neglected or abused people or animals from the home. Others may be granted the right of entry by the court to gather information needed to hear the case. Those who can be granted such a right include court-appointed housing inspectors, guardians *ad litem*, and lawyers. One caveat about warrants: although it is often expedient for different agencies (e.g., public health, child protective services) to share a warrant that grants entry to a particular home, we are aware of at least one case in which a family sued multiple agencies for overstepping their authority by not requesting separate warrants for each agency to enter the home.

The legal system also plays a role in enforcing an existing right of entry. Some authorities, such as fire officials, have the right under state law to enter a residence or other property without a warrant. However, if the dwellers deny these authorities access to the home, the legal system can be marshaled to enforce the right of entry, for example, through summons to appear before a judge and sanctions, such as fines, resulting from ongoing refusal to allow entry. Similarly, individuals and agencies (landlords, housing authority staff) that have the right to enter a property to inspect conditions pertinent to the lease can appeal to the court to enforce their right of access if it is denied. Likewise, in the case of private homes, public health officials can seek a legal warrant to enter when public health problems are visible from outside the home.

Another role of the legal system is to mandate change or to enforce change mandated by others. Certain authorities, such as the local fire or health department, routinely outline needed changes after inspection with a timeline for completion. For example, a tenant might be given 1 month to clear pathways to all doors and windows or to remove papers from the stove. If the tenant does not comply, these departments may appeal to the legal system to enforce the required changes, for example, through the threat of eviction or condemnation of the home. Similarly, protective service agencies can outline requirements that permit family member(s) to remain in or return to the home. Such legal mandates play an important role in motivating compliance through the threat of temporary and even permanent loss of child custody or guardianship of an elder or disabled adult. In cases of animal hoarding, prosecutors can appeal to the judge to limit or eliminate the offender's right to own animals. Individuals with hoarding problems of all kinds may also be legally mandated to engage in mental health treatment.

When intervention fails, the legal system has the ultimate responsibility of imposing sanctions or consequences for unresolved hoarding. In cases of lease violation, the lease is typically terminated and the tenant is evicted. Tenants who have a housing voucher may lose the voucher in addition to being evicted. For privately owned homes that continue to be in violation of fire or sanitation codes despite legal pressure to bring the home into compliance, the home is condemned. In cases involving abuse and neglect, the court removes custody permanently from the individual with a hoarding problem. For situations involving animal hoarding, the owner can be fined or, in extreme situations, sentenced to spend time in jail or prison. Thus, the consequences for failure to comply with legal regulations, especially repeated failure, can be severe.

KEY ROLES

Many individuals and agencies play key roles in the legal system. Because these roles differ across states, counties, and even municipalities, we offer a broad description and provide some examples of variations in the "Tips and Strategies" section below. The legal system becomes engaged in hoarding cases through the actions of individuals or agencies that trigger legal activity. One entry point is through first responders such as local and state police officers who often alert other agencies (e.g., fire, public health, child welfare) to the problem. In addition, police officers may be in a position to provide information to those who hoard about sources of help, such as human services. They can also serve as witnesses to the condition of the home or testify about the neglect or maltreatment of vulnerable people and animals. In some jurisdictions, the legal system is engaged when district attorneys and local prosecutors respond to reports of animal cruelty due to hoarding. These attorneys can bring criminal charges against the owner to both safeguard the abused animals and prevent the person from acquiring new animals.

Individuals and agencies who are not officers of the court can also serve as entry points for legal action. Among these are professionals working in protective services and public health and fire department personnel. The primary focus of these individuals and agencies is to safeguard vulnerable individuals and animals and to protect the community. In addition, they are often able to provide information and access to helpful resources and to monitor change. Housing providers are another point of entry for compliance or actions of eviction, and they may remain involved with tenants over an extended period as part of a reasonable accommodation to the person's disability (see "Hoarding and Federal and State Laws" below). Because of this extended contact, housing staff are often motivated to provide treatment information and resources to reduce clutter, such as home health aides or refuse removal services. Court-appointed assessors also play key roles in hoarding cases. Specialists employed through the housing court can conduct home inspections and provide information to the court about the condition of the home and changes over time. In potential cases of child abuse or neglect due to hoarding, a court-appointed *guardian ad litem* conducts an independent assessment of the home and the family context in the service of protecting the child's welfare.

Judges play a central role in cases involving hoarding. As mentioned earlier, they issue warrants that allow access to the home and make decisions about custody of children, guardianship of vulnerable adults, and ownership of animals. Judges also issue court orders to motivate change, particularly to bring homes into compliance with safety and sanitation standards and with the conditions of the lease in cases of rented homes. They can be instrumental in setting concrete goals with specific deadlines and in monitoring maintenance of gains following mandated interventions. For example, they can choose to continue a case rather than close it when maintenance is a concern. Judges also have the responsibility to mete out consequences when change does not take place or when the hoarding individual is charged with a criminal offense, as may be the case with animal hoarding.

Private and public attorneys (e.g., public prosecutors, public defenders, attorneys employed by legal service agencies) work alongside judges and play key roles by representing hoarding clients or opposing parties. Lawyers representing hoarding clients can advocate for a reasonable change plan, clarify the judges' orders, advise clients to seek support in overcoming their disorder, and help maintain their client's motivation for change between court dates. They can also help document the change process and advocate for their client's rights, as highlighted in the case study at the end of this chapter. Lawyers representing the opposing party can similarly advocate for a change plan with a timeline and specific benchmarks, as well as for mental health treatment and/or other services that promote change.

PITFALLS OF STANDARD INTERVENTIONS FOR HOARDING

The primary problem with standard legal interventions for hoarding is that they usually focus on the consequences of hoarding (removing clutter, cleaning the home) and neglect intervention for the underlying mental disorder. As a result, hoarding is currently a problem with a very high rate of recidivism. Individuals whose hoarding provokes legal action often have less power and resources than the plaintiff (for example, a building association, the town Board of Health). As a result, they are likely to lose the case and face serious negative consequences such as eviction. Because such legal outcomes do not resolve the underlying problem, these individuals may be evicted multiple times as the hoarding recurs when the person rents a different home, accumulates more possessions, and is again faced with legal action. Low-income individuals and families living in subsidized housing may become permanently homeless due to hoarding, usually because they lose their housing voucher or cannot obtain affordable housing after being evicted. Although shelters are often available to accommodate homeless people, as noted in Chapter 6, continued hoarding can interfere with their ability to remain in those safety net settings.

When family members or towns pay to clean out the hoarded home to forestall eviction or condemnation, the individual almost invariably reaccumulates possessions. Indeed, it is not unusual for the problem to worsen due to strong feelings of anger or loss evoked by the cleanout. Such consequences are especially problematic in cases of abuse and neglect when vulnerable individuals return to cleared out homes, only to have the problem recur. In the case of animal hoarding, the recidivism rate after removing animals approaches 100% (Berry, Patronek, & Lockwood, 2005). Because most individuals cannot overcome hoarding without treatment, mandating change in the home without appropriate mental health treatment virtually guarantees eviction, loss of custody of children, guardianship of disabled adults, or elderly relatives, or removal of animals.

Another serious problem with standard interventions for hoarding through the legal system is that those who hoard can suffer grave effects of having their homes forcibly cleaned out. The film, *My Mother's Garden*, documents the case of producer Cynthia Lester's mother Eugenia who has a severe hoarding disorder. The film captures the children's efforts during a 6-week-long cleanout of her home while Eugenia takes a trip with her daughter to another city. Although Eugenia consented to the cleanout, she is devastated on her return home. The film captures her protracted experience of loss and grief as a result of the clean out, an emotional crisis that leads to many weeks of psychiatric hospitalization for severe depression. In some cases, cleanouts are associated with even more severe consequences as in the case mentioned in Chapter 2 in which three homeowners who were cleaned out by the local Health Department died shortly after returning to their homes (Brace, 2007).

AN EMERGING ROLE OF THE LEGAL SYSTEM: PROMOTING ENDURING CHANGE

An emerging role of the legal system is to intervene effectively with hoarding, addressing the underlying problem and establishing enduring change. A growing number of judges and lawyers across the country are becoming aware that hoarding requires a more sophisticated approach than simply evicting the individual, mandating a cleanout, or removing vulnerable individuals from the home. Officers of the court have begun working together with human service providers to coordinate pressure on those who hoard to change and also to provide support in making necessary changes. This approach has the effect of resolving the hoarding problem in the long term and also mitigates the legislative power differential faced by many of those who hoard.

A key part of this process is generating a clear plan that clarifies essential changes in the home and gives a timeline for reaching the mandated benchmarks (Volunteer Lawyers Project, 2008). In contrast to the days or weeks budgeted by standard court orders, these plans often allow months for benchmarks to be completed, making the goals attainable by hoarding offenders and those supporting them. These plans often have reasonable expectations about reducing clutter and ensuring safety, prioritizing safety, and sanitation. For example, priority is given to removing flammable materials and garbage, creating access to critical appliances such as sinks, sanitizing kitchen and bathroom surfaces, clearing entryways, and creating broad pathways through the home (Volunteer Lawyers Project, 2008). Reducing possessions and organizing the home are the focus of the plan after the higher priority safety and sanitation tasks have been accomplished. Of course, vulnerable individuals may have to be removed from the home until it is rendered to be an acceptable living environment.

Officers of the court are also becoming aware that hoarding rarely resolves through a plan for clearing and organizing the home, as hoarding is a problem not only in the home, but also inside the individual. As described in Chapter 5, overcoming hoarding requires changes in beliefs, emotions, and behaviors that contribute to hoarding, as well as new skills that help clients organize and discard items and resist acquiring. Increasingly, judges are mandating psychological individual or group treatment for those who hoard to help address the underlying mental disorder. In addition, due to the complexity of hoarding and accompanying mental and physical problems, a team approach may be recommended with support from mental health providers, visiting nurses, occupational therapists, and "heavy chore" agencies.

Even when the person is motivated to overcome hoarding and receives state-of-the-art intervention, backsliding is still common. This is especially likely without a mandate for regular assessment of the home. Accordingly, some judges are requiring ongoing monitoring of gains through court-instigated assessments. This mandated longer-term support can be instrumental in maintaining motivation to change and building on improvements.

HOARDING AND FEDERAL AND STATE LAWS

Housing

Hoarding jeopardizes housing stability and can even lead to permanent homelessness, for example, due to the loss of subsidized housing or a subsidized housing voucher. However, because hoarding is a mental disorder, eviction based on hoarding may constitute discrimination under the federal Fair Housing Act (the Act, see 42 U.S.C. §§ 3601–3619 for the entire Act and 42 U.S.C. § 3604 (f)(3) for the section on discrimination under the Act). This act aims to promote equal access to housing and prohibits discrimination on the basis of race, national origin, religion, skin color, sex, familial status, and disability, including mental disability. To ensure that those with disabilities have an equal opportunity to enjoy a dwelling, the Act requires that housing providers make reasonable accommodations in their services, practices, rules and policies for such individuals and their families. (For examples of reasonable accommodations see the "Joint Statement of the Department of Housing and Urban Development and the Department of Justice," *Reasonable Accommodations Under the Fair Housing Act*, 2004.) A housing provider may not deny a request for a reasonable accommodation unless it would impose an excessive financial or administrative burden. However, even in such cases, housing providers are expected to engage in a dialogue with the person requesting accommodation to reach an agreement (Department of Housing and Urban Development & Department of Justice, 2004). As private landlords often have more limited resources than public housing providers, reasonable accommodations may differ for private or public housing providers (see Chapter 6).

As mentioned earlier, even mild to moderate hoarding may constitute a breach of the lease since hoarding can lead to unsanitary or unsafe conditions. Nonetheless, the Fair Housing Act makes clear that unless housing providers attempt to make a reasonable accommodation, they are guilty of discrimination on the basis of mental disability. Reasonable accommodation may involve delaying eviction proceedings and allowing the tenant to access mental health treatment or other services that would facilitate bringing the home into compliance with the lease (Volunteer Lawyers Project, 2008). It may also involve tolerating different or unusual behavior (for example, owning more possessions than usual), provided the behavior does not actually breach sanitation or safety codes. We note that laws regarding eviction and timetables for compliance vary from state to state.

Protection of Children, Disabled Adults, and Elders

As noted earlier, federal laws protect children from abuse and neglect (42 U.S.C. Ch. 132), as well as elders and adults with disabilities (42 U.S.C. Ch. 35, §3002). When hoarding interferes with normal caring for children, disabled adults, and elders, it may constitute neglect or abuse. In many states, self-neglect by an elderly or disabled person also constitutes an adult protection concern under the law. Most states consider a person under 18 years to be a child, whereas definitions of disability and eligibility for elder abuse prevention services vary across states. Most states, like the federal law, consider a person aged 60 years or older to be an elder who qualifies for elder services (Lawyers.com, 2010). Each state is mandated to have one or more agencies whose task it is to respond to reports of abuse and neglect. States also mandate reporting of suspected abuse or neglect to these agencies, although which individuals and agencies are mandated reporters differs across states. Law enforcement officers and medical and mental health providers are mandated reporters in most, if not all, states, and public health officials and even lawyers may be mandated reporters in some states.

Child welfare workers have a responsibility to act in the best interest of the child and must determine whether there is the need for the agency to seek custody or whether the child can remain safe living in the home. The child welfare agency works through the court to seek custody and may mandate mental health treatment for parents who hoard. The agency may make reunification with the child contingent on reduction of clutter in the home. Adult protective services differ from child protective services insofar as adults are entitled to make decisions for themselves. Accordingly, even if a disabled or elder adult is being abused or neglected because of hoarding (including self-neglect), adult protective services and the court generally cannot force him or her to accept help or leave the home. However, if protective service professionals have evidence that the disabled adult or elder is not competent to make his or her own decisions, they can petition the court for a competency evaluation and, if necessary, the appointment of a guardian. The guardian then has an obligation to safeguard the vulnerable adult and can be subject to criminal charges if he or she fails in this responsibility.

Animal Welfare

The Animal Welfare Act (7 U.S.C. §§ 2131–2159) is a federal statute that protects the rights of animals used in research, exhibition, and for commerce. It does not apply to the care of pets and also excludes birds, rats, and mice. As a result, there is wide variation in state animal welfare laws (Animal Legal Defense Fund, 2009). Nonetheless, each state has anticruelty laws and minimum standards of care for animals. All states require that animal owners and caretakers ensure that animals maintain their normal body weight through adequate nutrition, maintain normal body temperature through shelter from the elements, live in a clean and sanitary environment, and receive adequate veterinary care to treat illness or injury (Patronek et al., 2006). In addition to state laws, cities and towns may have animal care ordinances to further protect animals from cruelty.

The definition of animal hoarding is based on these animal welfare laws and ordinances such that animal neglect or cruelty is evident in inadequate food or shelter, squalid living conditions, and lack of veterinary care. Allegations of animal cruelty are investigated by different agencies depending on the state or county (e.g., humane society, animal warden). In some states and counties these investigators have the right to bring charges;

in other states and counties, these agencies alert the county or state prosecutor (e.g., District Attorney, State's Attorney, Prosecuting Attorney, or Commonwealth's Attorney) who then brings charges. Animal cruelty charges are criminal, and if the acts of neglect or abuse are serious enough, they can be deemed felonies. However, animal ownership is a right that only a judge can limit or eliminate with good cause. For this reason, investigators of animal hoarding must establish that animal cruelty has taken place by gathering admissible evidence (e.g., photographs, veterinary reports) and identifying reliable witnesses (Patronek et al., 2006). State or county prosecutors then advance animal cruelty charges, which can be followed by sanctions that include fines, jail or prison sentence, probation, elimination or limit of animal ownership, and mandated mental health treatment. Animal hoarding may also be reported to the local Health Department since it can lead to public health concerns (see next section).

Public Health and Safety

Public health and safety that affect homes and neighborhoods are primarily legislated at the state, county, and municipal levels. All states have detailed public health and safety codes that make unsanitary and unsafe conditions in the home or on properties an offense. Cities and towns often have additional ordinances to protect public health and safety. These codes and ordinances address dangerous and unsanitary conditions, such as improper storage of garbage, presence of animal feces and pest infestation, broken household plumbing, and fire hazards, such as flammable materials on stoves and near heaters. The codes and ordinances make provision for sanctions, such as fines, lease termination, or condemnation of properties, when violations are not addressed in a reasonable time frame. All communities have a health department whose mission is to prevent the spread of disease and a fire department to prevent and extinguish fires. These departments investigate complaints and ensure that property owners bring buildings and homes into compliance with health and safety codes and ordinances. Many cities also have other officials, such as building inspectors, who are charged with ensuring that properties are in compliance with state and local codes.

ASSESSMENT

Hoarding is an extreme behavior that falls outside the range of ordinary housekeeping. However, reasonable people may have different opinions about the severity of hoarding and the degree of change needed to render a home in compliance with relevant standards (e.g., safety, lease). Furthermore, individuals with hoarding who are ordered to declutter their homes can expend considerable effort but accomplish little improvement in the condition of the home because of the sheer volume of possessions and limited organizing skills. As a result, if the degree of change is not carefully documented, the hoarding individual may be unfairly judged to have put forth insufficient effort and may be unjustly penalized. Therefore, objective assessment of hoarding and especially clutter is critical to determine violations and compliance with laws.

A variety of hoarding assessment tools were described in Chapter 4. Among these the pictorial Clutter Image Rating (CIR, Frost et al., 2008) is one of the most useful for objectively recording change in clutter in the standard rooms of the home (living room, kitchen, bedroom). This simple measure requires no special training and is particularly well suited for use by court officers and agency staff reporting to the court to provide an objective baseline as well as a measure of change over time. Another means of assessing hoarding severity and change over time is photographs of the home; these can be supplied voluntarily by the dweller or may be ordered by the judge. Photographs can be taken by a range of individuals, including court-appointed inspectors, lawyers, and agencies reporting to the court, such as child and adult protective services. An important caveat, however, is to request that subsequent pictures be taken from the same location and angle as the baseline photos. The judge interprets this evidence and determines if sufficient progress has been made on clutter and sanitary conditions to forestall pending negative consequences (eviction, condemnation, loss of custody, etc.)

Testimony from eyewitnesses and from experts is another source of information about the severity of the hoarding problem and the degree of change achieved. Eyewitnesses should be reliable external evaluators (unbiased to the extent possible) and may include local and state law enforcement officers, medical first responders, fire department personnel, landlords, housing provider inspectors, housing subsidy agency inspectors, city housing inspectors, public health staff, protective service and animal welfare professionals, and guardians *ad litem*. At times, experts on hoarding may be needed to educate the court about hoarding severity and outcomes based on their clinical experience and on the use of standardized hoarding assessment tools. These professionals can also speak to the issue of reasonable change over time based on the size of the home, the quantity of possessions, the capacity of the individual, and other relevant factors.

By their nature, court cases are adversarial—an unresolved conflict has brought the case before a judge, the parties are assigned the role of plaintiff and defendant, and the goal is to determine guilt or innocence of the defendant. This adversarial style stands in contradiction to hoarding intervention efforts, which assume the client is ambivalent about change and must first resolve this ambivalence via a mental health service provider (see Chapter 2). Direct argument is avoided as it promotes resistance to change. Nonetheless, external pressure in the form of limits, consequences, and deadlines is often necessary to help individuals with limited motivation prioritize clutter removal. Thus, these conflicting goals and needs must be balanced to facilitate maximum improvement in the hoarding behavior.

Judges play a key role in courtroom intervention. A judge's authority to issue orders to evict a tenant, remove a housing voucher, or condemn a home can provide essential pressure toward change when pressure from others such as family members, landlords, and public health officials has failed. Similarly, judges make decisions about child protection, exerting pressure on the individual who hoards to retain or regain legal and physical custody. Judges can issue orders specifying decluttering goals and time frames and can mandate mental health treatment or other needed social services. In mandating services, judges should take into account the local availability of trained hoarding treatment providers and the need for sustained intervention that might require several months. Another problem may be payment for services. Mental health treatment for hoarding is currently billed as treatment for obsessive compulsive disorder (until hoarding disorder is included in the *DSM* as a separate billable mental health problem). Most health insurers cover such treatment, but creative solutions are needed for uninsured defendants and for other needed services that do not fall under a mental health service, such as heavy chore or clean-up work. By keeping cases open, judges have the opportunity to exert pressure over time and also monitor maintenance of gains.

TIPS AND STRATEGIES

- Develop creative strategies to intervene with hoarding. For example, California included a provision in its housing code for temporary receivership of properties to remedy code violations. The judge appoints a receiver who effectively becomes the guardian of the property, ordering necessary work, such as removing clutter and repairing plumbing and structural damage. The homeowner must fund this work, and the court can order the owner to make necessary arrangements, such as refinancing the home to pay for the needed changes. Once the home is brought into compliance, the receivership is dissolved. This strategy seems a humane and positive alternative to declaring the dweller incompetent based solely on the hoarding behavior.

- Establish a liaison agency to mediate between those with hoarding problems, landlords, and the court. The Tenancy Preservation Project (TPP) in Massachusetts plays such a role. TPP is part of MassHousing, a statewide agency that provides affordable housing to low and moderate income residents with a goal of preventing homelessness among those with disabilities. In addition to its mediation role, TPP staff members collaborate with many other agencies, including protective services, housing management companies, legal services, and so forth. TPP caseworkers can advocate for clients, locate resources, and coordinate services, helping scores of low-income tenants who hoard to remain stably housed.
- Develop standardized protocols for intervening with hoarding. In part this depends on the recognition that hoarding is a complex cognitive, emotional, and behavioral disorder. Federal statutes may be needed to standardize the practice of ordering mental health treatment for hoarding (cf. 42 U.S.C. Ch. 42).
- Consider adopting the International Property Maintenance Code (International Code Council, 2009) for the town or county to promote standardization across communities of both property maintenance requirements and code violations.
- Use conditional termination of a lease or housing voucher to exert pressure on individuals who hoard to initiate and maintain reductions in clutter. A judge who determines that the tenant is in violation of the lease or voucher can rule to terminate the lease or voucher but can then continue the case, allowing the tenant a designated period of time to bring the home into compliance and thereby reinstate the lease or voucher. A judge can also order specific benchmarks that must be accomplished by each court date. To monitor change, a city inspector or housing agency inspector can be appointed.
- Use photographs of the home as a communication tool to document baseline hoarding status and efforts for change. Those who hoard may resist this plan due to negative reactions to legal system involvement in their lives and embarrassment about the state of their home. To reduce these concerns, the attorney can request that they be placed under seal rather than being part of the public case record. If possible, two or three wide-angel photos should be taken of each room and repeated from the same angle at future evaluations of progress.

CASE STUDY: BRENDA

Brenda, a 49-year-old divorced white woman living on disability income, was using her housing voucher to rent one of four apartments in a building owned by a private landlord. In addition to hoarding, Brenda suffered from severe depression. Although she had been hospitalized several times in the past and had taken psychotropic medication, she was not receiving any mental health treatment at the time the case was active. As a result of hoarding, Brenda had been evicted twice in the previous 10 years. She acknowledged that she had too many possessions in her home, but she viewed her past evictions as major contributors to her hoarding because she had been forced to pack her belongings quickly without time to sort and organize them.

Brenda's landlord became aware of the excessive clutter when he talked to Brenda in her doorway about needed repairs. He noticed that Brenda had difficulty opening her door because of the piles and could see no obvious pathways through the rooms. He also complained to Brenda that she had too many things in her common area. Brenda responded that the area was not strictly "common" since she alone occupied the top floor of the building. The landlord became increasingly frustrated with her failure to make changes and called a lawyer. His lawyer sent Brenda a *Notice to Quit*, citing lease violations as the reason for terminating her lease. A 30-day *Notice to Quit* is the first step in evicting a tenant in the state in which Brenda lives. Once the notice period expired, the landlord's lawyer prepared a *Summary Process Eviction* complaint that was served to Brenda by a constable.

In response to the eviction complaint, Brenda sought help from the no-cost Lawyer of the Day program at the housing court serving her area and was able to prepare a *pro se* answer to the eviction complaint. In her answer, Brenda requested reasonable accommodation due to her disability and also made a request for discovery (that is, a request for the documents her landlord would present before the judge). Brenda also contacted her local legal services agency and was assigned a lawyer. At a hearing a few weeks later, Brenda and her attorney requested a bench trial to hear the case. As she told her lawyer, she had been through the pain of two previous evictions and had felt powerless. She said she wanted to fight for her right to a reasonable accommodation as a disabled person. Her trial date was set for 2 months after the hearing, and was ultimately postponed an additional month. Her attorney convinced Brenda of the importance of documenting the condition of her apartment and changes she made via photographs for use in the courtroom. Although Brenda was very anxious about others seeing images of her home, she consented to her lawyer's request.

Recognizing the challenges that Brenda faced due to depression and hoarding, as well as the risk of losing not only her apartment but also her housing voucher, Brenda's attorney urged her to seek professional help. Brenda agreed and began meeting with a mental health clinician who specialized in treating hoarding. She diagnosed Brenda with hoarding disorder and major depression, and also noted that Brenda had mild obsessions about germs and cleaning compulsions, as well as paranoid thoughts and some features of borderline personality disorder. The therapist visited Brenda's home and rated her hoarding as moderate according to the Clutter Image Rating. She also noted that unlike many people who hoard, some parts of Brenda's home were well organized (for example, most of her books were shelved in crates stacked against the walls) and overall her home was clean. The attorney met with Brenda and the therapist during the home visit to determine priorities such as creating safe pathways and reducing the number of possessions in the common area at the front and rear of the apartment. As part of Brenda's defense, the therapist agreed to provide expert testimony on her behalf.

The prospect of going to trial motivated Brenda to work on decluttering. She unpacked and organized some of her many possessions, created pathways in her home and cleared space around entrances and exits. However, Brenda often had days of back pain and low mood that interfered with this work. Her progress was also slowed by the care she took to wash or dust her many possessions, clean her home, and laboriously wash clothing (many of which she did not actually wear). The therapist observed that Brenda seemed more inclined to keep rather than to discard possessions that were of little value, such as broken items. She also realized that Brenda actively acquired objects such as others' discarded belongings. Nonetheless, Brenda was able to make observable progress in her home, and these changes were documented in a set of photographs taken by her attorney to present at the trial along with the photographs from before the start of treatment.

The therapist testified at Brenda's trial that hoarding is a complex cognitive, emotional, and behavioral disorder that usually requires mental health treatment and a systematic and detailed plan to make measurable progress. She stated that Brenda's hoarding was moderate and that her home was clean and had some well-organized sections, noting that this is uncommon among those who hoard. The clinician described Brenda's progress in her home over the previous 3 months and also clarified that substantial progress in overcoming hoarding typically requires several months and sometimes years. During the trial, the judge asked Brenda for a date by which she expected to bring her home into compliance with her lease, but Brenda refused to commit to a particular date. Accordingly, the judge found that although Brenda was disabled and entitled to reasonable accommodation, the open-ended nature of her request for accommodation was not reasonable.

Brenda's attorney filed an appeal of the court's decision, and as a condition of continuing the appeal, the judge requested that Brenda make her home clutter-free. In support of this, he ordered assessment of progress through inspections and photographs of the home by a housing specialist employed by the court. The appeal process unfolded over 6 months with two home inspections by the housing specialist and three appearances before the judge during that time. The judge gave Brenda very specific goals for her home. These included reducing the height and number of book crates lining her walls and clearing possessions from in front of her windows and around her radiators. During the appeal process, Brenda was very motivated to continue decluttering her home and was able to make many of the changes that the judge ordered. Because of the sheer number of possessions and her difficulty discarding them, the attorney advised Brenda to rent a storage unit to clear more possessions from her home. Brenda agreed to this just prior to her final home inspection. Ultimately, however, Brenda and her land-lord came to an agreement in which Brenda agreed to move and he agreed to pay her moving expenses.

Case Discussion

Brenda's case highlights the role of the legal system in motivating change when pressure from other sources fails. The threat of eviction alone was not sufficient to motivate Brenda to remove clutter, evident in past evictions due to unchecked hoarding behaviors. The prior evictions did not alter her hoarding behavior, and she contended that they may have worsened it by requiring rapid packing without time to sort and make decisions about her possessions. By contrast, during the 3-month period leading up to the trial, Brenda was very motivated and made clear progress on the established goals. She remained moti-vated and made more gains after the trial during the 6-month appeal process. Brenda also accepted her attorney's advice to obtain psychotherapy, and this appeared to contribute to her success in meeting benchmarks on time. Interestingly, Brenda's interactions with the judge also seemed to motivate her. Although she did not always agree with the goals he established, Brenda's comments to her clinician and lawyer suggested that his approval mattered to her. As a result, she worked very hard to meet the goals he set for her. In turn, the judge set reasonable goals that accommodated her disability.

Although Brenda worked very hard during the 9 months her case was in housing court, she also expressed ambivalence. She neither consistently acknowledged having a problem with hoarding, nor did she deny it. During home visits with her therapist Brenda agreed that she had too many things, but at other times, particularly in the pres-ence of certain possessions or in adversarial contexts (e.g., during a home inspection), she insisted she needed most of her things. It is possible that Brenda's poverty (she lived on very limited disability income) contributed to her attachment to her possessions, as she feared she would not be able to replace them in the future. Brenda was also ambiva-lent about accepting help. She canceled many meetings with her therapist and was reluc-tant to travel to office appointments, electing instead to speak by phone. Brenda's variable insight about her hoarding is not unusual. Without the pressure from the court to con-tinue removal of the clutter, Brenda would no doubt have used her time differently.

Even at its best, her home remained somewhat cluttered. Brenda loved knick-knacks, books, and household goods and enjoyed having two or three of the same items such as brooms and hairbrushes. She liked having counter spaces, shelves, and walls that were busy with favorite objects. Although she was able to meet safety goals for her home, it is unlikely she will ever have a home with minimal clutter. Those who hoard can often meet safety goals but are unlikely to sustain a completely uncluttered home.

Brenda's case was not a resounding success. When she settled with her landlord, her focus shifted from decluttering to packing up her possessions once again and moving to another apartment. Just prior to this, her attorney advised Brenda to rent a storage unit as a measure of last resort. Although this allowed Brenda to make observable progress in her home, renting a storage unit is not recommended because it is expensive, makes access to possessions for sorting and decision-making more difficult, and may encourage even more acquiring to fill the additional space. Although Brenda certainly made substantial strides in her home during the 9 months she was involved with the legal system, some important hoarding behaviors did not change. She continued to acquire new items on a weekly basis and to maintain beliefs about the usefulness and value of her things, leading to limited discarding. Brenda's capacity for decluttering was also slowed by her washing and cleaning compulsions, which remained relatively unchanged with treatment. It is clear that additional treatment and perhaps even legal restrictions would be needed to maintain the improvement this multiply challenged client managed to achieve.

CHAPTER 11

Medical Aspects of Hoarding

This chapter is intended to provide information and guidelines to those in the medical field, given the close relationship of hoarding to problems related to physical health. Individuals with hoarding behavior are significantly more likely to suffer from obesity and chronic medical concerns than are others with mental health problems (Tolin, Frost, Steketee, Gray, & Fitch, 2008). These chronic conditions range widely and include arthritis, hypertension, fibromyalgia, lung problems such as asthma and emphysema, autoimmune conditions such as lupus, and stomach conditions (Tolin et al., 2008). Many of these difficulties can limit a person's ability to declutter his or her home. For example, arthritis can make handling objects difficult, interfering with sorting and organizing. The exhaustion caused by emphysema or fibromyalgia can interfere with sustaining physical effort, attention, and decision making.

In addition, hoarding behavior itself can have adverse health effects. For example, unstable walking surfaces, dust, mold, and pest infestation, as well as broken heating and plumbing can provoke or exacerbate existing physical limitations and health problems. This is especially true for elderly clients for whom cluttered walkways and stairwells increase the likelihood of falling and the seriousness of the consequences. Likewise, dust and mold can worsen lung conditions, and plumbing and heating problems can stress vulnerable individuals who are sensitive to temperature extremes.

Medical personnel may be the first to encounter a hoarding problem and can be instrumental in persuading sufferers to seek help. Medical providers include emergency medical technicians (EMTs), primary care providers, medical specialists (e.g., orthopedic surgeons, oncologists), psychiatrists, nurses (in clinics, hospitals, rehabilitation facilities, or visiting nurse associations), social workers in medical settings, home health aides, personal care assistants, occupational therapists, and physical therapists.

These providers often play a role in detecting a hoarding problem (e.g., EMTs, nurses, primary care providers) or are involved in providing interventions for hoarding and related problems (e.g., visiting nurses, home health aides, personal care assistants). This chapter provides information to medical providers about detection, assessment of severity, referral, and intervention.

MEDICAL STAFF INVOLVEMENT WITH HOARDING

Emergency Medical Technicians

EMTs routinely enter patients' homes and are therefore more likely to encounter the manifestation of hoarding directly and unexpectedly. Moderate hoarding can impede the ability of EMTs to provide emergency care. The main entrance to the home may be partially or completely blocked by possessions making it difficult to fully open the door, or possessions may be stacked along hallways or stairs, making it difficult or impossible to bring in essential equipment such as a gurney or a defibrillator. In severe hoarding cases, EMTs may not be able to enter the patient's home at all. Delays in rendering treatment can lead to greater consequences from the emergency (e.g., more severe damage from a stroke) and even death. Whatever the extent of hoarding, in the course of their work, EMTs can play a vital role by engaging the patient in a dialog about the difficulty caused by the hoarding and in encouraging the use of services to address the hoarding problem. If they are able to enter the home, they can also provide assessment information to providers of treatment.

Visiting Nurses, Home Health Aides, and Personal Care Assistants

Visiting nurses and paramedical personnel who enter patients' homes in the course of their work encounter hoarding directly. Moderate to severe hoarding usually interferes with their work, endangers their safety, and the safety of their patients. Visiting nurses, home health aides and personal care assistants who enter the home can directly assess the severity of hoarding, health and safety risks, medication compliance, sanitation, and food safety (see Valente, 2009). They can also encourage patients to seek help for their problem and are in the unique position of being able to assist patients directly in working on the hoarding problem. For example, they might help the patient or the family clear space around the bed or in hallways to facilitate the use of a walker.

Medical Doctors, Nurses, Physician's Assistants, and Social Workers in Medical Settings

The majority of medical personnel usually encounter hoarding indirectly, as they typically see patients within a clinic, hospital, or rehabilitation setting. Nonetheless, these professionals can help assess the condition of the home as part of rendering care. Medical professionals who care for elderly patients routinely ask about activities of daily living, such as the patient's mobility within the home, ability to prepare food, and bathe. Medical social workers often include questions about patients' homes as part of aftercare planning. For example, discussions of patient self-care after surgery or chemotherapy may require discussion of alternative and adaptive strategies until patients are recovered. A simple question about whether there is any problem within the home (e.g., a readily accessible bathroom and running water, an easy path to the toilet) that would interfere with aftercare will help clarify special conditions that require attention. In addition, medical staff can be on the alert for signs of hoarding, such as patients who collect brochures from the waiting room or who carry overstuffed bags or one or more bags filled with assortments of objects (e.g., paper, containers). In addition, these providers are in a position to detect problems related to personal hygiene that might be indicative of hoarding or problems with squalor. Like EMTs, these individuals can play an important role in establishing a relationship that helps connect patients with services to address these problems.

Occupational and Physical Therapists

For older and disabled adults in particular, physical and occupational therapists often visit the home regularly until the health problem for which their services are required is alleviated. This puts these professionals in a good position to observe the impact on their patient when hoarding is present and to advocate for important changes that have direct health effects. For example, an adult who is seeking to regain the strength to walk without aids is likely to have strong motivation to discuss a clutter problem that impedes movement or increases the likelihood of a disastrous fall. Occupational therapists can be especially helpful in promoting recovery of everyday living skills such as manipulating objects, cooking, bathing, doing laundry, and completing basic housekeeping tasks. These professionals commonly work with patients in their homes to train them in these skills and in so doing have considerable leverage in providing direct assistance with sorting, organizing, and discarding, or in helping clients engage services to assist with these tasks. Both physical and occupational therapists can insist on the need for specific changes and encourage contact with an appropriate referral source to make this possible.

ASSESSMENT METHODS FOR MEDICAL SETTINGS

A number of assessments may be helpful to medical personnel, whether they encounter hoarding in the office or in the home. These assessment tools were described in detail in Chapter 4 and are provided in the Appendix. Below we highlight four instruments that are especially appropriate for medical personnel: the Hoarding Rating Scale, the Activities of Daily Living–Hoarding, the Clutter Image Rating Scale, and the Home Environment Index.

Hoarding Rating Scale (HRS)

Medical personnel can use this five-item scale to ask simple questions about the severity (0 to 8) of clutter, difficulty discarding, acquisition, distress, and impairment in the clinic setting if they suspect a problem may be present based on the patient's physical presentation or comments about the home. When inside the home, they can supplement their queries with personal observations. Scores that are moderate or above should trigger concerns and further discussion with the patient about how to address the hoarding problems.

Activities of Daily Living–Hoarding (ADL-H)

Two of the ADL-H subscales are relevant for medical professionals who are assessing hoarding inside the home or in the clinic. One measures basic self-care activities, such as preparing food and bathing, and the other rates the impact of hoarding on the person's safety, including the ability to move about the home and the ease with which medical personnel can enter the home.

Clutter Image Rating Scale (CIR)

Nurses, social workers, or physicians can use this pictorial instrument in the clinic to ask patients to point to the living room, kitchen, and bedroom pictures that best match their own rooms. In the home, occupational thera-pists, visiting nurses, and home health aides can complete the ratings them-selves. Again, moderate severity (4 or above on this 9-point set of pictures) in any room should trigger a discussion of how the clutter might interfere with the medical goals of the staff and the patient. If patients appear to be minimizing personal risk or interference with medical care, home visiting medical providers can ask the patient to also rate the CIR (as well as the HRS and ADL) to determine whether patients are underestimating the impact of their clutter. In turn, this can indicate whether to approach patients directly about intervention and referral for those with good insight, or more cautiously to avoid triggering defensive reactions for those with limited insight and commitment.

Home Environment Index (HEI)

This patient self-report questionnaire assesses squalor, self-care, cleanli-ness, and personal hygiene. However, it can also be used by medical provid-ers as the basis for a brief interview or in-home observations (for example to determine the frequency of doing laundry, observation of body odor, and wearing clean clothing).

An additional measure, the HOMES risk assessment tool, may prove suitable for assessing health and safety aspects of hoarding pertinent to medical care.

TALKING ABOUT MEDICAL RISK AND HOARDING

Medical providers have a special advantage in motivating patients to seek and accept help for hoarding. Patients often have positive feelings about medical providers who occupy a helping role with regard to a funda-mentally important aspect of patients' lives—their health. Because they often experience medical providers as being genuinely concerned about them, patients may be receptive to their provider's opinion and more inclined to follow their advice. Medical providers therefore can explain the risks associated with hoarding and raise patients' awareness about the relationship between hoarding and their health problem (e.g., mold and exacerbating a lung condition). By expressing concern for the patient, med-ical professionals can urge patients to accept help and even make very spe-cific recommendations about how to do this. Likewise, medical social workers can facilitate this discussion and identify appropriate resources to accomplish decluttering goals. For patients who are already seeking help for hoarding from medical or nonmedical staff, medical providers can encourage these efforts.

Despite the helping nature of the medical relationship, patients with hoarding may not be receptive to their provider's advice or concern. In such cases, further steps may be needed to safeguard the well-being of patients or vulnerable others. Many medical personnel are mandated reporters and therefore bear the legal responsibility of reporting risky situations to the relevant authorities, such as the abuse or neglect of children. In addition, because any concerned person can contact protective service agencies, even medical professionals who are not mandated reporters can alert the relevant agency to a potential problem stemming from hoarding. As indicated in Chapter 7, concern about elder self-neglect can be sufficient reason for elder protective services (a voluntary service) to become involved with the patient. Such involvement can motivate patients to accept help for their hoarding problem.

HOARDING INTERVENTION BY MEDICAL PROFESSIONALS

The primary form of intervention for the majority of medical personnel is referral of the patient to appropriate services for reducing hoarding behaviors. For receptive patients a referral for mental health treatment is needed to address the underlying mental disorder that contributes to the symptoms and manifestation of hoarding (see Chapter 5). Reluctant patients may be willing to accept other types of services. For example, a visiting nurse can assist eligible patients (typically those receiving Medicare or Medicaid, but also others, depending on the insurance carrier) on a short-term basis with personal safety. Examples of such medical needs are ensuring access to the bed or bathtub, creating and maintaining wide pathways throughout the home, and organizing medications and medical appointments. Other patients may be eligible for longer term care from a home health aide who can help with safety, organization, and ultimately with decluttering the home for cooperative patients. Patients can also benefit from working with an occupational therapist in the home who assists them in creating safe environments, accomplishing daily living tasks and learning practical skills such as organizing and problem solving.

MEDICAL INTERFACE WITH OTHER SYSTEMS

As discussed in Chapter 3, cases of hoarding often involve multiple agencies, systems, and/or service providers. Medical personnel can learn whether there is a hoarding task force or other hoarding initiative in their city or town that could serve as a resource. At the same time, the unique perspective of medical professionals makes them valuable members of or collaborators with hoarding initiatives. As mentioned earlier, medical personnel may need to contact protective services or public health staff. Conversely, protective service workers and public health officers may contact them about a patient. Visiting nurses, home health aides, and occupational therapists would ideally interface with other service providers, such as psychotherapists or professional organizers who are working directly on the hoarding problem. Medical doctors may need to assess adult patients with hoarding problems for competency to care for themselves and provide this information to adult protective services or to the court. Medical professionals who enter the patient's home, such as visiting nurses or EMTs, are witnesses to the condition of the home and may need to provide information about this to medical doctors and protective service workers. Providers who visit the home may also be called to testify in cases of hoarding in the legal system.

Medical personnel, as well as mental health providers, are subject to the privacy rule of the Health Insurance Portability and Accountability Act (HIPAA, see www.hhs.gov/ocr/hipaa and http://www.hhs.gov/ocr/privacy/ for online information about this legislation), which limits the sharing of protected health information, such as a patient's diagnosis and treatment. Determining the extent to which such information may be shared across agencies that are involved in addressing the hoarding or related problems (e.g., child and adult protection, public health) can be complex and is beyond the scope of this book. When such issues arise, medical personnel should discuss these questions with their supervisors to determine appropriate practices.

TIPS AND STRATEGIES

Given the close association of physical and mental health, the following suggestions can improve both physical and mental health care:

- Conduct initial screening in the clinic and/or the patient's home. This information will spark conversation about needed intervention and, with the patient's permission, can be shared with other care providers.
- Use potential medical complications to discuss hoarding and needed interventions. Imparting information about the effect of hoarding on the physical health of patients can help motivate them to begin to make their homes more safe and comfortable.

- Collaborate with other care providers to coordinate services for patients who hoard. When possible, share information about hoarding severity and its impact on activities of daily living to establish priorities for the patient and his or her other providers.
- Serve as a cheerleader and/or inspiration for addressing the hoarding problem. Even a question or two from a medical doctor can communicate to the patient both caring and the importance of the declutter work. Praise and other positive feedback strongly affirms the progress of patients and encourages them to continue their efforts to reduce clutter.

CASE STUDY: HOARDING EFFECTS ON MEDICAL CONDITIONS

This case illustrates the adverse effects of hoarding on existing medical problems and the struggles of a single mental health provider to resolve the situation in the absence of consultation with medical personnel. The discussion addresses some of the issues raised in this case.

Roger was a 75-year-old never married white man living on retirement income. He owned his home, a two-story single-family dwelling, in a small town outside a large metropolitan area. Due to the substantial accumulation of objects in his yard, Roger's neighbors contacted their public health department, which sent a staff member to investigate. Roger did not allow the public health worker to enter his home and received a citation for the condition of his property. The worker urged Roger to seek support for his difficulty with clutter, and Roger found a mental health therapist in his area who specialized in hoarding treatment.

After an initial office visit to begin the assessment, Roger's therapist completed an assessment at his home. She found severe problems that resulted in squalid conditions. Broken pipes had flooded the floor in the kitchen months previously during the winter and had not been repaired. The sink was unusable and was full of dirty dishes. In addition, water damage was not cleaned up so that mail and other papers were stuck to the floor and counters in the kitchen. The flooring itself buckled due to the flooding, and mold spread on the counters and in the kitchen cupboards. The broken plumbing meant there was no running water in either of the two bathrooms in the home. Roger eventually disclosed to his therapist that he filled a bucket from a tap in the basement to flush the toilet on the ground floor.

The central heating radiator system was also broken due to the ruptured pipes. Roger's brother had offered to pay for repairs to the plumbing and heating system, but Roger had not accepted his offer because hoarding impeded access to the pipes and the furnace. Roger acknowledged to his therapist that he slept on the couch in the living room and showed her bites on his arms from the many mice infesting his home.

The therapist rated Roger's home as a 6–7 overall on the CIR due to the accumulation of clutter such that only sideways paths existed through the passable areas of the home. Parts of the home were completely inaccessible, such as the bedrooms on the second floor, which were filled with furniture and other possessions.

Roger had a medical diagnosis of congestive-obstructive pulmonary disease (COPD) and was under medical advice to use oxygen at all times. He reported to his therapist that he used oxygen only part of the time because the limited space in his home prevented him from moving the oxygen tank. He often became fatigued from bending over and could work on the clutter for only short periods due to the COPD. Despite his physical limitations, Roger progressed well in the first months of treatment, canceling only one treatment session due to illness and working steadily on removing clutter from the main areas in his home. He made good progress in his kitchen and living room, but reported to his therapist that he struggled with exhaustion and was also bothered by the dust disturbed by the sorting and clutter removal because it affected his breathing.

A few months after treatment began, the weather became colder as winter approached, and the therapist noticed that the average temperature in the house began to fall. Roger reported using space heaters, but also acknowledged that the cold was making his COPD worse. His pace of decluttering slowed and his therapist expressed concern about Roger's health and the broken heating system. At this time, Roger elected to spend a month in a warmer state visiting extended family members. In the interim, his therapist sought consultation with other clinicians about Roger's situation and her role. She was particularly concerned about the extent to which the circumstances in Roger's home might call for forced intervention, for example, through a call to the public health department.

On Roger's return to the area, his therapist broached the topic of his health and safety and the need to repair his plumbing and heating. She suggested a solution that involved teaming up with a group of people for a structured clean out with the goal of gaining access to the plumbing and heating system so it could be repaired. She asked Roger to determine how to categorize items that would be sorted into piles of (1) keep, (2) donate, and (3) discard, and locations for the items to be kept. The team would sort the possessions according to his system, organize those he wanted to keep, and remove from his property those he chose to discard. Roger was initially upset by his therapist's raising health and safety concerns and the proposal to do a structured clean out. He stated that he did not wish others to see the state of his home. He also expressed his concern that his home might be condemned if the conditions were not improved since the public health department had already been alerted about a possible hoarding problem. Over two further treatment sessions, Roger and his therapist continued to discuss his dilemma, the possibility of a team clean out, and other options, such as Roger's spending the remainder of the winter in a warmer state. Roger decided to accept help in the form of a team clean out.

Roger's brother paid for four workers from a local cleaning company to work with Roger and the therapist in his home. The team was given the list of categories he developed and the rules for sorting all items into these categories. They were instructed that whenever there was any question, Roger would make the ultimate decisions about all items. The workers spent 4 hours in Roger's home and cleared space to permit a plumber and heating repair person to access the pipes and furnace. One worker also focused on items on the property outside the home, reducing the clutter that had led to public health involvement. The workers hauled away items for trash and items to donate. Roger expressed pleasure to his therapist about the results of the structured clean out. His brother paid for the plumbing and heating repairs and Roger was able to enjoy a warm home with running water. Although some clutter remained, it was not health threatening and could be addressed at a slower pace.

Case Discussion

Seniors are a particularly vulnerable population because they may have physical and health limitations that are exacerbated by hoarding. In Roger's case, his neighbors alerted the public health department and the resulting inspection prompted Roger to seek treatment. Alternatively, Roger's home situation might have come to the attention of medical personnel. For example, a social worker, geriatric nurse, or even his primary care provider could have evaluated the conditions in his home for their impact on his COPD. Questions about mold, dust, and clutter could have led to a productive conversation with Roger months or even years before neighbors were moved to call the public health department.

Involving medical personnel during the course of treatment might also have helped his therapist intervene sooner or more effectively with regard to the broken plumbing and heating. By collaborating with Roger's doctor, his therapist could have discussed who would raise this difficult topic and how to motivate Roger to address the issue. A team meeting might have permitted Roger to experience the concern of both his mental and physical health providers, including their fears about how to help him cope if his physical health worsened. In all of these discussions, Roger's medical providers serve as another source for motivating change and for generating possible solutions.

CASE STUDY: MEDICAL CONDITIONS THAT AFFECT HOARDING

This case illustrates the interference of existing medical problems in the work of a very motivated hoarding client. The case discussion addresses some of the issues raised.

Emily was a 63-year-old married white woman. She and her husband owned their home in an upper-middle-class urban neighborhood. Although in the past Emily worked as a full-time professional, for the past 18 years she was able to work only part-time. This change was necessary due Emily's fibromyalgia and to allow needed time to bring her son to appointments for his severe obsessive compulsive disorder (OCD) and learning difficulties. Emily had a moderate case of hoarding. Her overall CIR score was 5 at the outset of treatment, but the rooms in her home varied in the degree of clutter so that some rooms were unaffected whereas others (the bedroom and den) were rated at 7 and 8 (severe) on the CIR.

One of Emily's strengths was her interest in understanding her problems to the extent that she had extensively researched her symptoms on the web. She found substantial information about hoarding that led her to read several self-help books on organizing. Two years ago, she found a hoarding specialist in her area and began weekly treatment. Emily was very committed to treatment and rarely canceled appointments. She also complied well with assigned homework between therapy sessions and made good use of home visits to intensify her decluttering efforts.

However, Emily's fibromyalgia significantly interfered with her progress. Feelings of exhaustion reduced her motivation to work on the clutter, and muscle soreness made lifting or pushing objects virtually impossible. As an example, Emily described going into the bedroom to work on the closet and feeling the need to lie down "for a few moments" that became a few hours. Emily and her therapist scheduled home visits in the afternoon so that Emily could rest during the morning to prepare for the visit. Emily and her therapist determined that Emily's lethargy was not due to depression. Emily also suffered from sleep apnea and reported that she experienced irregular and uneasy sleep. Emily had her sleep apnea confirmed by a physician through a sleep study and used a breathing machine at night. The fibromyalgia, together with exhaustion caused by sleep apnea, limited her energy as well as her capacity to physically sort and move her possessions.

Fibromyalgia is considered by many to be a vague diagnosis and even Emily's husband was not convinced that she had this disorder. Because of this, Emily experienced guilt, shame, and embarrassment about her diminished capacities and found it difficult when her husband came home and asked her what she had done during the day. On some days, she was able to manage only basic errands like grocery shopping. Emily and her husband also experienced financial strain because she was unable to work full-time and her husband's income as an artist was limited. Emily also acknowledged to her therapist that she overate when she felt stressed.

Emily developed a good relationship with her primary care physician (PCP) and asked him many questions to deepen her understanding of fibromyalgia and obtain advice on how to best live with this condition. Some months ago, Emily's PCP told her about some research he had read suggesting that chronic Lyme disease may present as fibromyalgia. He referred Emily to a specialist to assess whether her symptoms of fibromyalgia might instead be due to Lyme disease. The specialist diagnosed Emily as just such a case and prescribed a course of multiple antibiotics to treat Lyme disease. This treatment was successful and Emily's symptoms improved, greatly reducing her pain, lethargy, and "brain fog," as she described it. She had more energy for daily activities, including decluttering, and made significantly faster progress in decluttering her home.

Case Discussion

Emily was able to receive care for her difficulties from various providers—her PCP treated her for fibromyalgia and sleep apnea, her mental health therapist treated her for hoarding, and more recently, a medical specialist treated her for Lyme disease. Because medical conditions can affect treatment for hoarding, as Emily's case illustrates, coordination of care among providers is optimal. Through sharing information, providers can gauge and help mitigate the effect of the treatment on the person's mental and physical health. Furthermore, care coordination can help patients feel supported in their efforts to manage their physical conditions while working to overcome hoarding, and may itself contribute to improved well-being.

It is not unusual for those with hoarding to have a chronic medical problem. Tolin et al. (2008) found that the incidence of fibromyalgia alone is 11% among those with clinical levels of hoarding and 8% among those with subclinical levels. To the extent that a chronic illness may respond to a change of treatment or better management of symptoms, with concomitant positive effects on hoarding intervention, we encourage providers and their patients to actively evaluate the effects of the current treatment and to pursue alternatives when appropriate.

CHAPTER 12

Role of Professional Organizers

This chapter is intended for professional organizers who work directly with people who hoard in their homes and for other professionals interested in understanding how professional organizing skills may be used to assist people with hoarding problems. Material in this chapter derives from interviews with several professional organizers and from books on clutter recommended by professional organizers (see below and the Resources section).

Individuals with hoarding problems may seek the services of a professional organizer because their clutter and difficulty discarding appear to stem from disorganization. For many people who hoard, engaging the services of a professional organizer does not carry the stigma that mental health treatment does, and so may be a preferred form of intervention. Some professional organizers have obtained specialized training in hoarding to extend their skills beyond merely helping organize to addressing some of the broader problems associated with hoarding. These include attention deficit disorder and decision making, as well as excessive acquiring and strong attachment to and beliefs about possessions that interfere with discarding. Professional organizers interested in learning more about working with those who hoard can review Chapter 5, which provides additional information about hoarding and mental health, along with other resources listed at the end of this book.

THE WORK OF PROFESSIONAL ORGANIZERS

Individual and business clients engage professional organizers to help them improve the organization in their homes and/or work places (see Kolberg & Nadeau, 2002). Although hoarding appears to be rarer or more often contained in the work place, a number of clients who maintain a home office or are sole proprietors of their own business have hoarding problems accompanied by serious disorganization. Professional organizers provide a range of services. They help clients sort and organize papers and objects and make decisions about what to keep or discard. They collaborate with clients to design and implement organizational systems (e.g., a paper filing system, closet and shelf storage, a system for managing appointments) and to establish routines (e.g., sorting mail daily, recycling regularly). They also help clients prioritize personal and professional activities (e.g., running errands early in the weekend to allow time for other activities and allocating sufficient time to prepare for an important meeting). As a result of working with a professional organizer and becoming more organized, clients may experience benefits such as wasting less time because they can locate needed items, generating more business or profit, and feeling less stress in their day-to-day lives. Professional organizers can be located through the National Association of Professional Organizers (NAPO) at www.napo.net and through the Institute for Challenging Disorganization (ICD) at www. challengingdisorganization.org. The latter group represents a specialization within the field of professional organizing that often encounters and works with hoarding problems. Members of the ICD specialize in chronic disor-ganization (CD), which is defined as (1) a history of disorganization in which efforts to get organized are not maintained, (2) undermining of the quality of life due to the disorganization, and (3) an expectation that dis-organization will continue (Kolberg, 1999). Although people with CD do not necessarily have a hoarding problem, the majority of people with hoard-ing do display CD. Both groups maintain geographically identified referral listings through their websites.

CHRONIC DISORGANIZATION AND HOARDING

Because professional organizers specialize in helping others sort, catego-rize, and make decisions about what to keep and what to discard, clients with serious disorganization that contributes to clutter can benefit from their help. An important determination is whether the clutter stems mainly from CD or whether it derives from multiple causes, including difficulty organizing. Terry Prince, co-founder of ICD and co-author of the Clutter Hoarding Scale© (described below), characterizes those with CD as having a history of disorganization that affects their daily lives and relationships. This chronic problem can be expected to continue into the future if no intervention is made. She suggests that major contributors to CD include creativity, bipolar disorder, attention deficit disorder (ADD), and physical challenges and limitations due to aging such as poor health and reduced living space.

In her book on professional organizing and hoarding, Kolberg (2008) notes that those with hoarding problems share common ground with the chronically disorganized, as hoarding can stem from similar contributors such as ADD and physical challenges. However, there are important differences. People with hoarding problems generally have stronger emotional attachment to their possessions than those who do not hoard (see Grisham et al., 2009) and their attachment appears to extend to a wider range of items. Although research on these distinctions is lacking, we suspect that people who hoard often feel more ambivalent about correcting their problem, both wanting and not wanting help, compared to those who are simply disorganized. Intense feelings of shame are part of this struggle, along with a strong attachment to possessions. These manifestations can signal to a professional organizer that the disorganized person also has hallmarks of hoarding. As commonly occurs in referrals to mental health professionals, this reluctance to seek help is often evident in the fact that family members or guardians, rather than the person with the problem, seek help from the professional organizer.

Another difference between those with CD and those with a hoarding problem is the nature of the possessions that are saved. Those who hoard often have an excessive number of items that others consider useless or of little value, whereas those with CD may have many objects that most people view as useful or valuable. For example, a person who hoards may have dozens of old newspapers and clothes that no longer fit, whereas someone with CD may have acquired dozens of office supplies because he or she has misplaced the ones already purchased. However, we note that researchers have not confirmed these hypothesized differences, and thus it is possible that chronically disorganized people may simply represent a subset or earlier stage of clinical hoarding problems.

THE PROFESSIONAL ORGANIZER'S ROLE

After assessing the problem, professional organizers must decide whether they have the expertise to work with a prospective client. If they judge that the client's organizing problem falls outside of their purview, they may refer the client to the ICD website to find a professional organizer with special expertise in this area. If the prospective client seems to have other difficulties likely to impede work on organizing, such as untreated depression, anxiety, or bipolar disorder, the professional organizer can refer the client to a mental health professional. Note that a few professional organizers are trained in both specializations (for example, clinical psychology and professional organizing) and must determine their role with the client. Our experience with moderate to severe hoarding is that concurrent mental health treatment is often vital to promoting enduring change in the chronic disorganization problem. Professional organizers can devote many hours to creating space and organizational systems only to have the area recluttered because the underlying disorder remains untreated. A frank conversation communicating this concern early in their work together helps clients have reasonable expectations and make informed decisions about the supports they may need. For clients who resist an additional referral, trial and error may persuade them of the need for mental health treatment.

Professional organizers can often work collaboratively with others to provide the range of services their clients need to overcome this complex and multifaceted problem. As other chapters in this book attest, many different professionals may be involved with hoarding problems, whether in a helper role (e.g., psychiatrist, psychotherapist, visiting nurse, home health aide) or an enforcement role (e.g., public health inspector, protective services worker, judge). Depending on the case, collaborations may include different combinations of individuals. For example, a professional organizer may work with a psychiatrist, who is managing medication needs for bipolar problems, as well as a social worker, who specializes in clinical treatment for hoarding. Likewise, the organizer may team up with a family member, a home health aide, and/or a housing services coordinator. Before communicating with other providers, professional organizers will need to clarify the nature of the communication, ask the client's permission, and ask for a written release to share information.

Collaborations involving therapists with specialized training in hoarding can be particularly helpful for promoting long-term change in hoarding behaviors. As described in Chapter 5, clients work with therapists on the underlying cognitive and emotional contributors to the disorder, challenging beliefs about saving possessions, overcoming fears associated with discarding, and modifying problematic behaviors such as excessive acquisition and churning piles of objects. Clients also receive help clarifying their values and goals for treatment and developing skills that assist in decision making and problem solving, as well as organizing. Specialized mental health clinicians typically use sorting of the client's personal items in the office as a basis for identifying mistaken beliefs and strong emotions that interfere with discarding and organizing; those able to make home visits do this work in the client's home. Professional organizers can play a key role in helping clients develop and implement organizational systems, as well as helping with structure and motivation to carry out the work at home. This often requires months of continuing effort and sometimes years in homes with substantial clutter.

Professional organizers may take different roles in cases of very severe hoarding when hoarding clients are forced to make changes because of the threat of eviction due to housing code or public health violations. They may also take a different role in cases in which clients are deemed incompetent to care for themselves—that is, when their client is not the person who hoards but an appointed legal guardian or family member (see Chapter 10). In such cases, professional organizers may be asked to assume the role of project manager, communicating with family members, other service providers, and health department or code enforcement personnel. The organizer might recruit and supervise staff who provide the necessary hours to declutter the home and render it safe and compliant with relevant codes. The professional organizer can also arrange for disposal of unwanted possessions through a dumpster service, sale, or other method.

The majority of professional organizing services are paid for privately, usually by the person with the hoarding problem or the family. In some states public funds can be tapped to pay for these services, for example, through agencies or departments that provide services for the disabled and the elderly. Professional organizers usually bill by the hour and their rates vary widely depending on factors such as professional experience and geographic region.

ASSESSMENT OF HOARDING

As they begin their work with clients, professional organizers need to assess the client's organizational skills and deficits, the severity of the clutter problem, and the associated features of the hoarding disorder. As for other professionals, two readily available tools for assessing hoarding severity are the pictorial Clutter Image Rating (CIR) and the Activities of Daily Living for Hoarding (ADL-H), described in Chapter 4 and included in the Appendix. Both measures can provide a baseline for comparison over time to track improvement. Clients with limited insight may rate themselves lower (less severe) on these measures than does the professional organizer, suggesting the need to work on motivation to overcome the problem (see Chapter 2 for suggestions on how to enhance motivation). The CIR can also help prioritize goals as rooms with higher scores might require immediate attention when they are critical household locations such as the kitchen or bedroom. Likewise, the ADL-H can prove useful for prioritizing safety concerns and the ability to complete important daily activities in the home.

A third tool, the Clutter Hoarding Scale©, distributed by the ICD, assesses aspects of clutter and home safety. This residential assessment scale developed by professional organizers with expertise in chronic disorganization measures clutter, as well as health and safety concerns on a single five-point scale. Level I characterizes an average home without clutter and no health or safety concerns. Level II indicates a home with some clutter but no health and safety concerns (a messy average home). A home scored at Level III has slight health and/or safety problems, such as mold or mildew. Clutter at this level is beyond average and reflects chronic disorganization or mild hoarding. Level IV characterizes a home with substantial disorganization or hoarding and/or significant health or safety problems, such as a blocked doorway. Level V represents severe disorganization and hoarding accompanied by health and safety problems that are code violations and could lead to the home being condemned. This includes significant structural problems, broken plumbing, and/or a broken heating system. The Clutter Hoarding Scale© is limited as a tool to assess hoarding per se insofar as a home rated at Level V because of serious health or safety concerns may have very little clutter.

ASSESSING ORGANIZATIONAL SKILLS

Safren, Perlman, Sprich, and Otto's (2005) manual on ADHD provides some useful methods for assessing attention problems, including self and family report forms that list the current symptoms of ADHD based on a mental health diagnosis of this problem. Although not a substitute for formal assessment and diagnosis of ADHD, these tools are useful in determining whether clients have significant problems with attention and/or hyperactivity. If they do and these difficulties interfere with the work, the professional organizer may encourage the client to seek further assessment and intervention from a psychiatrist or psychologist.

Organizational skills can be hard to discern on entering the homes of those with hoarding problems and chronic disorganization. However, strengths are often evident among organizational challenges. For example, it is almost a cliché that although a room appears to be a disaster, the occupant "knows where everything is." That is, the person is able to use spatial memory to find the possession, as in the case of a client who recalls that the article on pruning roses is in the pile by the sofa, about half way down. Although this might still take a little time to find, often the memory is accurate. As part of assessing organizational skills, professional organizers listen closely to identify existing systems, such as the visual memory above, file folders that hold important papers, and collections of similar items located in the same general area of a room.

In general, people who hoard have deficits in categorizing their possessions into practical groupings and thus have trouble sorting (Wincze et al., 2007). They also have difficulty making decisions about where to put items, what to keep, and what to discard. Difficulty processing information contributes to this. Those with hoarding disorder might attend to features of objects that do not produce useful categories. For example, color can be a good system for storing fabrics or spools of thread, but not office supplies or books. Disorganized individuals also tend to consider too many features of an object when making decisions. For example, there are many possible uses of a box (container, recycled cardboard, package for mailing future items, part of a craft project), but only the most important/relevant of these provides useful rules and categories for sorting, discarding, and storing (for example, "if I am almost out of mailing boxes, I will keep this and otherwise, I will recycle this and similar items").

Perfectionism also contributes to difficulty categorizing and making decisions, as the person with hoarding disorder develops categories that are too specific in order to "get it right," resulting in too many classifications to be practical. An example was evident in one woman who was faced with sorting 87 pieces of glassware on her dining room table. Instead of making a few simple groupings such as mugs, drinking glasses, and cups, she sorted them into 17 categories that included collector's items, souvenirs, everyday cups, and holiday use. This made it impossible to identify locations for storage and to determine what she could discard. In working with clients, then, professional organizers must assess their clients' capacity to sort, categorize, and make decisions to determine what interferes with creating practical systems (Kolberg, 2008).

INTERVENTION

Professional organizers can be immensely helpful to those who hoard. In fact, some aspects of the cognitive and behavioral treatment for hoarding (see Chapter 5) are drawn from the practices of professional organizers. Although organizers do not usually address the underlying contributors to hoarding, they can certainly help change the behavioral manifestation of unmanageable clutter. An important early determination is whether the organizer will do the bulk of the work or whether the client is able to do some or even most of the organizing, albeit with help. If the client is the guardian or responsible family member (e.g., adult child of a disabled parent) of the person with the problem, the professional organizer and hired assistants will likely do most of the work. Likewise, when safety concerns loom and reduction in clutter must be accomplished quickly, the professional organizer will likely take the lead in the work. When hired directly by clients who hoard, other factors determine if the professional organizer will do the bulk of the work, for example, if the client is elderly or ill and simply cannot physically or mentally carry out the needed work.

When working collaboratively with clients, professional organizers not only teach clients skills to create and maintain organizational systems, they also assist their clients by *motivating* them to carry out the declutter work. As indicated in Chapter 2, those with hoarding tend to have significant ambivalence about getting organized and especially about removing clutter. However, they often become more comfortable and motivated by the regular presence of a professional organizer who is coaching them to tackle the daunting work of sorting and de-cluttering. As clients learn skills and see progress, they often become more confident of their abilities and work harder and more steadily.

Professional organizers use both standard and specialized organizing strategies. One standard strategy is O.H.I.O. or Only Handle It Once. This strategy is designed to address the *churning* behavior that occurs when people with difficulty making decisions and inadequate organizing systems try to decide what to do with a given item. Clients begin to sort a pile of papers but are stymied by having to classify each item and decide whether to keep or discard it; their tendency is to put any challenging item aside (often this is most items) until new piles simply replace the original one. O.H.I.O. raises awareness of this churning behavior and encourages clients to choose an ultimate disposition for each item more quickly. Related to this is a key strategy of encouraging clients to sort into a small number of categories initially until they become more skilled and comfortable with new sorting systems. Typical early categories are "keep," "remove," and "unsure" (this last one allows discussion about decisions as described further below). Other important strategies are to identify a "home inside the home" for all items and to develop maintenance skills such as reading and sorting mail daily, immediately discarding or recycling peripheral items (empty envelopes, grocery bags), and putting items away shortly after use.

Work with disorganized hoarding clients must be specifically tailored to their difficulties. Tackling decision-making problems about whether to keep or remove items is a high priority for professional organizers. One strategy is to use a list of questions about possessions, such as "How many of these do I really need?" and "Do I already have other items like this one?" (see Steketee & Frost's 2007 manual for a longer list of such questions). Another strategy is to develop discarding rules tailored to the client, such as "For each item I buy, I must discard or use up a similar one" and "If I haven't used this in the past two years, it needs to go." Certain types of paper items have built-in limits. These include tax documents that need to be kept for only 7 years and credit card receipts that can be discarded as soon as the purchase appears on the statement. Web-based financial services have reduced even further the number of paper items clients need to retain.

To address attention problems, professional organizers first need to assess the client's attention span and then begin by working within that span. For clients with short attention spans of 5 to 10 minutes, sorting and organizing tasks can be broken down into small, manageable steps that intersperse more difficult cognitive effort (for example, 5 minutes of sorting paper) with more physical activity (getting up to take sorted papers to the box or shelf where they belong). Safren et al. (2005) suggest additional interventions and the ICD website offers numerous articles, books, and courses to increase knowledge about specific organizing, sorting, and storing strategies. The reference section at the end of this volume includes additional sources of information.

INTERFACE WITH OTHER SYSTEMS

During their work with clients, professional organizers may become keenly aware of risky situations in the home or ones in which they are concerned about the welfare of children or elders. This can lead them to feel concerned and even overwhelmed. Some clients lack insight about the degree of danger posed by the clutter and/or about the impairment and distress their hoarding causes others. Furthermore, clients may have goals different from the professional organizer, for example, in prioritizing efficient closet space over safety concerns about a blocked door or window. Similarly, clients might place their needs above those of vulnerable others in the home, for example, in sentimental saving of items from their adolescent child's infancy at the cost of space in the child's bedroom for age-appropriate studying and projects. Such misplaced priorities are often part of the hoarding disorder itself and may require intervention from mental health professionals.

Professional organizers are not mandated reporters and therefore may not be accustomed to seeking help when hoarding situations violate the rights of vulnerable individuals or violate safety and health codes. As noted in Chapter 8, federal law defines vulnerable individuals as those under age 18 years, those aged 60 years, and older, and those deemed mentally or physically disabled, and each state has established agencies to protect the rights of these individuals. Anyone can contact these agencies on behalf of a vulnerable individual, including a concerned professional organizer. When faced with such situations, professional organizers must resolve a basic dilemma—if they call the relevant state agency, they risk losing their client and the income from that work, but if they do not call, they permit a potentially dangerous situation to persist. Consultation with a colleague can help resolve this conflict. Our goal here is not to resolve this dilemma, but rather to raise awareness about the possibility of abuse or neglect due to hoarding and the resources available to protect vulnerable individuals.

TIPS AND STRATEGIES

- Ask permission before touching clients' possessions and accommodate their wishes to refrain if needed. Professional organizers who routinely handle their clients' possessions as part of their work should remember that clients who hoard are strongly attached to their possessions and may become very uncomfortable if others handle them. Failing to heed this sensitivity may lead to premature termination of the work.

- Teach decision-making strategies and help clients develop decision rules. Professional organizers may view the process of making decisions about clients' possessions as part of their work. After all, they are experts at discerning what is useful and what should be discarded, and most clients expect them to do just this as part of their services. However, because difficulty making decisions is a hallmark of hoarding, having others make choices for them does not remedy their disorganization problem in the long run. It is therefore important that professional organizers modify their work to facilitate this learning with hoarding clients. For more detail about implementing this suggestion, refer to Steketee and Frost's 2007 manual.

- Use the clients' language to refer to their possessions. Be careful to avoid terms such as "junk" or "trash," as clients instead may see these as treasures, or at least items of value. When clients refer to possessions as "my things" or "my collection," using the same words can help forge a good relationship and excellent cooperation.

- Don't overestimate what can be accomplished in a single session as clients learn to sort, make decisions, and tolerate emotions associated with discarding. Collaborative work with hoarding clients sometimes moves at a glacial pace. Organizing and decluttering can take a year or even longer.

- Be prepared for clients' expression of strong emotions that include anger, anxiety, sadness, and even grief while sorting possessions. Professional organizers may need education and support from experienced peers and mental health clinicians to handle these reactions and to know when and how to refer clients who require mental health treatment.

- Notice whether clients are bringing home new items on a regular basis and ask if they are willing to reduce or even eliminate this acquisition, at least temporarily. Purchased and free items add to the clutter, and successful organizing may depend on stemming this tide. Be aware that this effort may require help from a mental health clinician trained in cognitive and behavioral treatment for acquiring problems.

- Be prepared for slow progress if clients need to organize or empty their storage units. These units are often crammed so full that the only space for sorting is outside the unit (e.g., a hallway), requiring that possessions that are not discarded must be returned to the unit. To reduce discouragement, begin by generating creative ideas on how to work on such units to encourage problem solving and speed the evidence of progress. For example, once the client has acquired some sorting and decision-making skills, consider scheduling one or more marathon sessions (possibly with help from others) to sort and carry boxes of trash, recycle, sell, and give away items to another location.

CASE STUDY: GEORGE

George was a 46-year-old married white man who lived with his wife in a single family home in a suburb of a large northwestern city. He worked full time in information technology. In addition to hoarding, he had attention deficit disorder (ADD) and obsessive compulsive disorder (OCD), with fears of contamination and symptoms of checking. George was under the care of a psychiatrist who prescribed medication for his ADD and OCD. He also managed these mental health problems through self-care, such as exercise and getting sufficient sleep. In the past, he worked with an ADD coach for approximately 1 year and learned some systems to help him stay focused and organized, such as using a calendar and planner for appointments.

Three years ago, George took part in a 20-session group for hoarding. By the end of the group, he had reduced the clutter in his home and learned basic principles for sorting mail and for paper filing. However, he still felt the need for ongoing support to continue work on his hoarding and chose to attend a monthly support group with others who had also completed the hoarding treatment group. He also arranged to continue monthly individual sessions with one of the group facilitators.

Despite his progress during group treatment, it seemed clear that George needed the help of a professional organizer to implement and practice using the paper filing and mail sorting systems he developed during the group. He investigated a number of possible referrals and hired Jane because she had experience working with hoarding problems. Jane and George contracted to work for eight 2-hour sessions, meeting every 1–2 weeks. During the first session, Jane assessed George's greatest needs and identified his home office as the focal point for work on paper filing. Together, they set the goal of helping George establish a daily habit of sorting mail. Jane and George identified obstacles to implementing his paper filing system, such as having paper stacked in front of his filing cabinet and having already filled each drawer in the cabinet to capacity. They spent part of their first session and most of the second sorting the paper in front of the cabinets into categories, building on the filing categories George had already identified during group treatment. Jane coached George to promptly recycle unwanted paper, reducing the volume of paper in the room. Together, they cleared the area in front of the cabinet, making it accessible for the next organizing steps.

Jane helped George revamp his filing system, reviewing with him his major paper categories (medical, financial, hobbies, etc.) and subcategories (George's personal medical papers, his wife's medical papers, and so forth). When they encountered paper that did not fit into these categories, Jane asked George about his important needs and used the list of Questions about Possessions with him. This helped George decide whether to create a new paper category or simply discard the item. Jane guided George to update his master list of these categories to help him to remember his system and find the relevant files. She also guided him to use a temporary system (by using multicolored Post-it notes with the categories and subcategories written on them) to keep the papers sorted until they could be filed. The multiple bright colors helped maintain George's interest and more easily differentiated the categories, both challenges for people with ADD. Jane also helped George identify supplies he needed such as manila and hanging folders. He agreed to get these before the next visit and put this task on his calendar.

During the third session, Jane helped George decide which cabinet drawers would house the categories in his system and what labels to put on the drawers and on the folders. They used much of the remaining time in this session and most of the fourth session to sort the paper in each drawer, recycling unwanted paper and placing the sorted paper into the appropriate locations. Having reduced the paper in each drawer, George now had room to file the paper that had been in front of the cabinet. Jane and George used the four remaining sessions to tackle other areas cluttered with paper, such as the piles on the office floor and on his desk. George said that early in his work with Jane, he noticed that the new system was efficient and easy to use. He felt motivated to use the system on his own and was able to file paper between sessions.

To make progress toward the goal of sorting mail daily, Jane and George spent part of each session sorting recently arrived mail. Jane proposed a method for tracking important appointments and recommended that George buy a Personal Digital Assistant (PDA) as these had several features he might find helpful, such as an automatic warning signal to remind him of upcoming appointments. Jane helped George choose one location for new mail on one area of the kitchen counter. They agreed he needed to first sort the mail into two broad categories: mail for George and mail for his wife. George then practiced opening each envelope and immediately recycling unwanted items. For bills, George practiced writing the due date on the envelope and putting it on the part of the counter where he and his wife kept bills to pay. Using Questions about Possessions, Jane helped George determine that he did not wish to have more than a one-inch pile of "stuff to read" (or "stuff to deal with"). He practiced "dealing with" this pile between visits with Jane, by reading magazines, newspapers, or articles, entering important events into his PDA and discarding the original paper, and making final decisions about mail items by simply skimming (and usually discarding) them. This practice in making decisions helped George become "more ruthless," keeping fewer items for his "stuff to read/deal with" pile.

George found working with Jane immensely helpful and wished he had been able to afford to continue his work with her beyond their eight visits. At that time, his Clutter Image Rating score for his office had improved from 7 (severe but not extreme) to 4 (moderate). However, the limited number of visits left him with some continuing struggles with regular filing and avoidance of dealing with incoming paper and bill paying on his own. He enlisted the help of a volunteer from his church who came to his home every 1–2 weeks to act as a "body double," as George called it. This volunteer knitted or chatted with George while he worked, a companionable experience that he found far more motivating than trying to work on these tasks alone. George also benefitted from a supportive father who helped him complete household projects (another source of clutter) and sort nonpaper items such as empty boxes. Two years later, George had made good progress and was again poised to hire Jane to help him "fine tune" his filing system and tackle some remaining paper in his office and other parts of the house.

Case Discussion

George clearly benefitted from working with a professional organizer following his hoarding group treatment and alongside the other supports in his life. Although George acquired knowledge and skills during the group, including a "first pass" at his filing system, and made progress on decluttering his home, he saw the need for specialized help with organizing skills and developing strategies to circumvent problems keeping focused on everyday sorting tasks. At the same time, George's prior experience with specialized treatment for hoarding clearly facilitated Jane's work as she and George did not have to start at the beginning to help him learn these skills. Had George not had treatment previously, he and Jane would likely have made less progress, having to start with basic skills and motivational needs. George was an insightful and motivated client who was able to garner help (paid and volunteer), and yet he still needed more than 3 years of work to gain good control over the clutter his home.

George chose a professional organizer carefully. He was aware that his hoarding problem required specialized assistance, and therefore sought a professional organizer who understood hoarding and had experience working with this problem. Jane's use of Questions about Possessions illustrates this. She did not simply tell George what to keep and what to discard, but rather asked him specific questions to encourage decision making about what filing categories would work for his needs. George also benefitted from Jane's skill as she guided him in managing his filing system and the logistics of sorting paper in his office. She was knowledgeable about helpful tools for someone with attention deficit symptoms, such as color coding his temporary filing system and acquiring a PDA. George commented that he enjoyed working with Jane because she was patient, understanding, and sympathetic, as well as knowledgeable.

This case also illustrates that those with a hoarding problem often need and benefit from working with various professionals on their hoarding and co-occurring problems. In the past, George had sought behavioral help for his ADD and during the work with Jane, he received psychiatric medication to manage his ADD and OCD. He also had received assistance from an individual therapist who specialized in hoarding treatment. In addition, George benefitted from a compassionate and helpful father, a volunteer from his church, and a monthly support group for hoarding. Despite these multiple resources, George considered Jane's skills as a professional organizer who understood hoarding to be very useful indeed. Clients with fewer sources of assistance may need professional organizing help for more sessions and with a wider range of items. Professional organizers who are the first person on the scene may well recognize the need for additional client supports from other professionals.

CHAPTER 13

Next Steps in Services for Hoarding

It is our sincere hope that this book serves as a continuing resource and guide for human service professionals dealing with hoarding problems, especially among nonvoluntary clients whose hoarding is time-consuming and costly to resolve. Whether readers encounter hoarding regularly in their practice or are newly acquainted with it, our goal is to provide information and practical suggestions for how to conceptualize, assess, and intervene in serious hoarding problems. Many questions persist and much work remains to be done at both the research and practice levels. Nonetheless, many significant lessons about hoarding and important considerations for intervention have already been learned.

WHAT HAVE WE LEARNED?

During the past 15 years, research on hoarding has increased almost exponentially. Published articles in professional journals with a significant focus on hoarding have increased nearly four-fold since Frost and Hartl published a formal definition of the problem in 1996. Prior to this time, few systematic empirical studies were conducted, although the problem was certainly not new, even to social scientists (for a historical review of hoarding and related concepts see Chapter 2 in Frost & Steketee, 2010; also see Greenberg, 1987). The etiology, prevalence, demographics, characteristics, and manifestations of hoarding are now much better understood. Chapter 1 of this volume introduced a model of hoarding by Frost and Hartl (1996), illustrated in Steketee and Frost (2007). This model outlines potential causal and maintaining factors for hoarding behavior and leads to suggestions for intervention strategies. It also points to the likely role of executive brain functioning (e.g., Tolin, Kiehl, Worhunsky, Book, & Steketee, 2008), a recent and critical development in our understanding of hoarding. New knowledge in the fields of genetics and neurobiology is emerging (for a review see Pertusa et al., 2010a) and will undoubtedly provide new insights into the complexities of hoarding, its co-occurring features, and promising interventions.

While scientific knowledge is produced more slowly, practice wisdom abounds. Many professionals from a range of disciplines work daily with people who hoard, using strategies consistent with their professional discipline and adopting best practices from other fields as well. As is often true, professionals working in the field have valuable knowledge and learn through repeated trial and error; however, this collective knowledge concerning hoarding coming from across the human service professions is often untold. Unfortunately, the demands of human services work make it difficult to scientifically test many practices and to bring this knowledge together in a meaningful way to disseminate it broadly to others. However, one place in which hoarding interventions, practices, and queries are considered together is hoarding task forces, also called hoarding networks or collaborations. As discussed in Chapter 3, these task forces provide a mechanism for education, case consultation, and coordinated intervention. Many human service professionals report that task forces are a place to learn about the latest scientific findings and ground their intervention practices in a strong evidence base (Bratiotis, 2009).

In addition to facilitating the exchange of information and practice ideas, hoarding task forces are a mechanism for coordinating care for hoarding clients across multiple systems. Increasingly, the problem of hoarding is gaining recognition as both a private mental health problem and a matter of public health and safety. When conceptualized this way, hoarding is recognized as a social problem with social implications. This view suggests that the responsibility for intervention rests among many—those who hoard, human service professionals who interact with them, family members, neighbors, friends, and even faith communities. Task forces are currently a viable mechanism for addressing the multiple facets of hoarding and for involving all of these individuals. For example, people who hoard often have related problems with decision-making, organizing, difficulty discarding, acquisition, and, of course, clutter. They also suffer from other mental health problems such as depression and anxiety, as well as from physical health problems. By coordinating aspects of care across various human service professionals, no single provider assumes responsibility for assisting with every aspect of the problem. For example, a professional organizer can help clients with organizing and difficulty discarding, whereas a mental health professional can help reduce intense emotions and beliefs about collecting and discarding and manage comorbid mood problems.

Simultaneously, the fire chief addresses the practical structural and safety risks that stem from clutter, and the child protective service worker determines whether the children can remain in the home while the client is in treatment. In addition, medical professionals assist clients with health problems.

This example demonstrates that working with the multiple facets of hoarding can be resource-intensive. For example, if a single human service professional attempted to address all of these difficulties, the amount of time and agency resources required by a single professional would be quite extensive, not to mention overwhelming for the worker. Another lesson learned from the establishment of a hoarding task force, then, is the significant benefit of sharing the workload, resource allocations, and support systems for staff.

STRUGGLES AND SOLUTIONS

This section illuminates several common challenges related to hoarding intervention. Experience tells us that many human service professionals struggle intensely with common frustrations that emerge when a systematic infrastructure for hoarding intervention is lacking. Below we offer some suggested ways to address these challenges. Some of the proposed solutions can be implemented immediately, whereas others require collective capacity building efforts to find effective solutions.

Practical and emotional resources are scarce:

- **Triage cases with colleagues**. The demands of working with people who hoard are significant. It is important to recognize strong personal reactions to this work and seek consultation and support from colleagues who understand the challenges hoarding presents. As various chapters in the book suggest, talking through the multiple aspects of a hoarding case and brainstorming possible interventions, resources, and a plan of action can be particularly helpful on both a practical and an emotional level.
- **Increase the availability of evidence-based intervention trainings for human service professionals**. In communities throughout the United States, training on problems involving hoarding is becoming more available. Opportunities for training exist within and across some disciplines. For example, housing providers may be trained within their agencies in housing codes, regulatory procedures, and reasonable accommodation as applied to cases of hoarding. Cross-disciplinary training often showcases best practices from a range of

professions and highlights the benefits of collaborative work. Professionals attending such trainings can network with other human service providers to extend the opportunity for collaboration and learn more about their community services and professional groups.

- **Increase the number of mental health professionals trained in cognitive behavioral therapy (CBT) that is specialized for treating issues related to hoarding.** Unfortunately, the number of mental health clinicians trained in treating cases of hoarding is still small, making referrals to appropriate providers challenging, especially in smaller towns or rural communities. Mental health professional associations and organizations such as the Association for Behavioral and Cognitive Therapies (ABCT), the International Obsessive Compulsive Foundation (IOCDF), and the Anxiety Disorders Association of America (ADAA) maintain referral lists of mental health counselors, social workers, psychologists, psychiatrists, and psychiatric nurses who specialize in CBT and/or psychopharmacology. Some of these professionals have experience treating people who hoard, often those who are already trained and experienced in treating OCD because of the historical association of these two conditions.

- **Increase funding for hoarding intervention at the agency and community level.** At this time, only a handful of human service organizations allocate funds expressly for hoarding-related salaried positions and/or to support interventions such as mental health treatment and hoarding coaches. Task forces in some communities secure government or grant funds to implement collaborative hoarding interventions. In other parts of the world (for example, Australia), some government departments directly fund interventions for hoarding. Obviously, more efforts are needed to provide comprehensive services to those in need.

How to obtain reimbursement for hoarding services is unclear:

- **Educate yourself about the parameters for reimbursement.** The question of how to be compensated for interventions related to cases of hoarding is complicated by the kind of reimbursement sought and the services rendered. Unfortunately, there is no simple solution, and it is incumbent on the provider to understand what services are covered by contacting the insurance or relevant state or federal organization and asking questions. Sometimes private insurance, Medicare, or Medicaid will pay for some mental health services or services related to hoarding, such as occupational therapy, personal care assistants, home health aides, or visiting nurses. Currently, services provided by professional organizers are not reimbursable by insurance plans. Often it is difficult to obtain compensation for home visits, although some professionals working directly with insurance providers have been able to negotiate payment.

- **Advocate for changes to policy and clear guidelines for reimbursement.** It is certainly frustrating to many providers that they cannot get (adequate) compensation for treating cases of hoarding, especially as court-ordered evictions and clean outs can be very costly and the likelihood of recidivism is high (see Chapter 6). Although this situation may change when hoarding disorder is recognized in the *Diagnostic and Statistical Manual of Mental Disorders* (American Psychiatric Association, 2000), it is important to take every opportunity to advocate for insurance coverage and reimbursement for hoarding disorder. This can be accomplished at an individual level, with each client's insurance provider, and at a larger societal level, with legislation pertaining to mental health insurance coverage.
- **Choose creativity.** Approach the reimbursement or payment of treatment and intervention for hoarding creatively. Think differently about clients with hoarding problems as this can help identify ways to get needed services in place. For example, if a mental health clinician cannot be reimbursed for home visits but can bill insurance for in-office treatment, is there another organization or person who could collaborate to accomplish the in-home portion of the work?

Research on hoarding is still very limited:

- **Increase research to understand the causes of hoarding.** The number of researchers investigating hoarding disorder has increased in the past decade, as has the sophistication and specificity of the research. In general, the federal government has been relatively slow to fund behavioral science studies of hoarding; despite this, scientists have conducted research that is yielding important information about the nature of this complex problem and its response to some intervention efforts. Still, many aspects of hoarding need more study, including its occurrence in diverse populations, the manifestation in children and older adults, causal and maintaining biological factors, and its relationship to other disorders. Advocacy for more funding of methodologically rigorous studies is clearly needed.
- **Provide support and infrastructure for human service agencies to conduct research on best practices.** As previously noted, human service professionals and agencies have valuable practice experience with community-based hoarding interventions. Community agency and

university/research institution partnerships are an important way to study interventions and outcomes as universities provide research expertise and community human service agencies offer access to the clients for data collection. Such partnerships also facilitate a wider audience for the dissemination and discussion of results. These scientific and community collaborations are occurring in only a few communities; expansion could aid in the proliferation of timely research findings that influence interventions and outcomes.

Sharing of information across agencies is difficult; everyone has different rules:

- **Understand HIPAA regulations and its limitations.** The Health Insurance Portability and Accountability Act (HIPAA) is a system of protections for clients receiving particular kinds of services, including medical and mental health treatment. Some human service organizations are bound by HIPAA regulations, whereas others are not. It is important for human service professionals to understand the application of HIPAA regulations with regard to their settings and clients. When hoarding professionals are sharing information about a case, some organizations, such as fire and police departments, can divulge significant information, whereas other agencies, such as protective services, are more rule-bound. It is important that each organization discuss cases to the extent allowed by law and that other partnering organizations understand and respect these limitations.
- **Above all, respect the rights of the person who hoards.** When providers are uncertain about what information can be shared and the appropriate mechanisms for doing so, erring on the side of caution should be the standard of care. It is critical to recognize that people who hoard, like all human service clients, have the right to privacy. It can be easy to talk casually without intending harm and to thereby violate a person's right to privacy. Many human service professions have codes of ethics or standards of care that provide helpful guidelines. At the very least, human service professionals should put themselves in the place of the person who hoards and imagine how they would want their personal information protected.
- **Engage in creative problem solving.** Abiding by HIPAA regulations and professional codes does not mean that meaningful information about clients who hoard cannot be shared. It is often in everyone's best interest for appropriate information to be exchanged, as this is how hoarding clients will receive the best and most coordinated care. One approach taken by some community task forces is to use a

hypothetical case discussion; critical elements of the case are discussed without identifying information. For example, the details of where a person lives, their gender, age, family, and occupation information are not divulged. Instead, the focus of the case is on the details of the hoarding situation—the interference in daily life activities and threats to health and safety. Whether this approach or another is taken, human service professionals can creatively generate solutions that enable them to share information to the extent needed and implement the most promising interventions.

There is little information about the influence of culture and race on hoarding:

- **The scientific study of hoarding is limited by voluntary participants.** Most of the current information about hoarding derives from research studies conducted at academic institutions and research centers. Unfortunately, the voluntary participants in these studies often do not reflect a representative cross-sample of the population. Increasing community-based hoarding research may provide access to more diverse groups of people who hoard to better understand their challenges and needs.
- **Hoarding occurs in many cultures throughout the world.** In addition to North America, research and practice colleagues from Asia, Europe, and Australia recognize hoarding as a problem and use intervention methods similar to those outlined in this book. Nonetheless, almost no information about hoarding is available in most parts of Asia, as well as Africa and South America.
- **Avoid stereotyping and assigning meaning based on race or ethnicity alone.** Recognizing the influences of culture on behavior, thoughts, and emotions is critical to providing a sensitive and informed intervention for hoarding and its co-occurring conditions. Understanding the traditions and practices of particular racial and ethnic groups can be helpful in the assessment of and intervention for hoarding, but assigning meaning to hoarding behavior based on culture alone is unlikely to be useful. Professionals will be most helpful by discussing with clients the various influences on their collecting and saving behaviors as a necessary element for establishing a trusting relationship, the foundation on which effective intervention is built.

Early intervention and prevention are needed:

- **Identify the problem early—in childhood, adolescence, or young adulthood if possible.** Research suggests that the onset of hoarding occurs by early adolescence, around age 13 years (Grisham et al., 2006). At this stage, clutter has rarely amassed to the point of interference, but other features of the disorder may be identifiable such as difficulty parting with objects, assigning special meanings, strong emotional attachment, and indecision. Intervention during childhood and adolescence is currently being explored scientifically, but in the absence of research findings, early intervention might take the form of public education and broad training across professionals to identify problems early and prevent symptoms from worsening.

- **Intervene as early as possible.** Some human service professionals, especially providers who are in the home on a regular basis, first see cases of hoarding when they are at a mild or moderate state. For example, housing inspectors, occupational therapists, and home health aides may encounter hoarding symptoms before the clutter is severe. Given the chronic and worsening course of hoarding (Tolin, Meunier, Frost, & Steketee, 2010), it is in everyone's best interest to intervene at the first signs of daily life interference. Left untreated, clutter continues to amass and beliefs and emotions associated with possessions become more entrenched. Simultaneously clearing the clutter and attending to the underlying reasons for saving at the first sign of difficulty may forestall a more lengthy and laborious intervention later.

- **Educate the community to avoid simplistic solutions that can be harmful.** Although it is tempting for human service professionals to fall back on simply clearing out clutter to ameliorate the hoarding problem, evidence suggests that this approach is ineffective and even harmful (see Chapter 10). Home clean-outs require intensive fiscal and human resources and commonly lead to reaccumulation of clutter. In worst case scenarios, they lead to worsening health and even death. Slowly clearing the clutter through a systematic and therapeutically supported process promotes self-efficacy, maintains a trusting relationship with human service providers, and offers the most promise for sustained change. Even when additional intervention over time is needed, as several of the case examples in this book illustrate, clients are much more willing to seek further help when their experience with health and safety professionals has been positive.

A CALL FOR POLICY CHANGE AND DEVELOPMENT

The relative recency of the scientific study of hoarding means that systematic and coordinated responses have been slow to develop. This lack of standardization creates a situation in which communities address problems on a case-by-case basis as best they can and are sometimes overwhelmed by the number and severity of cases coming to their attention. Models of effective intervention are now surfacing as communities are beginning to talk to one another, sharing promising practices. This increased communication has the potential to lead to practice standards for hoarding and model-testing across different geographic regions. The information garnered through such efforts can be used to recommend policies that will best serve communities and clients.

Throughout this book, we have highlighted some areas in which policy change and development are needed. For example, the institutionalization of coordinated community responses such as those currently being advanced by hoarding task forces is an area ripe for policy development. At present, there are no overarching regulations at a community, state, or federal level that guide hoarding intervention. Organizations are not mandated to participate on task forces and task forces do not have special authority or power. Likewise, these efforts are not independently funded or staffed and therefore can dissolve quickly when interest and voluntary commitment wane.

Recognition of hoarding as a mental health disorder and the ability to bill for clinical treatment and other intervention services are other areas for policy development. To date, researchers have generally advanced knowledge about the damage hoarding can do and the need for intervention; however, practitioners from various disciplines are essential to this effort. As mentioned earlier, proposing policy change can happen through individual cases or at a larger system level, but efforts gain momentum when more than one practitioner is advancing this cause.

A FINAL WORD

This book is an outgrowth of repeated conversations among colleagues about the many challenges of working on the problem of hoarding. Our understanding that hoarding and its complexities require the expertise and experience of a wide range of any community's human service agencies led us to the writing of this book. None of the several professions that address hoarding—housing, fire, public health, animal control, professional organizing, and mental health—alone has the expertise to resolve the problem. Instead, it is the collective and shared wisdom and practice among these professions that provide the greatest hope for interventions that respect the person who hoards and that effect change over the long term.

We have been amazed and inspired by the countless human service professionals who contact us on a daily basis, searching for ideas, resources, and promising practices. These professionals are sincerely devoted to their work and to the hoarding clients they serve. They are empathic, motivated, and tenacious. For every one we have spoken to or corresponded with, we know there are hundreds, if not thousands, more in communities large and small making a significant difference in the lives of those who hoard.

If this book provides information, insight, and new perspectives or provokes reflection, contemplation, or conversation, our goal has been achieved. Of course, knowledge about hoarding and its interventions is constantly changing. As society continues to recognize hoarding as a problem requiring a systemic response, and as research and provision of human services continue to advance, the promise of policy institutionalization and change will hopefully be realized. Until then, each of us must strive to implement state-of-the-art hoarding interventions that are client-centered, sensitive to others who are affected, and evidence-based. So too, we must be willing to absorb and creatively utilize new information, grounded in our commitment to helping those who have problems with hoarding.

Hoarding Interview
(Modified for General Use By Non-mental Health Professionals)

Client Name_____   Date _____

Assessor Name_____

Current Living Situation

1. What type of home do you live in?

Single Family _____ Apartment_____ Single Room_____ Other _____

2. Who lives in your house and what are their ages, sex, and relationship to you?

Name	Age	Sex	Relationship

3. How many children do you have? _____

4. How many grandchildren do you have? _____

5. Can you tell me how difficult it is for you to use the various rooms in your home? For example, sitting down, moving around, finding things, having visitors present, and otherwise using it the way most people do. Let's use a scale that ranges from 0 meaning not at all difficult to 8 meaning extremely difficult to use.

[Show the client the scale below:]

0	1	2	3	4	5	6	7	8	N/A
Not at all Difficult		Mild		Moderate		Severe		Extremely Difficult	Not Applicable

Let's start with your _____

a) Living Room   (how hard is it to sit, move around, have visitors)   _____
b) Dining Room   (sitting, moving around, using the table)   _____
c) Bedroom   (sleeping, moving around)   _____
d) Kitchen   (cooking, eating, moving around)   _____
e) Bathroom   (bathing, using toilet)   _____
f) Hallways   (move without danger of falling)   _____
g) Stairways   (move without danger of falling)   _____
h) Basement   (find things, moving around)   _____
i) Attic   (find things, moving around)   _____
j) Porch   (sitting, moving around, etc.)   _____
k) Garage   (find things, moving around)   _____
l) Car   (drive, find things, carry passengers)   _____
m) Outdoors   (avoid complaints from neighbors, etc.)   _____
n) Place of work   (find things, work efficiently)   _____
o) Storage area   (find things, move around)   _____
p) Other   (specify:_____)   _____
q) Other   (specify:_____)   _____

6. In general, because of the clutter and the number of possessions in your home, how difficult is it for you to use the rooms in your home?

0	1	2	3	4	5	6	7	8
Not at all Difficult		Mild		Moderate		Severe		Extremely Difficult

7. How distressing or upsetting is it for you to have your home in its current state?

0	1	2	3	4	5	6	7	8
Not at all		Mild		Moderate		Severe		Extreme

8. Have other people or agencies ever tried to intervene because of home clutter?

a) Housing/landlord   Yes   No
b) Fire Department   Yes   No
c) Child protective service   Yes   No
d) Adult protective service   Yes   No
e) Animal protection   Yes   No
f) Police Department   Yes   No

If so, what happened?

9. To what extent do you have difficulty getting rid of (discarding, recycling, selling, giving away) ordinary things that other people would get rid of?

0	1	2	3	4	5	6	7	8
None		Mild		Moderate		Severe		Extreme/unable to discard

10. To what extent do you have difficulty organizing the things in your home?

0	1	2	3	4	5	6	7	8
None		Mild		Moderate		Severe		Extreme/unable to organize

11. When you try to get rid of things (discard, recycle, sell, give away, etc.), how much distress or emotional upset do you experience?

0	1	2	3	4	5	6	7	8
None		Mild		Moderate		Severe		Extreme

12. Are you afraid of *losing important information* when you try to throw something out? That is, you are afraid you will mistakenly throw out information that you will need someday.

0	1	2	3	4	5	6	7	8
Never		Rarely		Occasionally		Frequently		Nearly always

13. Do you save things because they are *sentimental or emotionally significant* to you? That is, you are so emotionally attached that you do not want to part with them.

0	1	2	3	4	5	6	7	8
Never		Rarely		Occasionally		Frequently		Nearly always

14. Are you afraid of *wasting a potentially useful object* when you try to discard something? That is, you are concerned about being wasteful because the object could eventually be put to good use.

0	1	2	3	4	5	6	7	8
Never		Rarely		Occasionally		Frequently		Nearly always

15. How often do you save things because the object is *beautiful or aesthetically pleasing* regardless of its monetary or sentimental value?

0	1	2	3	4	5	6	7	8
Never		Rarely		Occasionally		Frequently		Nearly always

16. Are there any other reasons why you have difficulty throwing things out?

17. Have you ever had a problem with collecting or buying more things than you need or can use or can afford?

0	1	2	3	4	5	6	7	8
No problem		Mild		Moderate		Severe		Extreme

18. Do you acquire things (free or purchased) because they contain *information* that you consider important? That is, you obtain the item because it might have information you need someday.

0	1	2	3	4	5	6	7	8
Never		Rarely		Occasionally		Frequently		Nearly always

19. Do you acquire things (free or purchased) because they are *sentimental or emotionally significant* to you? That is, you become so emotionally attached to items you see that you feel you must acquire them.

0	1	2	3	4	5	6	7	8
Never		Rarely		Occasionally		Frequently		Nearly always

20. Do you acquire things (free or purchased) because are you afraid of *wasting a potentially useful object* if you don't get it? That is, it seems wasteful to you not to get it because the object may eventually be put to good use.

0	1	2	3	4	5	6	7	8
Never		Rarely		Occasionally		Frequently		Nearly always

21. Do you acquire things (free or purchased) because the object is *beautiful or aesthetically pleasing* regardless of its monetary or sentimental value?

0	1	2	3	4	5	6	7	8
Never		Rarely		Occasionally		Frequently		Nearly always

22. Are there any other reasons why you acquire free or purchased items?

23. Do you think the clutter presents a problem for your health or safety? Yes No

For instance, does it present a problem for:

a) Falling　　　　　　　　　Yes　No
b) Fire hazard　　　　　　　Yes　No
c) Hygiene　　　　　　　　Yes　No
d) Nutrition　　　　　　　 Yes　No
e) Medical problems　　　　Yes　No
f) Insect infestation　　　　Yes　No

24. Do other people think the clutter presents a problem for your health or safety? Yes No

For instance, do they think it presents a problem for:

a) Falling　　　　　　　　　Yes　No
b) Fire hazard　　　　　　　Yes　No
c) Hygiene　　　　　　　　Yes　No
d) Nutrition　　　　　　　 Yes　No
e) Medical problems　　　　Yes　No
f) Insect infestation　　　　Yes　No

Use this scale to rate the following items:

0	1	2	3	4	5	6	7	8	N/A
Not at all		Mild		Moderate		Severe		Extreme	Not applicable

25. Because of clutter, acquiring, or difficulty discarding, to what extent do you experience problems with general living? For example:
   a) Difficulties on the job or at school (e.g., not keeping things organized) _____
   b) Social activities (e.g., not inviting people to the house) _____
   c) Daily routine (e.g., bathing, cooking) _____
   d) Family activities (e.g., unable to engage in desired activities) _____
   e) Financial burden (e.g., money spent on purchases, credit card debt, storage fees, purchase of second home due to hoarding) _____
   f) Family conflict (e.g., arguments) _____

26. In what other ways has clutter, difficulty discarding (recycling, selling, giving away), or buying or acquiring things interfered with your life?

27. When, as far as you can remember, was the first time that you noticed that you had trouble acquiring too many things, throwing things away, or had a lot of clutter in your home?

28. Tell me about that time and why you think the trouble developed.

[Ask about possible losses (moving, job loss, death of family member), deprivation (not enough food or clothing, few toys, no money), or other problems that might have occurred at this time.]

29. Did anyone in your family have a hoarding problem? Yes No

If yes, who?

Do you think their hoarding had an influence on you? How so?

30. Do family members or friends or others visit you at your home?

[Ask who and how often to get a picture of home life and social life.]

31. Do you visit other people in their homes?
32. Observational Ratings of the Participant.
   a) Was there an unpleasant body odor?   0   1   2   3   4

                                      none   overpowering

   b) Personal physical appearance: 0   1   2   3   4

               very clean/neat   very dirty/unkempt

General comments:

Adapted from Steketee, G., & Frost, R. O. (2007). *Compulsive hoarding and acquiring: Therapist guide*. New York: Oxford University Press.

Hoarding Rating Scale (HRS)
(Interview Format)

1. Because of the clutter or number of possessions, how difficult is it for you to use the rooms in your home?

0	1	2	3	4	5	6	7	8
Not at all difficult		Mild		Moderate		Severe		Extremely difficult

2. To what extent do you have difficulty discarding (or recycling, selling, giving away) ordinary things that other people would get rid of:

0	1	2	3	4	5	6	7	8
No difficulty		Mild		Moderate		Severe		Extremely difficult

3. To what extent do you currently have a problem with collecting free things or buying more things than you need or can use or can afford?

0	1	2	3	4	5	6	7	8
No problem		Mild, occasionally (less than weekly) acquires items not needed, or acquires a few unneeded items		Moderate, regularly (once or twice weekly) acquires items not needed, or acquires some unneeded items		Severe, frequently (several times per week) acquires items not needed, or acquires many unneeded items		Extreme, very often (daily) acquires items not needed, or acquires large numbers of unneeded items

4. To what extent do you experience emotional distress because of clutter, difficulty discarding, or problems with buying or acquiring things?

0	1	2	3	4	5	6	7	8
None/not at all		Mild		Moderate		Severe		Extreme

5. To what extent do you experience impairment in your life (daily routine, job/school, social activities, family activities, financial difficulties) because of clutter, difficulty discarding, or problems with buying or acquiring things?

0	1	2	3	4	5	6	7	8
None/not at all		Mild		Moderate		Severe		Extreme

Reproduced from Tolin, D. F., Frost, R.O., & Steketee, G. (2010). A brief interview for assessing compulsive hoarding: The Hoarding Rating Scale. *Psychiatry Research*, with permission from Elsevier. doi.org/10.1016/j.psychres.2009.05.001.

Clutter Image Rating

Using the three series of pictures (CIR: Living Room, CIR: Kitchen, and CIR: Bedroom), please select the picture that best represents the amount of clutter for each of the rooms of your home. Put the number on the line below.

Please select the picture that is closest to being accurate, even if it is not exactly right.

If your home does not have one of the rooms listed, just put NA for "not applicable" on that line.

Room _Number of closest corresponding picture (1–9)_

Living Room   _____

Kitchen   _____

Bedroom #1   _____

Bedroom #2   _____

Also, please rate other rooms in your house that are affected by clutter on the lines below.

Use the _CIR: Living Room_ pictures to make these ratings.

Dining room   _____

Hallway   _____

Garage   _____

Basement   _____

Attic   _____

Car   _____

Other_____   Please specify: _____

TARGET ROOM RATING FORM (BASED ON CIR RATINGS)

Rate up to three rooms that are the main target areas of intervention. Note the CIR pictures used to rate the target room or area. For rooms other than the living room, kitchen, or bedroom (e.g., hallway, attic, basement, walk-in closet, garage, storage area), the living room pictures will generally be used.

Target Room #1 _____

CIR picture set used: LR BR Kit Score:_____

Target Room #2 _____

CIR picture set used: LR BR Kit Score:_____

Target Room #3 _____

CIR picture set used: LR BR Kit Score:_____

Reproduced from Steketee, G., & Frost, R. O. (2007). *Compulsive hoarding and acquiring: Therapist guide.* New York: Oxford University Press.

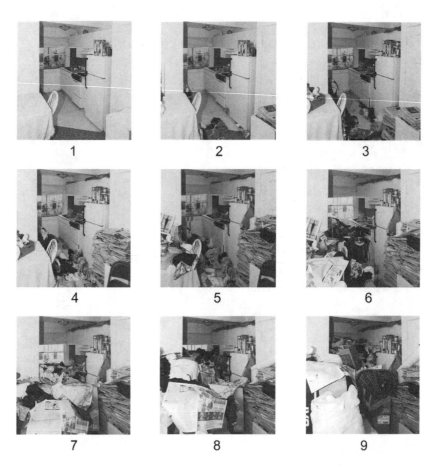

Figure A.1 Clutter Image Rating Scale: Kitchen.

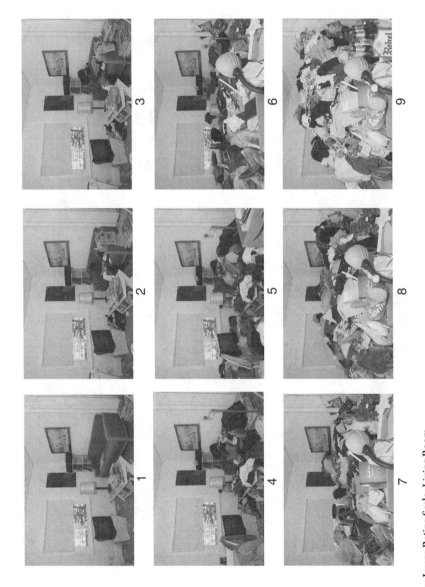

Figure A.2 Clutter Image Rating Scale: Living Room.

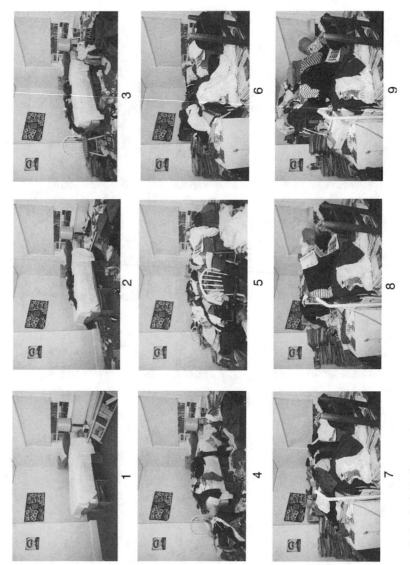

Figure A.3 Clutter Image Rating Scale: Bedroom.

Activities of Daily Living–Hoarding (ADL-H) Scales

A. ACTIVITIES OF DAILY LIVING

Sometimes clutter in the home can prevent you from doing ordinary activities. For each of the following activities, please circle the number that best represents the degree of difficulty you experience in doing this activity because of the clutter or hoarding problem. If you have difficulty with the activity for other reasons (for example, you are unable to bend or move quickly due to physical problems), do not include this in your rating. Instead, rate only how much difficulty you would have due to hoarding. If the activity is not relevant to your situation (for example, you don't have laundry facilities or animals), check the Not Applicable (N/A) box.

Activities affected by clutter or hoarding problem	Can do it easily	Can do it with a little difficulty	Can do it with moderate difficulty	Can do it with great difficulty	Unable to do it	N/A
1. Prepare food	1	2	3	4	5	NA
2. Use refrigerator	1	2	3	4	5	NA
3. Use stove	1	2	3	4	5	NA
4. Use kitchen sink	1	2	3	4	5	NA
5. Eat at table	1	2	3	4	5	NA
6. Move around inside the house	1	2	3	4	5	NA
7. Exit home quickly	1	2	3	4	5	NA
8. Use toilet	1	2	3	4	5	NA
9. Use bath/shower	1	2	3	4	5	NA

10. Use bathroom sink	1	2	3	4	5	NA
11. Answer door quickly	1	2	3	4	5	NA
12. Sit in sofa/chair	1	2	3	4	5	NA
13. Sleep in bed	1	2	3	4	5	NA
14. Do laundry	1	2	3	4	5	NA
15. Find important things (such as bills, tax forms)	1	2	3	4	5	NA
16. Care for animals	1	2	3	4	5	NA

B. LIVING CONDITIONS

Please circle the number below that best indicates how much of a problem you have with the following conditions in your home:

Problems in the home	None	A little	Somewhat/ moderate	Substantial	Severe
17. Structural damage (floors, walls, roof, etc.)	1	2	3	4	5
18. Presence of rotten food items	1	2	3	4	5
19. Insect infestation	1	2	3	4	5
20. Presence of human urine or feces	1	2	3	4	5
21. Presence of animal urine or feces	1	2	3	4	5
22. Water not working	1	2	3	4	5
23. Heat not working	1	2	3	4	5

C. SAFETY ISSUES

Please indicate whether you have any concerns such as those described below in your home.

Type of problem	Not at all	A little	Somewhat/ moderate	Substantial	Severe
24. Does any part of your house pose a fire hazard (for example, stove covered with paper, flammable objects near the furnace, etc.)?	1	2	3	4	5
25. Are parts of your house unsanitary (bathrooms unclean, strong odor)?	1	2	3	4	5
26. Would medical emergency personnel have difficulty moving equipment through your home?	1	2	3	4	5
27. Are any exits from your home blocked?	1	2	3	4	5
28. Is it unsafe to move up or down the stairs or along other walkways?	1	2	3	4	5
29. Is there clutter outside your house (porch, yard, alleyway, common areas, if apartment or condo)?	1	2	3	4	5

SCORING KEY

The Hoarding ADL yields three scores:

A. *Activities of Daily Living*: Sum items 1–16, excluding items with NA (not applicable) ratings. Divide by the number of items that are given a numerical rating to yield an average score that ranges from 1.0 to 5.0.

B. *Living Conditions*: Sum items 17–23 and divide by 7 to yield an average score ranging from 1.0 to 5.0.

C. *Safety Issues*: Sum items 24–29 and divide by 6 to yield an average score ranging from 1.0 to 5.0.

Reproduced from Steketee, G., & Frost, R. O. (2007). *Compulsive hoarding and acquiring: Therapist guide*. New York: Oxford University Press.

Saving Inventory–Revised

For each question below, circle the number that corresponds most closely to your experience

DURING THE PAST WEEK

	0	1	2	3	4
	None	A little	A moderate amount	Most/ much	Almost all/ complete
1. How much of the living area in your home is cluttered with possessions? (Consider the amount of clutter in your kitchen, living room, dining room, hallways, bedrooms, bathrooms, or other rooms.)	0	1	2	3	4
2. How much control do you have over your urges to acquire possessions?	0	1	2	3	4
3. How much of your home does clutter prevent you from using?	0	1	2	3	4
4. How much control do you have over your urges to save possessions?	0	1	2	3	4
5. How much of your home is difficult to walk through because of clutter?	0	1	2	3	4

For each question below, circle the number that corresponds most closely to your experience

DURING THE PAST WEEK

	0	1	2	3	4
	Not at all	Mild	Moderate	Considerable/ severe	Extreme
6. To what extent do you have difficulty throwing things away?	0	1	2	3	4
7. How distressing do you find the task of throwing things away?	0	1	2	3	4
8. To what extent do you have so many things that your room(s) are cluttered?	0	1	2	3	4
9. How distressed or uncomfortable would you feel if you could not acquire something you wanted?	0	1	2	3	4
10. How much does clutter in your home interfere with your social, work, or everyday functioning? Think about things that you do not do because of clutter.	0	1	2	3	4
11. How strong is your urge to buy or acquire free things for which you have no immediate use?	0	1	2	3	4

DURING THE PAST WEEK

	0	1	2	3	4
	Not at all	Mild	Moderate	Considerable/ severe	Extreme
12. To what extent does clutter in your home cause you distress?	0	1	2	3	4
13. How strong is your urge to save something you know you may never use?	0	1	2	3	4

For each question below, circle the number that corresponds most closely to your experience

14. How upset or distressed do you feel about your acquiring habits?	0	1	2	3	4
15. To what extent do you feel unable to control the clutter in your home?	0	1	2	3	4
16. To what extent has your saving or compulsive buying resulted in financial difficulties for you?	0	1	2	3	4

DURING THE PAST WEEK

	0	1	2	3	4
	Never	Rarely	Sometimes/ occasionally	Frequently/ often	Very Often
17. How often do you avoid trying to discard possessions because it is too stressful or time consuming?	0	1	2	3	4
18. How often do you feel compelled to acquire something you see, e.g., when shopping or offered free things?	0	1	2	3	4
19. How often do you decide to keep things you do not need and have little space for?	0	1	2	3	4
20. How frequently does clutter in your home prevent you from inviting people to visit?	0	1	2	3	4
21. How often do you actually buy (or acquire for free) things for which you have no immediate use or need?	0	1	2	3	4

22. To what extent does the clutter in your home prevent you from using parts of your home for their intended purpose, for example, cooking, using furniture, washing dishes, cleaning, etc.?	0	1	2	3	4
23. How often are you unable to discard a possession you would like to get rid of?	0	1	2	3	4

SI-R (MODIFIED) SCORING SUBSCALES:

Clutter Subscale (9 Items):

Sum items: 1, 3, 5, 8, 10, 12, 15, 20, 22

Difficulty Discarding/Saving Subscale (7 items):

Sum items: 4 (reverse score), 6, 7, 13, 17, 19, 23

Acquisition Subscale (7 items):

Sum items: 2 (reverse score), 9, 11, 14, 16, 18, 21

Total Score = sum of all items

	Average Score	High Score
Total Score	24	40
Clutter Subscale	9	15
Difficulty Discarding/Saving Subscale	8	16
Acquisition Subscale	6	10

Reproduced from Frost, R.O., Steketee, G., & Grisham, J. (2004). Measurement of compulsive hoarding: Saving Inventory-Revised. *Behaviour Research and Therapy, 42,* 1163–1182, with permission from Elsevier.

Home Environment Index

To what extent are the following things present in the home?

1. Structural damage

0	=	All walls, ceilings, floors, and beams (both weight-bearing and non-weight-bearing) are intact and in good repair
1	=	All vital components of the infrastructure are intact; slight damage to paint or other surfaces
2	=	Most vital components of the infrastructure are intact; widespread surface damage
3	=	Infrastructure is in poor repair (e.g., rotten beams or sinking floor)

2. Blocked exits

0	=	No exits blocked.
1	=	Some stuff in front of one exit
2	=	Stuff blocking some but not all exits
3	=	All exits seriously clogged or blocked

3. Fire hazard

0	=	No fire hazard exists
1	=	Some risk of fire (e.g., lots of flammable material)
2	=	Moderate risk of fire (e.g., flammable materials near heat source)
3	=	High risk of fire (e.g., flammable materials near heat source; electrical hazards, etc.)

4. Moldy or rotten food

0	=	None
1	=	A few pieces of moldy or rotten food in the kitchen
2	=	Some moldy or rotten food spread throughout the kitchen
3	=	Large quantity of moldy or rotten food in the kitchen and elsewhere

5. Standing water (in sink, tub, other container, or basement)

0	=	No standing water
1	=	Some water in sink/tub
2	=	Water in several places, especially if dirty water
3	=	Water in numerous places, especially if dirty

6. Human/animal waste/vomit

0	=	No human/animal waste/vomit visible
1	=	No human waste/vomit; no animal waste/vomit outside the cage or box
2	=	Some animal/human waste/vomit visible (e.g., in unflushed toilet)
3	=	Animal/human waste/vomit on floors or other surfaces

7. Dirty or clogged sink

0	=	Sink empty and clean
1	=	A few dirty dishes with water in the sink
2	=	Sink full of water, possibly clogged
3	=	Sink apparently clogged with evidence that it has overflowed onto counters, etc.

8. Mildew or mold

0	=	No mildew/mold is detectable
1	=	Small amount of mildew/mold in limited amounts and in expected places (e.g., on the edge of the shower curtain or on the refrigerator seal)
2	=	Considerable, noticeable mildew/mold
3	=	Widespread mildew/mold on most surfaces

9. Dirty food containers

0	=	All dishes washed and put away
1	=	A few unwashed dishes
2	=	Many unwashed dishes
3	=	Almost all dishes are unwashed

10. Dirty surfaces (floors, walls, furniture, etc.)

0	=	Surfaces are completely clean
1	=	A few spills, some dirt or grime
2	=	More than a few spills, perhaps a thin covering of dirt or grime in living areas
3	=	No surface is clean, dirt or grime covers everything

11. Piles of dirty or contaminated objects (e.g., bathroom tissue, hair, sanitary products, etc.)

0	=	No dirty/contaminated objects on floors, surfaces, etc.
1	=	Some objects (e.g., toilet paper or sanitary product wrappers) may be present around trash cans or toilets
2	=	Many contaminated objects fill the bathroom or the area around trash cans
3	=	Contaminated objects are all over the floors and surfaces in most rooms

12. Insects

0	=	Absence of insects: none visible/discernible
1	=	A couple of insects may be visible; cobwebs and/or insect droppings present
2	=	Many insects and droppings are visible; cobwebs in the corners
3	=	Swarms of insects; high volume of droppings; many cobwebs on household items

13. Dirty clothes

0	=	Hamper may contain dirty clothes; none outside the hamper
1	=	Hamper may be full; a few dirty clothes lie around; inhabitant is wearing dirty clothes
2	=	Hamper is overflowing; many dirty clothes lie around; inhabitant is wearing dirty clothes
3	=	Clothes cover the floor and other surfaces; inhabitant is wearing dirty clothes

14. Dirty bed sheets/linens

0	=	Bed coverings are very clean
1	=	Bed coverings are relatively clean
2	=	Bed coverings are dirty and in need of washing
3	=	Bed coverings are very dirty and soiled

15. Odor of house

0	=	No odor
1	=	Slight odor
2	=	Moderate odor; strong in some parts of the house
3	=	Strong odor throughout the house

16. Body odor

0	=	No odor
1	=	Slight to moderate odor
2	=	Strong odor when standing close
3	=	Strong odor even at a distance

BEHAVIOR

During the past month, how often did you do each of the following?

17. Do the dishes

0	=	Never (0 times/month)
1	=	Every other week (up to 2 times/month)
2	=	1–2 times a week (up to 8 times/month)
3	=	Every other day/every day (up to 30 times/month)

18. Open the refrigerator

0	=	Never (0 times/month)
1	=	Every other week (up to 2 times/month)
2	=	1–2 times a week (up to 8 times/month)
3	=	Every other day/every day (up to 30 times/month)

19. Clean the bathroom

0	=	Never (0 times/month)
1	=	Every other week (up to 2 times/month)
2	=	1–2 times a week (up to 8 times/month)
3	=	Every other day/every day (up to 30 times/month)

20. Shower or bath

0	=	Never (0 times/month)
1	=	Every other week (up to 2 times/month)
2	=	1–2 times a week (up to 8 times/month)
3	=	Every other day/every day (up to 30 times/month)

21. Do laundry

0	=	Never (0 times/month)
1	=	Every other week (up to 2 times/month)
2	=	1–2 times a week (up to 8 times/month)
3	=	Every other day/every day (up to 30 times/month)

22. Change clothes

0	=	Never (0 times/month)
1	=	Every other week (up to 2 times/month)
2	=	1–2 times a week (up to 8 times/month)
3	=	Every other day/every day (up to 30 times/month)

HOMES© Multidisciplinary Hoarding Risk Assessment

INSTRUCTIONS FOR USE

- **HOMES** Multidisciplinary Hoarding Risk Assessment provides a structural measure through which the level of risk in a hoarded environment can be conceptualized.
- It is intended as an *initial* and *brief* assessment to aid in determining the nature and parameters of the hoarding problem and organizing a plan from which further action may be taken—including immediate intervention, additional assessment, or referral.
- **HOMES** can be used in a variety of ways, depending on needs and resources. It is recommended that a visual scan of the environment in combination with a conversation with the person(s) in the home be used to determine the effect of clutter/hoarding on the **H**ealth, **O**bstacles, **M**ental Health, **E**ndangerment, and **S**tructure in the setting.
- The Family Composition, Imminent Risk, Capacity, Notes, and Postassessment sections are intended for additional information about the hoarded environment, the occupants, and their capacity/strength to address the problem.

©Bratiotis (2009).

❏ Health

❏ Cannot use the bathtub/shower	❏ Cannot prepare food	❏ Presence of spoiled food	❏ Presence of insects/rodents
❏ Cannot access toilet	❏ Cannot sleep in the bed	❏ Presence of feces/ urine (human or animal)	❏ Presence of mold or chronic dampness
❏ Garbage/trash overflow	❏ Cannot use the stove/refridgerator/ sink	❏ Cannot locate medications or equipment	

Notes:_____

_____

❑ **Obstacles**

❑ Cannot move freely/safely in home	❑ Unstable piles/avalanche risk
❑ Inability for EMT to enter/gain access	❑ Egresses, exits, or vents blocked or unusable

Notes:_____

_____

❑ **Mental health** (Note that this is not a clinical diagnosis; use it only to identify risk factors)

❑ Does not seem to understand the seriousness of the problem	❑ Defensive or angry	❑ Unaware, not alert, or confused
❑ Does not seem to accept the likely consequences of the problem	❑ Anxious or apprehensive	

Notes:_____

_____

❑ **Endangerment** (evaluate threat based on other sections with attention to the specific populations listed below)

❑ Threat to the health or safety of a child/minor	❑ Threat to health or safety of a person with disability
❑ Threat to the health or safety of an older adult	❑ Threat to the health or safety of an animal

Notes:_____

_____

❑ **Structure and Safety**

❑ Unstable floorboards/stairs/porch	❑ Leaking roof	❑ Electrical wires/cords exposed	❑ No running water/plumbing problems
❑ Flammable items beside heat source	❑ Caving walls	❑ No heat/electricity	❑ Blocked/unsafe electric heater or vents
❑ Storage of hazardous materials/weapons			

Notes:_____

_____

©Bratiotis (2009).

HOMES© Multidisciplinary Hoarding Risk Assessment

Household Composition

of Adults _____ # of Children _____

and kinds of Pets _____

Ages of adults: _____ Ages of children: _____

Person who smokes in home ❑ Yes ❑ No

Person(s) with physical disability_____

Language(s) spoken in home_____

Assessment Notes: _____

_____

_____

_____

Risk Measurements

❑ Imminent harm to self, family, animals, public: _____

❑ Threat of eviction: _____

❑ Threat of condemnation: _____

Capacity Measurements

Instructions: Place a check mark by the items that represent the strengths and capacity to address the hoarding problem

❑ Awareness of clutter

❑ Willingness to acknowledge clutter and risks to health, safety, and ability to remain in home/impact on daily life

❑ Physical ability to clear clutter

❑ Psychological ability to tolerate intervention

❑ Willingness to accept intervention assistance

Capacity Notes: _____

_____

_____

_____

©Bratiotis (2009)

Post assessment

Plan/Referral _____

_____

_____

_____

_____

_____

Date: _____ Client name: _____

Assessor: _____

©Bratiotis (2009).

Metropolitan Boston Housing Partnership, Inc. Inspections Hoarding Referral Tool©

Instructions: For each room in the unit, draw the window/door locations and shade the area that is cluttered. If possible note the location of large pieces of furniture. Use the notes section to rate the severity of the clutter on a scale of 1–10 where 1 = no clutter and 10 = no access; also note the types of possessions causing clutter.

Example:

Room Type: Living Room

6-foot stacks of newspapers and mail; doorway opens but very narrow egress path; books and board games stacked throughout the unit. See the attached inspection report for compliance.

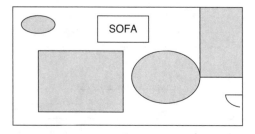

Unit Address: _____

Tenant Name: _____

Tenant Telephone: _____

Referred To: _____ Date: _____

Inspector Name: _____ Telephone: _____

©Jesse Edsell-Vetter (2009).

Living Room:

Kitchen:

Bathroom:

Bedroom #1:

Bedroom #2:

Basement:

Tufts Animal Care and Condition Scale

Tufts Animal Care and Condition* (TACC) scales for assessing body condition, weather and environmental safety, and physical care in dogs

*A tool developed for veterinarians, animal control officers, police, and cruelty investigators by Tufts Center for Animals and Public Policy. Published in: Patronek, GJ. Recognizing and reporting animal abuse ~ a veterinarian's guide. Denver, CO:American Humane Association, 1997.

I. Body condition scale (Palpation essential for long-haired dogs; each dog's condition should be interpreted in light of the typical appearance of the breed)

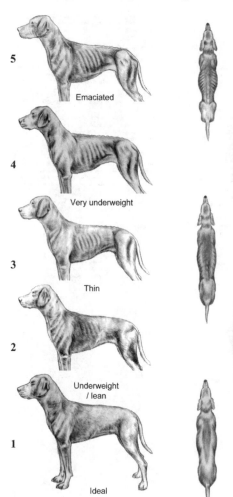

5 — Emaciated
- All bony prominences evident from a distance
- No discernible body fat
- Obvious loss of muscle mass
- Severe abdominal tuck and extreme hourglass shape

4 — Very underweight
- Ribs, lumbar vertebrae, and pelvic bones easily visible
- No palpable body fat
- Some loss of muscle mass
- Prominent abdominal tuck and hourglass shape to torso

3 — Thin
- Tops of lumbar vertebrae visible, pelvic bones becoming prominent.
- Ribs easily palpated and may be visible with no palpable fat
- Obvious waist and abdominal tuck
- Minimal loss of muscle mass

2 — Underweight / lean
- Ribs easily palpable with minimal SQ fat
- Abdominal tuck evident
- Waist clearly visible from above
- No muscle loss
- May be normal for lean breeds such as sighthounds

1 — Ideal
- Ribs palpable without excess SQ fat
- Abdomen tucked slightly when viewed from the side
- Waist visible from above, just behind ribs

Body condition scale adapted from Laflamme, DP. Proc. N.A. Vet Conf 1993, 290-91; and Armstrong, PJ., Lund, EM. Vet Clin Nutr 3:83-87; 1996. Artwork by Erik Petersen.

II. Weather safety scale

Read score off diagonal bars, by dog size:

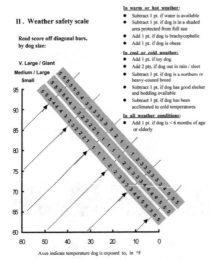

V. Large / Giant
Medium / Large
Small

Axes indicate temperature dog is exposed to, in °F

To determine score, draw a line up from the current temperature and parallel to the dotted lines, and read score on bars. Common sense must be used to take into account the duration of exposure to any given temperature when assessing risk; even brief periods of high heat can be very dangerous, whereas a similar duration of exposure to cold temperatures would not be life-threatening.

In warm or hot weather:
- Subtract 1 pt. if water is available
- Subtract 1 pt. if dog is in a shaded area protected from full sun
- Add 1 pt. if dog is brachycephalic
- Add 1 pt. if dog is obese

In cool or cold weather:
- Add 1 pt. if toy dog
- Add 2 pts. if dog out in rain / sleet
- Subtract 1 pt. if dog is a northern or heavy-coated breed
- Subtract 1 pt. if dog has good shelter and bedding available
- Subtract 1 pt. if dog has been acclimated to cold temperatures

In all weather conditions:
- Add 1 pt. if dog is < 6 months of age or elderly

Interpretation of the TACC score from scales I - IV:

The Tufts Animal Condition and Care (TACC) score is assessed from the number of points read off either the **Body Condition, Weather Safety, Environmental Health,** or **Physical Care** Scale. When multiple scales are evaluated, the highest score on any scale should be used to determine the risk of neglect. Multiple high scores are indicative of greater neglect, risk, or inhumane treatment than a single high score.

Score	Body condition, physical care, environ. health scales	Weather safety scale
≥ 5	Severe neglect and inhumane treatment. An urgent situation that justifies an assertive response to protect the animal.	Potentially life-threatening risk present. Immediate intervention to decrease threat to the animal required (provide water, shelter).
4	Clear evidence of serious neglect and / or inhumane treatment (unless there is a medical explanation for the animal's condition). Prompt improvement required.	Dangerous situation developing. Prompt intervention required to decrease risk (e.g. provide water, shade, shelter, or bring indoors). Warn owner of risk and shelter requirements.
3	Indicators of neglect present. Timely assessment; correction of problems and/or monitoring of situation may be required.	Indicators of a <u>potentially</u> unsafe situation, depending on breed, time outdoors. Inform owner of risk and proper shelter requirements.
2	A lapse in care or discomfort may be present. Evaluate, and discuss concerns with owner. Recommend changes in animal husbandry practices, if needed.	Risk unlikely, but evaluate the situation, and if warranted, discuss your concerns with the owner for proper shelter with the owner.
≤ 1	No evidence of neglect based on scale (s) used	No evidence of risk

Disclaimer: The TACC score is intended to be a simple screening device for determining when neglect may be present, for prioritizing the investigation of reported animal cruelty cases, and as a system for investigative agencies to use to summarize their case experience. The TACC score is not intended to replace definitive assessment of any animal by a veterinarian or law enforcement agent. A low TACC score does not preclude a diagnosis of abuse, neglect, or a dog requiring veterinary care upon more careful examination of an animal and its living situation.

III. Environmental health scale

5 **Filthy** - many days to weeks of accumulation of feces and / or urine. Overwhelming odor, air may be difficult to breathe. Large amount of trash, garbage, or debris present; inhibits comfortable rest, normal postures, or movement and / or poses a danger to the animal. Very difficult or impossible for animal to escape contact with feces, urine, mud, or standing water. Food and / or drinking water contaminated.

4 **Very unsanitary** - many days of accumulation of feces and / or urine. Difficult for animal to avoid contact with waste matter. Moderate amount of trash, garbage, or clutter present that may inhibit comfortable rest and / or movement of the animal. Potential injury from sharp edges or glass. Significant odor makes breathing unpleasant. Standing water or mud difficult to avoid.

3 **Unsanitary** - several days accumulation of feces and urine in animal's environment. Animal is able to avoid contact with waste matter. Moderate odor present. Trash, garbage, and other debris cluttering animal's environment but does not prohibit comfortable rest or normal posture. Clutter may interfere with normal movement or allow dog to become entangled, but no sharp edges or broken glass that could injure dog. Dog able to avoid mud or water if present.

2 **Marginal**- As in #1, except may be somewhat less sanitary. No more than 1-2 day's accumulation of feces and urine in animal's environment. Slight clutter may be present.

1 **Acceptable** - Environment is dry and free of accumulated feces. No contamination of food or water. No debris or garbage present to clutter environment and inhibit comfortable rest, normal posture and range of movement or pose a danger to the animal.

"Environment" refers to the kennel, pen, yard, cage, barn, room, tie-out or other enclosure or area where the animal is confined or spends the majority of its time. All of the listed conditions do not need to be present in order to include a dog in a specific category. The user should determine which category best describes a particular dog's condition.

IV. Physical care scale

5 **Terrible** - extremely matted haircoat, prevents normal motion, interferes with vision, perineal areas irritated from soiling with trapped urine and feces. Hair coat essentially a single mat. Dog cannot be groomed without complete clipdown. Foreign material trapped in matted hair. Nails extremely overgrown into circles, may be penetrating pads, causing abnormal position of feet and make normal walking very difficult or uncomfortable. Collar or chain, if present, may be imbedded in dog's neck.

4 **Poor** - substantial matting in haircoat, large chunks of hair matted together that cannot be separated with a comb or brush. Occasional foreign material embedded in mats. Much of the hair will need to be clipped to remove mats. Long nails force feet into abnormal position and interfere with normal gait. Perineal soiling or irritation likely. Collar or chain, if present, may be extremely tight, abrading skin.

3 **Borderline** - numerous mats present in hair, but dog can still be groomed without a total clip down. No significant perineal soiling or irritation from waste caught in matted hair. Nails are overdue for a trim and long enough to cause dog to alter gait when it walks. Collar or chain, if present, may be snug and rubbing off neck hair.

2 **Lapsed** - haircoat may be somewhat dirty or have a few mats present that are easily removed. Remainder of coat can easily be brushed or combed. Nails in need of a trim. Collar or chain, if present, fits comfortably.

1 **Adequate** - dog clean, hair of normal length for the breed, and hair can easily be brushed or combed. Nails do not touch the floor, or barely contact the floor. Collar or chain, if present, fits comfortably.

All of the listed conditions do not need to be present in order to include a dog in a specific category. The user should determine which category best describes a particular dog's condition. This scale is not meant for assessment of medical conditions, e.g., a broken limb, that clearly indicate a need for veterinary attention.

RESOURCES

ANIMAL HOARDING
See the Appendix for the Tufts Animal Care and Condition Scale (TACC) for assessing animal neglect.

- Hoarding of Animals Research Consortium (HARC)
  www.tufts.edu/vet/cfa/hoarding/
- *Animal hoarding: Structuring interdisciplinary responses to help people, animals and communities at risk* (Patronek, G. J., Loar, L., & Nathanson, J. N., 2006, Eds.). Boston, MA: Hoarding of Animals Research Consortium. Also known as the Angell Report.
  www.tufts.edu/vet/cfa/hoarding/pubs/AngellReport.pdf
- Animal Legal Defense Fund, www.aldf.org

This organization works to protect the lives and advance the interests of animals through the legal system.

ATTENTION DEFICIT (HYPERACTIVITY) DISORDER (ADD/ADHD)

- Safren, S. A., Perlman, C. A., Sprich, S., & Otto, M. W. (2005). *Mastering your adult ADHD*. New York: Oxford University Press.
- Kolberg, J., & Nadeau, K. (2002). *ADD-friendly ways to organize your life*. New York: Brunner-Routledge.

COGNITIVE-BEHAVIORAL THERAPISTS
Referral information for mental health practitioners can be found at the following organizations:

- Anxiety Disorders Association of America (ADAA)
  www.adaa.org/findatherapist
- Association for Behavioral and Cognitive Therapies (ABCT)
  www.abct.org/Members/?m=FindTherapist&fa=FT_Form&nolm=1
- International Obsessive Compulsive Foundation (IOCDF)
  www.ocfoundation.info/treatment-providers-list.php

COGNITIVE BEHAVIORAL TREATMENT FOR HOARDING

- Steketee, G., & Frost, R. O. (2007). *Compulsive hoarding and acquiring: Therapist guide*. New York: Oxford University Press.
- Steketee, G., & Frost, R. O. (2007). *Compulsive hoarding and acquiring: Workbook*. New York: Oxford University Press.

FAMILIES AND HOARDING

- Tompkins, M. A., & Hartl, T. (2009). *Digging out: Helping your loved one manage clutter, hoarding and compulsive acquiring.* Oakland, CA: New Harbinger.

FEDERAL AND STATE LAWS AFFECTING HOARDING AND HOARDING INTERVENTION
Animal Welfare

- The federal Animal Welfare Act does not apply to pets, birds, mice, and rats. However, every state has laws protecting animals. The Animal Legal Defense Fund, www.aldf.org, is another resource about animal welfare.

Children

42 U.S.C. Ch. 132—Federal law seeking to protect children from abuse and neglect. Text of the law can be found at http://uscode.house.gov/download/pls/42C132.txt

Elders and Adults with Disabilities

- The definition of an adult with a disability is determined by federal law and can be found by consulting the website for Americans with Disabilities, www.ada.org.
- 42 U.S.C. Ch. 35, §3002—Federal law seeking to protect elders and adults with disabilities from abuse and neglect. Text of the law can be found at http://uscode.house.gov/download/pls/42C35.txt.

Housing

- Fair Housing Act—42 U.S.C. §§ 3601–3619 is the entire Act and 42 U.S.C. § 3604 (f)(3) is the section on discrimination under the Act. The text of the Fair Housing Act can be found at http://uscode.house.gov/download/pls/42C45.txt.
- Reasonable Accommodation

See "Joint Statement of the Department of Housing and Urban Development and the Department of Justice, *Reasonable Accommodations Under the Fair Housing Act*" at www.hud.gov/offices/fheo/library/huddojstatement.pdf.

Health Insurance Portability and Accountability Act (HIPAA)

- For online information about HIPAA see www.hhs.gov/ocr/privacy/.

FIRE

- Lucini, G., Monk, I., & Szlatenyi, C. (2009). *An analysis of fire incidents involving hoarding households.* Report of fire incidents involving hoarding in Sydney, Australia at www.wpi.edu/Pubs/E-project/Available/E-project-052209-111725/unrestricted/WPI_MFB_Hoarding_IQP_Report_22.5.09.pdf.

HOARDING ASSESSMENT

Assessment tools useful for human service professionals are listed below. The following are included in the Appendix to this book:

- Hoarding Interview
- Hoarding Rating Scale (HRS)

- Activities of Daily Living–Hoarding (ADL-H)
- Home Environment Index (HEI)
- Clutter Image Rating (CIR)
- Tufts Animal Care and Condition Scale (TACC)
- HOMES Multidisciplinary Hoarding Risk Assessment
  (also found at www.masshousing.com/hoarding)
- Saving Inventory-Revised (SI-R)
- Inspections Hoarding Referral Tool (developed by Jesse C. Edsell-Vetter, Metropolitan Boston Housing Partnership, Inc. Boston, MA)

Other assessment instruments:

- The Clutter Hoarding Scale© developed by the Institute for Challenging Disorganization is available at www.challengingdisorganization.org/node/58.

HOARDING CASE STUDIES

- Frost, R. O., & Steketee, G. (2010). *Stuff: Compulsive hoarding and the meaning of things.* New York: Houghton Mifflin Harcourt.

HOARDING FILMS

All the films listed below are documentaries.

- *My Mother's Garden* by filmmaker Cynthia Lester
  www.mymothersgardenmovie.com
- *Stuffed* by filmmakers Arwen Curry and Cerissa Tanner
- *Packrat* by filmmaker Kris Britt Montag
  www.packratthemovie.com
- *Grey Gardens* (1975) directed by Ellen Hovde, Albert Maysles, David Maysles, and Muffie Meyer.

HOARDING TASK FORCES

- www.hoardingtaskforce.com

This website provides an international listing of hoarding task forces and their current activities. Task force members can gain permission to access the site and participate in resource and idea sharing.

HOUSING
Low Income Housing Resources

- U.S. Department of Housing and Urban Development (HUD)
  www.hud.gov/offices/pih/programs/ph/programs.cfm
  www.hud.gov/offices/pih/programs/hcv/about/fact_sheet.cfm
  http://portal.hud.gov/portal/page/portal/HUD/topics/rental_assistance/local

Policy and Code Standardization

- Schwartz, A. F. (2010). *Housing policy in the United States.* New York: Routledge Press.
- International Code Council. (2009). *2009 International Property Maintenance Code.* Washington, DC: International Code Council.
  www.iccsafe.org/pages/default.aspx

MOTIVATIONAL INTERVIEWING
Books

- Miller, W. R., & Rollnick, S. (2002). *Motivational interviewing, 2nd ed.: Preparing people for change.* New York: Guilford Press.

Training Materials

- Motivational Interviewing Resources for Clinicians, Researchers, and Trainers
  http://motivationalinterview.org

ONLINE HOARDING INFORMATION

- International Obsessive Compulsive Foundation (IOCDF) Virtual Hoarding Center
  www.ocfoundation.org/hoarding/welcome.aspx
- OCD Chicago
  www.ocdchicago.org (search for "hoarding")
- San Francisco Bay Area Internet Guide for Extreme Hoarding Behavior
  www.hoarders.org

PROFESSIONAL ORGANIZERS
Books

- Kolberg, J. (2008). *What every professional organizer needs to know about hoarding.* Decatur, GA: Squall Press, www.squallpress.net.

Organizations

- National Association of Professional Organizers (NAPO)
  www.napo.net

Founded in 1985, this organization for professional organizers has a membership of over 4,000, including members from 12 countries outside the United States. NAPO's mission is to raise awareness about the profession, encourage members' development as professional organizers, and promote the profession.

- The Institute for Challenging Disorganization (ICD)
  www.challengingdisorganization.org

The mission of the ICD, founded in 1992, is to benefit people affected by chronic disorganization. The ICD explores, develops, and communicates information, organizing techniques and solutions to professional, organizers, related professionals, and the public. ICD members include professional organizers as well as mental health professionals, medical professionals, social workers, educators, researchers, municipal planners and code enforcers, ADD coaches, and other related professionals (ICD, 2011).

SELF-HELP FOR HOARDING
Online Information

- The International Obsessive Compulsive Foundation website has self-help information at
  www.ocfoundation.org/hoarding/self_help.aspx

Books

- Neziroglu, F., Bubrick, J., & Yaryura-Tobias, J. (2004). *Overcoming compulsive hoarding: Why you save and how you can stop.* Oakland, CA: New Harbinger.
- Tolin, D. F., Frost, R. O., & Steketee, G. (2007). *Buried in treasures: Help for compulsive acquiring, saving, and hoarding.* New York: Oxford University Press.

Support Groups

- Clutterer's Anonymous
  http://sites.google.com/site/clutterersanonymous
- Messies Anonymous
  www.messies.com

Online Support Groups

- Messies Anonymous self-help group
  http://health.groups.yahoo.com/group/Messiness-and-Hoarding
- Moderated self-help group
  http://health.groups.yahoo.com/group/H-C

GLOSSARY

Assessment: Process of gathering information about a client's problem with the purpose of diagnosing and determining the severity of the condition or planning intervention. Often involves the use of standardized measures.

Assessor: Qualified person who conducts an assessment; may be a researcher or other agency staff member trained in the specific area being assessed.

Board of Health: Public agency with multiple divisions that organize and carry out regulations and programs that protect and improve the public's health; sometimes called a Department of Public Health, Health Department, or Health Service.

Case management: Planning and implementation of a range of services on behalf of a client, such as those related to housing, poverty, and physical and mental health; usually provided by a social worker or other human service agency staff member.

Change talk: Derived from motivational interviewing methods, this refers to clients' comments about their desires, reasons, ability, and/or need to change their behavior.

Chronic disorganization (CD): Habitual lack of systems and behaviors for organizing and managing objects and tasks that adversely affects the person's quality of life.

Churning: Process of resorting papers or objects from one pile into new piles without effectively organizing or discarding the items.

Code of ethics: Set of moral guidelines that govern the behaviors of a profession or members of an organization.

Code violation: Failure to meet the minimum standard established by federal, state, or local fire, safety, sanitation, or subsidized housing regulations; can result in fines, sanctions, or other penalties.

Cognitive disability: Substantial difficulty with one or more mental capacities such as communication, social skills, or functional academics; usually due to biological, genetic, or chemical causes or can be the result of physical injury.

Comorbidity: Presence of one or more mental or physical disorders (or diseases) in addition to a primary disorder or disease of interest.

Convergent validity: Research term related to survey instruments or psychometric tests; the degree of agreement between measurements of the same trait obtained by different approaches intended to measure the same trait.

Department of Social Services (DSS): Public agency that provides services and programs for children and families; also known as the Department of Children and Families (DCF), Child Protective Services (CPS), or other names depending on the state in which it is located.

Diagnostic and Statistical Manual of Mental Disorders (DSM): Published by the American Psychiatric Association to provide a common language and standard criteria for the classification of mental disorders.

Discriminant validity: Research term indicating the lack of relationship among measures that are theorized to be unrelated.

Egress: Place or means of exit (e.g., windows, doors).

Euthanize: Put to death painlessly, usually to relieve suffering.

Evidence-based: Based on research evidence showing the statistically significant effectiveness of a treatment for a specific problem; also known as empirically supported.

Fire load: Amount of combustible material in a specific space that could become fuel for a fire.

First responder: Generic term referring to human service providers who are usually the first on the scene in response to a request for help; usually police, fire, and emergency medical technicians. Can be the first person to encounter a crisis situation.

***Folie à deux*:** French term referring to a psychiatric condition wherein delusional beliefs are shared between two individuals forming a common reality.

Functional Magnetic Resonance Imaging (fMRI): Brain scan that measures the change in blood flow related to neural activity during particular tasks. fMRI produces a three-dimensional image of the areas of the brain that are most active during the tasks.

Guardian *ad litem*: Person appointed by the court to represent the interests of another person, usually a child, with respect to litigation; Guardians *ad litem* usually provide an assessment to the court or report information relevant to the case to the court. In child custody cases, a Guardian *ad Litem* for the child may present information related to the suitability of each parent to have custody of the child.

Health Insurance Portability and Accountability Act (HIPAA): National standards governing health care transactions among which is the Privacy Rule, which protects individually identifiable health information (e.g., name, diagnosis); this rule governs the sharing of protected information between health care providers and may also affect other human service professionals.

Heavy chore service: Assistance with routine maintenance tasks and household chores such as washing floors, cleaning windows, and moving heavy items.

Home health aide: A person who provides home-based basic, personal care, and health-related services to individuals who need assistance; also known as a home caregiver, patient care technician, or certified nursing assistant (CNA).

Human service: Range of professionals and disciplines that provide direct services to people; examples are social workers, psychologists, medical/health care staff (doctors, nurses, physician assistants), and emergency medical technicians.

Imminent risk: Immediate threat of danger or harm to self or others.

Insight: Awareness of illness; contrasted with anosognosia or lack of awareness of illness, a syndrome commonly seen in people with serious mental illness and some neurological disorders. Insight may range from none to full awareness.

Internal consistency: Research term referring to the extent to which all questions or items on a survey or assessment instrument measure the same characteristic, skill, or quality.

Interrater reliability: Research term referring to a statistical measure of the extent to which two or more individuals agree on a survey or assessment rating of intensity/severity; a measure of the consistency of a particular rating system.

Mandated reporter: Professional who is required by law to report suspected instances of abuse or neglect (physical, sexual, financial) in relation to vulnerable populations (children, older adults, people with disabilities).

Medicaid: U.S. federally funded state-administered health insurance program for eligible individuals who qualify for medical care because of low income.

Medicare: U.S. health insurance program for people age 65 years or older, some disabled people under age 65 years, and people of all ages with end-stage renal disease.

Personal care assistant: Person who provides assistance with hygiene, exercise, eating, and medication. Works as part of a medical team and is usually supervised by a registered nurse (RN); also known as a nurse's aide, nurse's assistant, or personal care worker.

Point of entry: Human service profession or system that first becomes aware of and intervenes with a problem.

Probate court: Specialized court that hears cases related to estates and distribution of assets, wills, guardianship, and conservatorship; also called Surrogate Court.

Psychosis: Psychiatric term meaning loss of contact with reality. Usually includes false beliefs about personal identity and/or events (delusions) and seeing or hearing things that are not real (hallucinations).

Receivership: Judicial appointment of a person (receiver) to collect and conserve assets and make distributions according to direction by the court.

Reliability: Research term referring to the dependability of a measure, procedure, or instrument. In practice, more reliable surveys or assessment instruments are preferred as these are likely to yield similar results when used by different assessors or at different times.

Resident service coordinator (RSC): Professional who works as part of a housing management team to ensure that residents comply with the terms of their lease; provides services to support tenants in maintaining their housing.

Right to Enter (of entry): Legal term referring to the right of a landlord or other authority (e.g., Fire Marshall, Board of Health Inspector) to enter a property.

Self-neglect: Intentional or unintentional inability to meet one's basic needs; behaviors (especially among the elderly) that threaten health or safety.

Serotonergic Reuptake Inhibitors (SRIs): Class of medications used to treat mood disorders such as major depression; also prescribed to treat some anxiety disorders such as obsessive compulsive disorder. Examples include Zoloft (sertraline), Paxil (paroxetine), Prozac (fluoxetine), Celexa (citalopram), and Lexapro (escitalopram).

Squalor: Filthiness or degradation from neglect; can be domestic (in the home) and/or personal (characterized by lack of personal hygiene).

Standardized measure: Survey or assessment instrument administered and scored in a consistent manner, usually determined to be reliable and valid according to research studies.

Task force: Group of people who work together on a defined task or activity; usually people from community organizations who engage in social planning, policy change, advocacy, and social change efforts; also referred to as collaborative or network.

Test–retest reliability: Research term indicating that the same test repeated at two different points in time with the same group of respondents yields similar results.

Validity: Research term indicating that a survey or assessment instrument measures what it intends to measure. In practice, instruments with high validity are preferred.

Voucher: Assistance for low income families, the elderly, and people with disabilities to afford safe and sanitary housing. Usually refers to the U.S. federal Housing Choice Voucher Program formerly known as Section 8 housing.

Warrant: Order of the court that provides authorization to the holder of the warrant to engage in a specified activity, for example, a search of someone's home.

REFERENCES

Abramowitz, J. S., Franklin, M. E., Schwartz, S. A., & Furr, J. M. (2003). Symptom presentation and outcome of cognitive-behavioral therapy for obsessive-compulsive disorder. *Journal of Consulting and Clinical Psychology, 71,* 1049–1057.

Abramowitz, J. S., Wheaton, M. G., & Storch, E. A. (2008). The status of hoarding as a symptom of obsessive–compulsive disorder. *Behaviour Research and Therapy, 46,* 1026–1033.

American Psychiatric Association. (APA, 2000). *Diagnostic and statistical manual of mental disorders (DSM-IV-TR),* Washington, DC: American Psychiatric Association.

Andersen, E., Raffin-Bouchal, S., & Marcy-Edwards, D. (2008). Reasons to accumulate excess: Older adults who hoard possessions. *Home Health Care Services Quarterly, 27,* 187–216.

Anderson, S. W., Damasio, H., & Damasio, A. R. (2005). A neural basis for collecting behavior in humans. *Brain, 128,* 201–212.

Andrews, K. (19 June 1999). Women charged with abusing cats. *The Calgary Herald,* B14.

Animal Legal Defense Fund. (2009). *Animal Bill of Rights.* Retrieved December 20, 2009 from http://www.aldf.org/section.php?id=148.

Arluke, A. (1998, February). *An ethnographic approach to animal hoarding.* Paper presented at the annual meeting of the Humane Society of the United States, Orlando, FL.

Arluke, A., Frost, R., Steketee, G., Patronek, G., Luke, C., Messner, E., Nathanson, J., & Papazian, M. (2002). Press reports of animal hoarding. *Society and Animals, 10,* 113–135.

Ayers, C. R., Saxena, S., Golshan, S., & Wetherell, J. L. (2009). Age at onset and clinical features of late life compulsive hoarding. *International Journal of Geriatric Psychiatry, 25*(2), 142–149.

Berry, C., Patronek, G., & Lockwood, R. (2005). Long-term outcomes in animal hoarding cases. *Animal Law, 11,* 167–194.

Brace, P. B. (2007). Hoarding becomes a health, safety issue. *The Nantucket Independent.* Retrieved January 11, 2010 from http://www.nantucketindependent.com/news/2007/1121/front_page/001.html.

Bratiotis, C. (2009). Task force community response to compulsive hoarding cases. Ph.D. dissertation, Boston University, Boston, MA. Retrieved August 24, 2010 from Dissertations & Theses @ Boston University. (Publication No. AAT 3363599.)

Bratiotis, C., & Flowers, K. L. (2010). Community-based cognitive behavioral interventions for elders who hoard. *Journal of Geriatric Care Management, 20*(2), 5–20.

Calamari, J. E., Wiegartz, P. S., Riemann, B. C., Cohen, R. J., Greer, A., Jacobi, D. M., Jahn, S. C., & Carmin, C. (2004). Obsessive-compulsive disorder subtypes: An attempted replication and extension of a symptom-based taxonomy. *Behaviour Research and Therapy, 42,* 647–670.

Centers for Disease Control. (2007, October). Lymphocytic Choriomeningitis Fact Sheet. http://www.cdc.gov/ncidod/dvrd/spb/mnpages/dispages/lcmv/qa.htm.

Cullen, B., Brown, C. H., Riddle, M. A., Grados, M., Bienvenu, O. J., Hoehn-Saric, R., Shugart, Y. Y., Liang, K. Y., Samuels, J., & Nestadt, G. (2007). Factor analysis of the Yale-Brown Obsessive Compulsive Scale in a family study of obsessive-compulsive disorder. *Depression and Anxiety, 24,* 130–138.

Danet, B., & Katriel, T. (1989). No two alike: Play and aesthetics in collecting. *Play and Culture, 2,* 253–277.

Frost, R. O., & Hartl, T. (1996). A cognitive-behavioral model of compulsive hoarding. *Behaviour Research and Therapy, 34,* 341–350.

Frost, R. O., & Steketee, G. (2010). *Stuff: Compulsive hoarding and the meaning of things.* New York: Houghton Mifflin Harcourt.

Frost, R. O., Steketee, G., & Grisham, J. (2004). Measurement of compulsive hoarding: Saving Inventory-Revised. *Behaviour Research and Therapy, 42,* 1163–1182.

Frost, R. O., Steketee, G., Tolin, D., & Brown, T. (2006). *Diagnostic issues in compulsive hoarding.* Paper presented at the European Association of Behavioral and Cognitive Therapies, Paris, France.

Frost, R. O., Steketee, G., Tolin, D., & Glossner, K. (2010). Comorbidity in hoarding disorder. Paper presented at the World Congress of Behavioral and Cognitive Therapies, Boston, MA.

Frost, R. O., Steketee, G., Tolin, D., & Renaud, D. (2008). Development and validation of the Clutter Image Rating. *Journal of Psychopathology and Behavior Assessment, 30,* 193–203.

Frost, R. O., Steketee, G., & Williams, L. (2000). Hoarding: A community health problem. *Health and Social Care in the Community, 8,* 229–234.

Frost, R. O., Steketee, G., Williams, L., & Warren, R. (2000). Mood, personality disorder symptoms and disability in obsessive compulsive hoarders: A comparison with clinical and nonclinical controls. *Behaviour Research and Therapy, 38,* 1071–1081.

Frost, R. O., Tolin, D. F., Steketee, G., Fitch, K. E., & Selbo-Bruns, A. (2009). Excessive acquisition in hoarding. *Journal of Anxiety Disorders, 23*(5), 632–639.

Greenberg, D. (1987). Compulsive hoarding. *American Journal of Psychotherapy, 41,* 409–416.

Grisham, J. R., Brown, T.A., Liverant, G.I., & Campbell-Sills, L. (2005). The distinctiveness of compulsive hoarding from obsessive-compulsive disorder. *Journal of Anxiety Disorders, 19*(7), 767–779.

Grisham, J. R., Frost, R. O., Steketee, G., Kim, H.-J., & Hood, S. (2006). Age of onset in compulsive hoarding. *Journal of Anxiety Disorders, 20,* 675–686.

Grisham, J. R., Kim, H.-J., Frost, R. O., Steketee, G., Tarkoff, A., & Hood, S. (2009). Formation of attachment to possessions in compulsive hoarding. *Journal of Anxiety Disorders, 23*(3), 357–361.

Harris, J. (2010, July). Household hoarding and residential fires. Paper presented at the International Congress of Applied Psychology, Melbourne, Australia.

Hartl, T. L., Frost, R. O., Allen, G. J., Deckersbach, T., Steketee, G., Duffany, S. R., & Savage, C. R. (2004). Actual and perceived memory deficits in individuals with compulsive hoarding. *Depression and Anxiety, 20,* 59–69.

Hoarding of Animals Research Consortium. (2000). People who hoard animals. *Psychiatric Times, 17,* 25–29.

Hoarding of Animals Research Consortium. (2002). Health implications of animal hoarding. *Health and Social Work, 27,* 125–132.

International Code Council. (2009). *2009 International Property Maintenance Code.* Washington, DC: International Code Council.

Kolberg, J. (1999). *Conquering chronic disorganization.* Decatur, GA: Squall Press.

Kolberg, J. (2008). *What every professional organizer needs to know about hoarding.* Decatur, GA: Squall Press.

Kolberg, J., & Nadeau, K. (2002). *ADD-friendly ways to organize your life*. New York: Brunner-Routledge.

Kyrios, M., Frost, R. O., & Steketee, G. (2004). Cognitions in compulsive buying and acquisition. *Cognitive Therapy and Research, 28,* 241–258.

Lawyers.com. (2010). Elder Abuse. Retrieved January 14, 2010 from http://elder-law.lawyers.com/Elder-Abuse.html.

Lockwood, R. (1994). The psychology of animal collectors. *American Animal Hospital Association Trends Magazine, 9*(6), 18–21.

Lockwood, R., & Cassidy, B. (1988). Killing with kindness? *Humane Society News, Summer,* 14–18.

Marx, M., & Cohen-Mansfield, J. (2003). Hoarding behavior in the elderly: A comparison between community-dwelling persons and nursing home residents. *Psychogeriatrics, 15,* 289–306.

Mataix-Cols, D., Baer, L., Rauch, S. L., & Jenike, M. A. (2000). Relation of factor-analyzed symptom dimensions of obsessive-compulsive disorder to personality disorders. *Acta Psychiatrica Scandinavica, 102*(3), 199–202.

Mataix-Cols, D., Grayton, L., Bonner, A., Luscombe, C., Taylor, P., & van den Bree, M. B. M. (2011). Prevalence and correlates of compulsive hoarding in a representative sample of homeless people. In preparation.

Mataix-Cols, D., Wooderson, S., Lawrence, N., Brammer, M. J., Speckens, A., & Phillips, M. L. (2004). Distinct neural correlates of washing, checking, and hoarding symptom dimensions in obsessive-compulsive disorder. *Archives of General Psychiatry, 61*(6), 564–576.

Mathews, C. A., Nievergelt, C. M., Azzam, A., Garrido, H., Chavira, D. A., Wessel, J., Bagnarello, M., Reus, V. I., & Schork, N. J. (2007). Heritability and clinical features of multigenerational families with obsessive-compulsive disorder and hoarding. *American Journal of Medical Genetics B: Neuropsychiatric Genetics, 144*(2), 174–182.

Meunier, S., Maltby, N., & Tolin, D. (2008). Compulsive hoarding. In M. Hersen (Ed.), *Handbook of psychological assessment, case conceptualization and treatment* (pp. 782–752). Hoboken, NJ: Wiley.

Miller, W. R., & Rollnick, S. (2002). *Motivational interviewing, 2nd ed.: Preparing people for change*. New York: Guilford Press.

Moore, E. (19 July 1991). Addicted to animals. *The Houston Chronicle*, 8–12.

Muroff, J., Bratiotis, C., & Steketee, G. (2010). Treatment for compulsive hoarding: A review. *Clinical Social Work Journal*. DOI 10.1007/s10615-010-0311-4

Muroff, J., Steketee G., Rasmussen, J., Gibson, A., Bratiotis, C., & Sorrentino, C. (2009). Group cognitive and behavioral treatment for compulsive hoarding: A preliminary trial. *Depression and Anxiety, 26,* 634–640.

Murphy, B. C., & Dillon, C. (2010). *Interviewing in action*, 4th ed. Belmont, CA: Brooks/Cole.

Nathanson, J. (2009). Slipping into the darkness of comorbid animal and self neglect. *Journal of Elder Abuse and Neglect, 21,* 307–324.

Patronek, G. J. (1999). Hoarding animals: An under-recognized public health problem in a difficult-to-study population. *Public Health Reports, 114,* 81–87.

Patronek, G. J. (2004). Animal cruelty, abuse, and neglect. In L. Miller & S. Zawistowski (Eds.), *Shelter medicine for veterinarians and staff* (pp. 427–452). Ames, IA: Iowa State University Press.

Patronek, G. J., & the Hoarding of Animals Research Consortium. (2001). The problem of animal hoarding. *Municipal Lawyer, 42*(3), 6–19.

Patronek, G. J., Loar, L., & Nathanson, J. N. (2006). *Animal hoarding: Structuring interdisciplinary responses to help people, animals and communities at risk*. Boston, MA: Hoarding of Animals Research Consortium.

Patronek, G. J., & Nathanson, J. N. (2009). A theoretical perspective to inform assessment and treatment strategies for animal hoarders. *Clinical Psychology Review, 29,* 274–281.

Pertusa, A., Fullana, M.A., Singh, S., Alonso, P., Menchon, J., Mataix-Coles, D. (2008). Compulsive hoarding: A symptom of OCD, a distinct clinical syndrome, or both? *The American Journal of Psychiatry, 165,* 1289–1298.

Pertusa, A., Frost, R., Fullana, M. A., Samuels, J., Steketee, G., Tolin, D., Saxena, S., Leckman, J. F., & Mataix-Cols, D. (2010a). Refining the diagnostic boundaries of compulsive hoarding: A critical review. *Clinical Psychology Review, 30,* 371–386.

Pertusa, A., Frost, R. O., & Mataix-Cols, D. (2010b). When hoarding *is* a symptom of OCD: A case series and implications for DSM-V. *Behaviour Research and Therapy, 48,* 1012–1020.

Rasmussen, S. A., & Eisen, J. L. (1992). The epidemiology and differential diagnosis of obsessive compulsive disorder. *Journal of Clinical Psychiatry, 53,* 4–10.

Rasmussen, J. L., Steketee, G., Brown, T. A., Frost, R. O., & Tolin, D. F. (2011). Assessing squalor in hoarding: The Home Environment Index. In preparation.

Safren, S. A., Perlman, C. A., Sprich, S., & Otto, M. W. (2005). *Mastering your adult ADHD.* New York: Oxford University Press.

Samuels, J., Bienvenu, O.J., Grados, M.A., Cullen, B.A., Riddle, M.A., Liang, K.Y., Eaton, W.W. & Nastadt, G. (2008). Prevalence and correlates of hoarding behavior in a community-based sample. *Behaviour Research and Therapy, 46,* 836–844.

Samuels, J., Bienvenu, O. J., Riddle, M. A., Cullen, B. A., Grados, M. A., Liang, K. Y., Hoehn-Saric, R., & Nestadt, G. (2002). Hoarding in obsessive compulsive disorder: Results from a case-control study. *Behaviour Research and Therapy, 40,* 517–528.

Saxena, S. (2007). Is compulsive hoarding a genetically and neurobiologically discrete syndrome? Implications for diagnostic classification. *American Journal of Psychiatry, 164*(3), 380–384.

Saxena, S. (2008a). Recent advances in compulsive hoarding. *Current Psychiatry Reports, 10,* 297–303.

Saxena, S. (2008b). Neurobiology and treatment of compulsive hoarding. *CNS Spectrums, 13,* 29–36.

Saxena, S. A., Brody, A. L., Maidment, K. M., Smith, E. C., Zohrabi, N., Baker, S. K., & Baxter, L. R. (2004). Cerebral glucose metabolism in obsessive-compulsive hoarding. *American Journal of Psychiatry, 161,* 1038–1048.

Saxena, S., & Maidment, K. M. (2004). Treatment of compulsive hoarding. *Journal of Clinical Psychology, 60,* 1143–1154.

Schwartz, A. F. (2010). *Housing policy in the United States.* New York: Routledge Press.

Seedat, S., & Stein, D. J. (2002). Hoarding in obsessive-compulsive disorder and related disorders: A preliminary report of 15 cases. *Psychiatry and Clinical Neuroscience, 56,* 17–23.

Sheppard, B., Chavira, D., Azzam, A., & Grados, M. A. (2010). ADHD prevalence and association with hoarding behaviors in childhood-onset OCD. *Depression and Anxiety, 27,* 667–674.

Snowdon, J., Shah, A., & Halliday, G. (2007). Severe domestic squalor: A review. *International Psychogeriatrics, 19,* 37–51.

Steketee, G., & Frost, R. O. (2003). Compulsive hoarding: Current status of the research. *Clinical Psychology Review, 23,* 905–927.

Steketee, G., & Frost, R. O. (2007). *Compulsive hoarding and acquiring: Therapist guide.* New York: Oxford University Press.

Steketee, G., Frost, R., & Kyrios, M. (2003). Cognitive aspects of compulsive hoarding. *Cognitive Therapy and Research, 27,* 463–479.

Steketee, G., Frost, R. O., Tolin, D., Rasmussen, J., & Brown, T. (2010a). Waitlist controlled trial of cognitive behavioral therapy for hoarding disorder. *Depression and Anxiety, 27,* 476–484.

Steketee, G., Frost, R. O., Wincze J., Greene, K. A. I., & Douglas, H. (2000b). Group and individual treatment of compulsive hoarding: A pilot study. *Behavioral and Cognitive Psychotherapy, 28,* 259–268.

Steketee, G., Gibson, A., Frost, R. O., Alabiso, J., Arluke, A., & Patronek, G. (2011). Characteristics and antecedents of animal hoarding: A comparative interview study. In preparation.

Tolin, D. F., Fitch, K. E., Frost, R. O., & Steketee, G. (2010). Family informants' perception of insight in compulsive hoarding. *Cognitive Therapy and Research, 34,* 69–81.

Tolin, D. F., Frost, R. O., & Steketee, G. (2010). A brief interview for assessing compulsive hoarding: The Hoarding Rating Scale. *Psychiatry Research, 30,* 147–152. doi.org/10.1016/j.psychres.2009.05.001

Tolin, D. F., Frost, R. O., Steketee, G., & Fitch, K. E. (2008). Family burden of compulsive hoarding: Results of an internet survey. *Behavior Research and Therapy, 46,* 334–344.

Tolin, D. F., Frost, R. O., Steketee, G., Gray, K. D., & Fitch, K. E. (2008). The economic and social burden of compulsive hoarding. *Psychiatry Research, 160,* 200–211.

Tolin, D. F., Frost, R. O., Steketee, G. (2007). An open trial of cognitive-behavioral therapy for compulsive hoarding. *Behaviour Research and Therapy, 45*(7), 1461–1470.

Tolin, D. F., Kiehl, K. A., Worhunsky, P., Book, G. A., & Maltby, N. (2008). An exploratory study of the neural mechanisms of decision making in compulsive hoarding. *Psychological Medicine, 39,* 1–12.

Tolin, D. F., Meunier, S. A., Frost, R. O., & Steketee, G. (2010). The course of compulsive hoarding and its relationship to life events. *Depression and Anxiety, 27,* 829–838.

Tolin, D. F., Meunier, S. A., Frost, R. O., & Steketee, G. (2011). Hoarding among patients seeking treatment for anxiety disorders. *Journal of Anxiety Disorders, 25*(1), 43–48.

Tompkins, M. A., & Hartl, T. (2009). *Digging out: Helping your loved one manage clutter, hoarding and compulsive acquiring.* Oakland, CA: New Harbinger.

Valente, S. M. (2009). The Hoarding Syndrome: Screening and treatment. *Home Healthcare Nurse, 7,* 432–440.

Volunteer Lawyers Project. (2008). *Hoarding and the Law* (White Paper). Boston, Massachusetts.

Wincze, J. P., Steketee, G., & Frost, R. O. (2007). Categorization in compulsive hoarding. *Behaviour Research and Therapy, 45,* 63–72.

INDEX

resident service coordinator (RSC), 219
resistance, 20–22
resources, self-help, 214–15
respectful language, 17–18, 173
retirement, 149
right of entry, 126–27
right to enter, 219
risk to self/others, 45–56
rodent infestations, 75, 79, 91
Rollnick, S., 25, 63, 66, 94, 223
rotting food, 199
RSC. *See* resident service coordinator

safety, 19
    in ADL-H, 193
    in HOMES Multidisciplinary Risk
      Assessment, 204
    maintaining, 28
    nets, 129
    personal, 147
    weather, 210
safety professionals, 89–90
Safren, S. A., 162, 211, 224
    on ADHD, 159
Samuels, J., 11, 13, 22, 222, 224
sanitation, 39, 81
    inoperable facilities, 92
Saving Cognitions Inventory (SCI), 51, 62
Saving Inventory-Revised (SI-R), 50, 62,
    194–97
Saxena, S., 8, 12, 58, 67, 106, 224
schizophrenia, 58
Schmalisch, Cristina Sorrentino, xii
Schwartz, A. F., 213, 224
Schwartz, S. A., 58, 221
SCI. *See* Saving Cognitions Inventory
Section 8, 74, 101, 121–22, 219
Seedat, S., 13, 224
Selbo-Bruns, A., 9, 222
self-assessment, 48–49
self-determination, 81–82
self-efficacy, 72
self-help resources, 214–15
self-neglect, 219
    elder, 147
sentimentality, 14
sertraline, 219
serotonergic reuptake inhibitors (SRIs),
    67, 219
service delivery systems, 30–44
    case studies, 40–44

severity, assessment of, 45–56, 62–63,
    82–83
    case studies, 54–56
Shah, A., 10, 224
Sheppard, B., 58, 224
shower cleaning, 202
SHPs. *See* subsidized housing providers
sink, clogged, in HEI, 199
SI-R. *See* Saving Inventory-Revised
skin care, 104
sleep apnea, 152–53
smoke alarms, 76
Snowdon, J., 10, 224
social isolation, 113
social phobia, 58, 63
social workers, 31, 91
    delivering CBT, 67
    in medical settings, 144
Society for Prevention of Cruelty to
    Animals (SPCA), 115
Sorrentino, C., 223
spatial memory, 159
SPCA. *See* Society for Prevention of Cruelty
    to Animals
spouses, 22–23
Sprich, S., 211, 224
    on ADHD, 159
squalor, 10–11, 219
SRIs. *See* serotonergic reuptake
    inhibitors
standardized assessment instruments,
    48–50
standardized measure, 219
standards of care, 173
standing water, in HEI, 199
state laws
    animal welfare, 133–34
    child protection, 132–33
    housing, 131–32
    public health, 134
    resources, 212
state prosecutors, 134
Stein, D. J., 13, 224
Steketee, Gail, xii, xiv, 4, 9, 13–14,
    48–52, 58–60, 111, 113, 142, 215,
    222–25
    on animal hoarding, 114
    on course of hoarding, 175
    on decision-making strategies, 163
    model introduced by, 168
    therapist guide, 25, 65, 66, 161